MW00640188

MARRIAGE RECORDS

OF THE

CITY OF FREDERICKSBURG

AND OF

ORANGE, SPOTSYLVANIA

AND

STAFFORD COUNTIES

VIRGINIA

1722-1850

Second Edition

Compiled and Edited by
Therese A. Fisher

HERITAGE BOOKS
2007

HERITAGE BOOKS
AN IMPRINT OF HERITAGE BOOKS, INC.

Books, CDs, and more—Worldwide

For our listing of thousands of titles see our website
at
www.HeritageBooks.com

Published 2007 by
HERITAGE BOOKS, INC.
Publishing Division
65 East Main Street
Westminster, Maryland 21157-5026

Copyright © 1990 Therese A. Fisher

All rights reserved. No part of this book may be reproduced or
transmitted in any form or by any means, electronic or mechanical,
including photocopying, recording or by any information storage
and retrieval system without written permission from the author,
except for the inclusion of brief quotations in a review.

International Standard Book Number: 978-1-55613-345-9

TABLE OF CONTENTS

iii

INTRODUCTION

Genealogical research in Virginia is made both easy and difficult by the large number of books published on various county records in the Commonwealth. It seems easy because so much information is available to the researcher. It proves to be difficult because all that information is deceiving. While there seems to be a bounty of documentation on marriages, I have found that even that large amount available is incomplete. Some books will contain marriage bonds only, some will contain marriage licenses, some will contain ministers' returns. These three means of documenting marriages in the early counties of Virginia were not necessarily equal either in their accuracy or in their completeness.

There is also the difficulty of sorting out who lived in what county. County borders changed for most counties. A family could live on the family spread for three generations and be listed in two, or in some cases, three different counties during that time frame.

Family members were not always cooperative when it came to marrying people from the same county, either. Brothers and sisters married into families in adjoining counties as well as counties quite distant from the family center.

Having experienced these types of frustrations and problems, I felt it was time to take a more original approach to compiling county records. In this volume I have included four political jurisdictions: Spotsylvania County, Stafford County, Orange County and the independent city of Fredericksburg. I have also made the attempt to use more than one type of documentation. I have included ministers' returns, marriage bonds, some newspaper notices, and in the case of Stafford, marriages implied from early land deeds, family Bible records and cemetery records, as well as the marriages recorded in Overwharton and St. Paul's parishes. These two churches were mandated by the early colonial governments to maintain vital-statistic information for the population within their geographic areas, regardless of religious affiliation. I have also included the minister's returns from the records of Jeremiah Chandler, the Baptist minister who presided over Piney Branch church in Spotsylvania County. While it appears that the marriages he performed were performed well within the Spotsylvania County limits, there are numerous entries in the Orange County records that bear his name. I have included his minister's returns under Spotsylvania records except where he indicated that the marriage took place in another location. In that case, I included an entry where he said it took place. In the cases where the marriage bond was issued in Orange County, I have made a separate entry showing the Orange marriage bond.

Researchers familiar with Virginia records recognize that Stafford County records were among those burned or stolen during the War Between the States. This explains the absence of Stafford County marriage bond records and the scarcity of Stafford county marriage records other than those provided by the records from Overwharton and St. Paul's and the miscellaneous minor sources available.

Ministers' returns, that is, the account of the marriages in the Overwharton and St. Paul parishes in Stafford County, account for approximately 94% of the Stafford marriage records (StM) between the years 1715 and 1798 found in this book. Earlier marriages (earlier than 1715) recorded in Stafford County were obtained from deeds that exist in the Stafford County Court House. Marriage records from family Bibles account for the other approximately 6% of marriages between 1715 and 1798, as well as many of the marriages after 1800. A number of family Bibles are on microfilm in the Virginia State Archives in Richmond, Virginia. Marriages after 1800 are also found on tombstones in the Aquia Church (the old Overwharton Parish) Cemetery, Stafford County, Virginia. A number of marriages from Stafford County as well as the city of Fredericksburg are noted in the *Virginia Herald and Fredericksburg Advertiser* located in the Library of Congress, Washington, D.C., and in the Virginiana Room of the Rappahannock area library in Fredericksburg, Virginia.

The observant researcher will also notice occasional discrepancies between marriage bond records and ministers' returns. These are not brought about by inaccurate research on my part (not that I am perfect!). In most cases, minor differences in name spellings or the use of nicknames in place of full legal names can be attributed to the time period with which these records deal. There was not the standardization of spellings we are accustomed to. A clerk of the court or minister could spell the name any way he chose. There are some obvious attempts to spell an unusual name the way it sounded to them. There are also spelling differences that seem to have come about through local accents. The wise researcher will talk to him- or herself, saying the possible variation out loud. This will occasionally provide insight into what the scribe was trying to spell. For the purpose of this book I have recorded the names as they appeared in the original document. I have not attempted to standardize or correct any spellings.

In this record of marriages I have made separate entries for marriage bonds and ministers' returns, even when this meant a double entry for a couple. Fortunate are the researchers who have these double entries because they provide additional clues to the origins of the families. In Virginia, marriage bonds had to be issued in the town of the bride's residence. This usually can point to the residence of the bridal family. Ministers could perform the marriage ceremony anywhere they wanted but the minister's return was supposed to be returned to the jurisdiction that issued the license.

I have not differentiated between marriage licenses and marriage bonds in this record. There was not a profusion of licenses that either were issued or that survived until today. In either case, they were a record of intent to marry, not the record of a marriage that had been performed.

In researching this book, I have examined the actual document whenever possible. In some cases, the original documents were in such jeopardy of deterioration that microfilm copies were all that were available for research. In one case, officials were unsure of the exact location of the original document, having only the microfilmed copy. Most of the sources can be found in the Virginia State Archives. I have found additional records in the Wallace Library's Virginiana collection in Fredericksburg, and a few records that have not been microfilmed or indexed in Spotsylvania and Stafford Counties. For researchers who feel that they could find more information by examining the source records, or for those who have inconsistencies between the marriage bond and the ministers' returns, I suggest you begin your search in Richmond at the state archives. While you may find the same uncertainties of spelling or indecipherable handwriting that I encountered, you may feel better for having taken that additional step yourself.

I hope that by including several jurisdictions that have numerous links in culture and geographic proximity, I have provided a more complete picture of family relationships. I would have liked to include King George County to make Stafford County records complete, and Green County to provide a more complete picture of Orange County, but I had to stop somewhere. These four areas today show the same close bonds established in the infancy of their colonization, particularly Spotsylvania, Stafford and Fredericksburg. Road and building names in these three localities reflect the names found in these early marriages. The vast progeny still living in this area today provide a testimony to the deep roots put down by these early pioneers: family names such as Fitzhugh, Lee, Chewning, Taliaferro, Clark, Minor, Collins and Lewis.

I once heard a genealogist remark (I think it was meant humorously) that everyone can trace an ancestor back to Virginia. If so, this book should provide a valuable tool for those with roots on the banks of the Rappahannock River.

HISTORY

Spotsylvania County was formed in 1721 from Essex County, which had its origins in 1692. Essex County was formed from the old Rappahannock County. Lancaster County was the parent county of Rappahannock County, and Northumberland County was the parent of Lancaster.

Orange County was split from Spotsylvania in 1734. Records for early Orange County were maintained in Spotsylvania County.

Stafford County was formed in 1664 from Westmoreland County which was formed from within Northumberland County.

Fredericksburg was formed in 1728 by an act of the Virginia General Assembly. In 1732 Fredericksburg was designated the site of the court of Spotsylvania County.

The British Empire, as well as the American colonies, used the Julian or Old Style calendar until 1752. This dating system had a year that began on March 25. In 1752 the colonies switched to the use of the Gregorian calendar, which has been used ever since. This change in calendars accounts for some of the ambiguities in year dates in the earlier records.

Some significant dates in the history of the area include:

1608: Captain John Smith discovers the falls of the Rappahannock River.

1664: Stafford County formed from Westmoreland County.

1671: Governor Berkeley grants John Buckner and Thomas Royston two thousand acres of land on the Rappahannock River near the falls discovered by Captain John Smith.

1714: Governor Spotswood established Germanna in Orange County as the earliest settlement in the area. Its original purpose was for the mining of iron. Its name was derived from the Germans who originally were brought to work the mines. A majority of these families eventually moved from this settlement.

1716: Governor Spotswood and his Knights of the Golden Horseshoe explore this area on their famous expedition over the Blue Ridge Mountains.

1721: Spotsylvania County formed from Essex County.

1732: County court moves from Germanna to Fredericksburg.

1734: Orange County is formed from Spotsylvania County.

ABBREVIATIONS

FB	Fredericksburg Marriage Bond
FM	Fredericksburg Marriage (usually minister's return)
OB	Orange County Marriage Bond
OM	Orange County Marriage (usually minister's return)
SpB	Spotsylvania County Marriage Bond
SpM	Spotsylvania County Marriage (usually minister's return)
StB	Stafford County Marriage Bond
StM	Stafford County Marriage
fpc	free person of color (to differentiate from a slave)
d/o	daughter of
s/o	son of
w/o	widow of
w/o ?	There was a statement that the bride was a widow but no mention is made of the name of the previous husband or husbands.
b.d.	birth date
b.p.	birth place
d.d.	death date
aka	also known as (This abbreviation was used when the original record designated "aka" to indicate that the person named was known by another name in the same group of documents.)
Co.	County

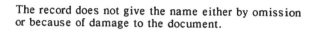 The record does not give the name either by omission or because of damage to the document.

Occasionally, a portion of the name was decipherable, while part could not be determined because of illegibility or destruction of the document.

ABBOTT, James & Fanny McDaniel; 10 Jun 1803 (SpM)

ABBOTT, John & Margaret Lyon; 15 Jan 1758 (StM)

ABBOTT, William C. & Martha L. Campbell; 12 Jun 1834 (SpM)

ABEL, John & Margaret Tinder; 5 Oct 1777 (OB)

ABELL, John S. & Sally King; 30 Jul 1805 (OB)

ABELL, Theopolis & Elizabeth Talley; 3 Dec 1850 (SpM)

ABRAHAM, Francis & Jestin Mallory; 20 Nov 1804 (OB)

ABRAHAM, Francis & Jestin Mallory; 21 Nov 1804 (OM)

ACORS, Hezikiah & Elizabeth Waller; 6 Apr 1848 (SpM)

ACRE, James & Elizabeth Acre; 21 Dec 1798 (OB)

ACRE, James & Elizabeth Acre; 21 Dec 1798 (OM)

ACREE, William & Rebecca Morris; 24 Dec 1804 (OB)

ACRES, John & Dully Griffin; 28 May 1798 (StM)

ADAMS, Benjamin & Milly Coleman; 7 Apr 1781 (OB)

ADAMS, Elisha & Delia Smith (d/o James Smith); 22 Dec 1795 (OB)

ADAMS, Elisha & Delia Smith (d/o James Smith); 22 Dec 1795 (OM)

ADAMS, James & Eley Welch; 3 May 1773 (OB)

ADAMS, James & Mary Chambers (d/o Thomas Chambers); 16 May 1782 (OB)

ADAMS, James & Patsey Harper; 17 may 1810 (OB)

ADAMS, John & Honora Carty; 23 Sep 1750 (StM)

ADAMS, Richard & Lucy W. Thornton; 18 Jul 1829 (SpM)

ADAMS, Thomas & Katherine Skinner; 18 Oct 1738 (StM)

ADAMS, Thomas B. & Judith Burnley (d/o Frances Burnley); 20 Jun 1807 (OB)

ADDISON, John & Mary Anne Findleston; 17 Apr 1761 (StM)

ADDISON, John & Monica Bryant; 19 Mar 1789 (StM)

ADIE, William & Elizabeth Parender; 25 Jul 1754 (StM)

AERY, George & Elizabeth Shiflett; 17 Nov 1808 (OB)

AHART, Abram Jr. &
Judith Kirk; 25 Mar
1793 (OB)

AHART, Jacob & Mary
Bruce; 21 Sep 1777 (OB)

AHART, John & Peggy
Pearson (d/o Robert
Pearson);12 Dec 1783
(OB)

AIRY, William & Mary
Stowers; 16 Aug 1788
(OB)

ALCOCK, Abner R. &
Elizabeth Hazegrove; 25
May 1816 (SpM)

ALCOCK, Robert & Mary
Bell(widow); 13 Jan
1786 (OB)

ALCOCK, William & Catey
Bell; 15 Mar 1785 (OB)

ALDRIDGE, John & Anne
Hamilton; 11 Jun 1738
(StM)

ALER, John & Elizabeth
Brown; 28 Jan 1808
(SpM)

ALEXANDER, James &
Franky Ahart; 14 Jun
1792 (OM)

ALEXANDER, James &
Jerusa Townsend; 10 Apr
1776 (OB)

ALEXANDER, John &
Susannah Pearson; 15
Dec 1734 (StM)

ALEXANDER, Lewis &
Elizabeth Patterson; 1
Aug 1808 (SpB)

ALEXANDER, Philip &
Sarah Hooe; 11 Nov 1726
(StM)

ALEXANDER, Robert (s/o
Robert Alexander) & Ann
Fowke (d/o Gerard Fowke
of Maryland); 1710
(StM)

ALEXANDER, Thomas C. &
Betsey Innes; Jun 1805
(FM)

ALEXANDER, William &
Sigismunda Mary Massey;
18 Apr 1765 (StM)

ALIAS, John & Mary
ONeal; 17 Sep 1722
(StM)

ALLAN, Archibald &
Penelope Skinner; 26
Dec 1722 (StM)

ALLAN, Francis &
Katherine Campbell; 17
Nov 1747 (StM)

ALLASON, William & Anne
Hooe; 26 Jun 1772 (StM)

ALLEN, Andrew & Alice
Sebastian; 12 Feb 1750
or 1751 (StM)

ALLEN, James & Betsy
Smith (d/o William
Smith); 24 Jul 1800
(FM)

ALLEN, James & Patsy
Woolfolk; 23 Sep 1787
(OB)

ALLEN, James & S. Hurst
(w/o Kemp Hurst); 1 May
1800 (FM)

ALLEN, John & Sarah
Head; 22 Dec 1808 (OM)

ALLEN, Richard & Nancy
Jones; 4 Feb 1788 (StM)

ALLEN, William &
Bridget Withers; 15 Feb
1743 (StM)

ALLEN, William &
Elizabeth Wallace (d/o
James Wallace); 12 Aug
1801 (OB)

ALLEN, William &
Elizabeth Wallace (d/o
James Wallace); 13 Aug
1801 (OM)

ALLEN, William &
Souritia A. Badger; [No
Date] (SpM)

ALLENTHORPE, Benjamin &
Elizabeth Fletcher; 19
Aug 1746 (StM)

ALLENTHORPE, John & Ann
Sebastian; 16 Apr 1723
(StM)

ALLISON, William & Ann
Fitzhugh; 21 Nov 1740
(StM)

ALLMAN, James & Mary
Faulconer; 26 May 1834
(SpM)

ALMOND, Henry & Joica
Faulcaner; 9 Feb 1810
(SpM)

ALMOND, Henry & Josea
Faulconer; 8 Feb 1810
(SpB)

ALSOP, Elliott &
Rebecca Alsop; 19 Dec
1801 (SpM)

ALSOP, James A. &
Elizabeth Mitchell; 14
Dec 1815 (SpM)

ALSOP, James M. & Susan
T. Beazley; 10 Feb 1848
(SpM)

ALSOP, John & Elizabeth
Conway; 30 Dec 1739
(StM)

ALSOP, John & Mary
McDonald; 20 Aug 1737
(StM)

ALSOP, John & Polly
Leavell; 23 Dec 1819
(SpM)

ALSOP, John T. & Martha
F. Holladay; 21 Dec
1848 (SpM)

ALSOP, Robert &
Elizabeth Mardus; 3 Jan
1791 (StM)

ALSOP, Thomas &
Elizabeth Wharton; 1
May 1815 (SpM)

ALSOP, William R. &
Martha D. Sadoy; 21 Nov
1850 (SpM)

ALVIS, Henry & Agnes
Armstrong; 19 Oct 1798
(OM)

AMISS, Elijah & Ann
Eliza Leavell; 20 Nov
1833 (FM)

AMMON, Thomas & Sarah
Edrington; 24 Jan 1733
or 1734 (StM)

AMOS, Joseph & Ann
Marr; 18 Apr 1798 (OB)

AMOS, Joseph & Ann
Marr; 18 Apr 1798 (OM)

AMUS, Benjamin & Nancy
Acre; 26 Feb 1796 (OB)

AMUS, Benjamin & Nancy
Acre; 26 Feb 1796 (OM)

ANCELL, Henry & Nancy
Beazley; 28 Dec 1801
(OB)

ANCELL, Robert &
Frances Pereson; 27 Aug
1804 (OB)

ANCELL, Robert &
Frances Pereson; 27 Aug
1804 (OM)

ANCROM, John & Mary
Thomas; 27 Jan 1726 or
1727 (StM)

ANDERSON, Albert &
Louisa Ann Day; 15 Jan
1829 (SpM)

ANDERSON, Benjamin &
Mary Miller (d/o John
Miller); 14 Oct 1807
(OM)

ANDERSON, Benjamin &
Mary Miller (d/o John
Miller); 14 Oct 1807
(OB)

ANDERSON, Benjamin &
Rachel Walden; 26 Nov
1812 (SpM)

ANDERSON, James &
Margaret Troy; 28 Jul
1746 (SpB)

ANDERSON, Joel & Lucy
Reddish; 30 May 1805
(OM)

ANDERSON, John & Sarah
Carney; 28 Nov 1752
(StM)

ANDERSON, John M. &
Eliza Ann Alsop; 22 Nov
1826 (SpM)

ANDERSON, Joseph & Mary
Ann Garner; 13 Apr 1795
(SpM)

ANDERSON, Nathan D. &
Milley Bell; 24 Oct
1798 (OB)

ANDERSON, Nathan D. &
Milly Bell; 24 Oct 1798
(OM)

ANDERSON, Nathaniel &
Lucy Crawford; 21 Aug
1805 (SpM)

ANDERSON, Thomas W. &
Jane P. Alsop; 23 Apr
1827 (SpM)

ANDERSON, William &
Lucy Hawkins (d/o
Reubin Hawkins); 22 May
1809 (OB)

ANDERSON, William &
Lucy Hawkins (d/o
Reubin Hawkins);25 May
1809 (SpM)

ANGELL, John & Milly
Harvey; 5 Oct 1750
(StM)

ANGELL, Samuel & Anne
Hornbuckle; 14 Aug 1745
(StM)

ANKRUM, Joel & Verlinda
Suttle; 12 Sep 1745
(StM)

ANKRUM, William &
Margaret Colvin; 24 Dec
1734 (StM)

ANTHONY, Mark & Polly
Bowling; 17 Jun 1815
(SpB)

ANTHONY, Mark & Polly
Bowling; 20 Jun 1815
(SpM)

ARHART, Jacob & Nanny
Ballard; 21 Dec 1773
(OB)

4

ARNALL, William B. &
Jane Martin (d/o
William H. Martin); 10
Sept 1809 (OM)

ARNALL, William B. &
Jane Martin (d/o
William H. Martin); 9
Sept 1809 (OB)

ARNOLD, James &
Elizabeth Atkins; 8 Feb
1790 (OB)

ARNOLD, Anthony & Nancy
Willoughby; 4 Aug 1801
(SpM)

ARNOLD, George & Sarah
White (of King George
Co.); 9 Nov 1758 (StM)

ARNOLD, Thomas & Peggy
Sanford; 27 Jan 1802
(OB)

ARNOLD, Thomas & Peggy
Sanford; 28 Jan 1802
(OM)

ARNOLD, Willis &
Margeret Golden; 23 Jul
1804 (OB)

ASBERRY, John & Jean
Boalin; 25 Feb 1745
(StM)

ASBURY, Thomas & Martha
Jennings; 1 Dec 1751
(StM)

ASBURY, William & Jean
Ankerum; 13 Jan 1749
(StM)

ASHBURN, John & Susanna
Arnold; 29 Jan 1804
(SpM)

ASHBY, Elias & Winifred
Million; 4 Sep 1745
(StM)

ASHBY, John & Jean
Combs; 11 May 1741
(StM)

ASHBY, John & Sarah
McCullough; 26 Feb 1756
(StM)

ASHBY, Thomas & Mary
McCullough; 14 Nov 1751
(StM)

ASHMORE, William &
Nancy Edrington; 14 Jan
1781 (StM)

ASHTON, Charles & Sarah
Butler; 22 Sep 1733
(StM)

ASHTON, Henry & Jane
Alexander; 23 Feb 1748
or 1749 (StM)

ASHTON, John &
Elizabeth Jackson; 16
May 1766 (StM)

ASHTON, Lawrence &
Elizabeth Ashton; 19
Apr 1768 (StM)

ASHTON, Lawrence &
Hannah Gibbons Dade
(d/o Horatio & Mary
Dade); Feb 1779 (StM)

ATCHISON, Adam &
Elizabeth Byram; 20 Oct
1742 (StM)

ATKINS, Edward &
Frankie Wisdom; 25 Jan
1780 (OB)

ATKINS, Gentre &
Frankey Chiles; 24 Dec
1801 (OB)

ATKINS, Gentry &
Frankey Giles; 24 Dec
1801 (OM)

ATKINS, Hezekiah &
Sally Chiles ; 23 Nov
1788 (OB)

ATKINS, James & Amey
Pigg; 29 Apr 1777 (OB)

ATKINS, James &
Elizabeth Poe; 6 Apr
1792 (OB)

ATKINS, James &
Elizabeth Poe; 6 Apr
1792 (OM)

ATKINS, James & Fanny
Atkins; 2 Nov 1803 (OM)

ATKINS, James & Lucy
Reynold; 1811 (SpM)

ATKINS, James Jr. &
Fanny Atkins; 22 Nov
1803 (OB)

ATKINS, John & Ann
Burrass (d/o Edmund
Burrass) ; 9 Feb 1778
(OB)

ATKINS, John & Ann
Burrus (d/o Edmund
Burrus); 11 Feb 1778
(OM)

ATKINS, John & Peggy
Campbell; 20 Dec 1806
(OB)

ATKINS, John & Peggy
Campbell; 20 Dec 1806
(OM)

ATKINS, Jonathan &
Milley Quisenberry; 10
Dec 1812 (OB)

ATKINS, Jonathan &
Milly Quisenberry; 10
Dec 1812 (SpM)

ATKINS, Jonathan &
Milly Quisenberry (d/o

George Quisenberry); 7
Feb 1813 (OM)

ATKINS, Joseph & Ann
Atkins; 9 Jan 1787 (OB)

ATKINS, Joseph & Mary
M. Dickenson; 21 Nov
1813 (SpM)

ATKINS, Joseph & Milly
James; 22 Sept 1775
(OB)

ATKINS, Mallachi &
Sally Montacue; 7 Jun
1797 (OB)

ATKINS, Mallachi &
Sally Montague; 7 Jun
1797 (OM)

ATKINS, Silence &
Frances Jennings (d/o
John Jennings); 1 Mar
1786 (OB)

ATKINS, Waller & Sally
Atkins; 16 Jan 1803
(OB)

ATKINS, Waller & Sally
Atkins; 16 Jan 1803
(OM)

ATKINS, William &
Wintifred Bryant; 4 Feb
1777 (OB)

ATKINS, Wisdom & Nancy
Atkins; 24 Oct 1800
(OM)

ATKINS, Wisdom & Nancy
Atkins; 24 Sep 1800
(OB)

ATKINSON, Thomas &
Sally Sylvie (d/o Sarah
Silby); 19 Jan 1802
(OB)

ATWOOD, Barnard &
Francel Conaor; 6 Aug
1805 (SpM)

AUSBUM, Robert & Milly
Cudden; 27 Feb 1775
(OB)

AUSTIN, David & Fanny
Williams; 22 Dec 1810
(OB)

AUSTIN, David (s/o
Nancy Austin of
Albemarle Co., Va) &
Fanny Williams (d/o
John Williams); 27 Dec
1810 (OM)

AUSTIN, John & Gestina
Burrus; 24 Dec 1807
(OM)

AUSTIN, John, & Justina
Burrus; 24 Dec 1807
(OM)

AUSTIN, RIchard & Mary
Snow; 25 Dec 1804 (OM)

BABER, Benjamin &
Mildred Berry (of King
George Co.); 10 Nov
1791 (StM)

BABER, Robert & Nancy
Spradling (d/o David
Spradling); 17 Dec 1782
(OB)

BABER, Robert & Nancy
Spradling (d/o David
Spradling);9 Jun 1797
(OB)

BABER, Robert & Nancy
Spradling; 9 Jun 1797
(OM)

BÄECKMAN, John &
Rebecca Hancock (d/o
William Hancock); 24
Jun 1809 (OB)

BAILEN, Peter & Martha
Parker; 6 Aug 1738
(StM)

BAILES, Joseph & Cency
Olliver (d/o Frances
Olliver); 14 Oct 1807
(OB)

BAILES, Joseph & Cency
Olliver; 16 Oct 1807
(OM)

BAILEY, John & Sarah
Frank; 6 Jan 1745 or
1746 (StM)

BAILEY, Lewis & Lucy
Mallory; 18 Nov 1801
(OM)

BAILEY, Thomas T. &
Catherine L.
Wiglesworth; 14 Oct
1829 (SpM)

BAILEY, William P. &
Mary L. Grimes (21
years old); 28 Oct 1800
(OB)

BAILEY, William P. &
Mary Lee Grymes; 28 Oct
1800 (OM)

BAILY, James & Nancy
Mallory; 2 Jun 1805
(OM)

BAKER, John & Rebecca
Sansford; 8 Jun 1747
(StM)

BAKER, John & Sarah
Walker; 30 Oct 1725
(StM)

BALL, George C. & Eliza
Jane Pollard; 28 Sep
1835 (SpM)

BALL, James C. &
Elizabeth C. Pulliam; 3
Jun 1840 (SpM)

7

BALLAD, Medley & Jane Dehoney (d/o Thomas & Hannah Dehoney); 25 Ddec 1797 (OM)

BALLARD, Larkin & Elizabeth Gaines (d/o Sally Gaines); 13 Jan 1786 (OB)

BALLARD, Medley & Jane Dehoney (d/o Thomas & Hanner Dehoney); 25 Dec 1797 (OB)

BALLARD, Thomas & Elizabeth Smith; 8 Mar 1778 (OB)

BALLARD, Washing & Elizabeth Thornhill; 5 Oct 1802 (OM)

BALLARD, William & Mary Snow; 7 Mar 1795 (OM)

BALMAINE, Alexander & Lucy Taylor (d/o Erasmus Taylor); 30 Oct 1786 (OB)

BANKS, Gerard James (s/o Adam Banks of Madison Co., Va) & Ann Davis; 17 Jan 1805 (OM)

BANNISTER, Nathan & Anne Eaves; 24 May 1752 (StM)

BANTON, William & Sarah Hamm; 1 Dec 1730 (StM)

BARBEE, Thomas & Margaret Fant; 29 Sep 1748 (StM)

BARBER, James & Susannah Dickerson; 5 Sep 1779 (StM)

BARBER, Robert & Penelope Gorman; 26 Oct 1747 (StM)

BARBER, Thomas & Mary Taylor; 22 Mar 1787 (OB)

BARBOUR, Ambrose & Catharine Thomas; 24 Sep 1773 (OB)

BARBOUR, James & Lucy Johnson; 15 Oct 1795 (OB)

BARBOUR, James & Lucy Johnson; 20 Oct 1795 (OM)

BARBOUR, Philip C.S. & Peggy Pollock (d/o William Pollock); 28 Nov 1808 (OB)

BARBOUR, Philip C.S. & Peggy Pollock; 29 Nov 1808 (OM)

BARBOUR, Philip Pendleton & Frances T. Johnson; 24 Sep 1804 (OB)

BARBOUR, Philip Pendleton & Frances T. Johnson; 4 Oct 1804 (OM)

BARBOUR, Richard & Mary Moore; 22 Mar 1796 (OB)

BARBOUR, Richard & Mary Moore; 22 Mar 1796 (OM)

BARBOUR, Thomas & Mary Thomas; _____ between 1771 & 1774 (OM)

BARKER, James & Sarah Mazes (w/o ?); 12 Jul 1791 (OM)

BARKER, Leonard &
Keturah Robinson (d/o
Francis Robinson); 29
Jan 1810 (SpM)

BARKER, Leonard &
Keturah Robinson; 29
Jan 1810 (OB)

BARKSDALE, Nathaniel &
Anne Douglas; 24 Sep
1772 (OB)

BARKSDALE, Nathaniel &
Anne Douglas; 24 Sep
1772 (OM)

BARLEY, George & Hannah
Jenkins; 27 Mar 1805
(SpM)

BARNETT, William &
Elizabeth Carrer; 1771
(OM)

BARNFATHER, Rehobeth &
Elizabeth Leg; 31 Dec
1724 (StM)

BARRADALL, Edward &
Sarah Fitzhugh; 5 Jan
1735 or 1736 (StM)

BARRET, Richard & Joyce
Duncan; 21 Sep 1729
(StM)

BARRETT, William & Mary
Hudson; 30 Dec 1785
(StM)

BARRINGTON, Timothy &
Mary Robins; 15 Oct
1731 (StM)

BARRY, Thomas &
Catherine Jones; 5 Aug
1749 (StM)

BASNIT, Isaac & Mary
Rhodes; 18 May 1745
(StM)

BATEMAN, John & Ann
Williams; 4 Feb 1740 or
1741 (StM)

BATEMAN, Thomas &
Winifred Kelly; 7 Feb
1771 (StM)

BATES, Reuben & Sarah
Pestridge; 4 Dec 1757
(StM)

BATES, William & Nancy
Hewlett; 17 Nov 1840
(FB)

BATEY, Simson &
Elizabeth McCarty; 24
Dec 1747 (StM)

BATLEY, Alford & Mishel
Wright; 26 Feb 1810
(OB)

BATTAILE, Lawrence &
Ann Hay Taliaferro; 9
Jun 1790 (OB)

BATTALEY, Morley &
Elizabeth Taliaferro;
22 Oct 1728 (SpB)

BATTOO, James & Winny
Holliday; 12 Feb 1747
(StM)

BAXTER, Alexander &
Mary Byram; 28 Nov 1751
(StM)

BAXTER, James & Anne
Brisse; 7 Jun 1767
(StM)

BAXTER, James & Sally
Payne; 31 Jul 1812 (OB)

BAXTER, James & Sally
Payne; 31 Jul 1812
(SpM)

BAXTER, James & Sarah
Sims; 20 Oct 1764 (StM)

BAXTER, John &
Elizabeth McCalley; 16
Dec 1819 (SpB)

BAXTER, John &
Elizabeth McCalley; 17
Dec 1819 (SpM)

BAXTER, John & Salley
Holloway; 5 Jan 1816
(SpM)

BAXTER, John & Sally
Holloway; 4 Jan 1816
(SpB)

BAXTER, William & Mary
Rallings; 1 Apr 1735
(StM)

BAYLIS, John & Mary
Baylis; 8 Oct 1747
(StM)

BAYLOR, Richard & Ann
T. Richards; 4 Apr 1810
(SpB)

BAYNE, Thomas & Sarah
Bowling; 21 Jan 1825
(SpM)

BAYNHAM, William &
Polly DeBaptist; 13 Jul
1815 (FB)

BAYSE, Thomas Pope & H.
Tuberville; May 1804
(FM)

BEACH, Bailey & Nancy
Vaughn (d/o James
Vaughn); 12 Jan 1793
(OB)

BEACH, George &
Susannah Duke; 23 Dec
1753 (StM)

BEACH, Henry & Delila
True (d/o Martin True);
21 Dec 1803 (OB)

BEACH, Henry & Delila
True; 27 Dec 1803 (OM)

BEADLES, John Jr. &
Lucinda Haynes (d/o
Jasper Haynes); 17 Dec
1810 (OB)

BEADLES, Robert M.
Sarah Winslow; 12 Jan
1807 (OB)

BEALE, William C. &
Jane B. Harrison; 17
Feb 1834 (FB)

BEALE, William Jr. &
Hannah Gordon (d/o John
& Hannah Gordon); 30
Mar 1786 (OB)

BEASLEY, Addison &
Frances Beasley; 3 Jun
1835 (SpM)

BEASLEY, Bennett & Mary
Bryan; 24 Jul 1797 (OB)

BEASLEY, Henry &
Elizabeth Clemons; 3
Nov 1835 (SpM)

BEASLEY, John & Sally
Eaves; 9 Jun 1791 (OM)

BEASLEY, John (s/o
Augustine Beasley) &
Sally Eaves (d/o
William Eaves); 8 Jun
1791 (OB)

BEATTIE, Daniel &
Susannah Rogers; 2 Aug
1781 (StM)

BEATTIE, John & Ann
Whiting; 10 Sep 1779
(StM)

BEAZLEY, Addison &
Frances Beazley; 3 Jun
1835 (SpM)

BEAZLEY, Augustine &
Jane Carnal; 7 Feb 1826
(SpM)

BEAZLEY, Charles &
Belindia McKenney; 7
Apr 1817 (SpM)

BEAZLEY, Charles &
Elizabeth Wait; 1 Oct
1792 (OB)

BEAZLEY, Charles &
Elizabeth Wait; 30 Oct
1792 (OM)

BEAZLEY, Charles &
Julianna Mitchell; 25
Dec 1818 (SpM)

BEAZLEY, Charles A. &
Mary S. Alsop; 3 Aug
1848 (SpM)

BEAZLEY, Henry &
Elizabeth Duerson; 1807
(SpM)

BEAZLEY, Henry &
Harriet A. Weber; 6 Dec
1849 (SpM)

BEAZLEY, James M. &
Mary B. Carpenter; 6
Mar 1827 (SpM)

BEAZLEY, John & Lucy
Porter (d/o Abner
Porter); 18 Dec 1802
(OB)

BEAZLEY, John & Lucy
Porter; 23 Dec 1802
(OM)

BEAZLEY, John George &
Sarah E. Long; 24 Jul
1845 (SpM)

BEAZLEY, Thomas & Ann
Beazley; 1 Jan 1835
(SpM)

BEAZLEY, Valentine &
Franky Powell (d/o
Joice Powell); 21 Jun
1803 (OB)

BEAZLEY, Valentine &
Franky Powell; 30 Jun
1803 (OM)

BEAZLEY, Walter A. &
Catharine E. Abbott; 24
Dec 1845 (SpM)

BEAZLEY, William &
Betsy Powell (d/o
Benjamin Powell); 25
Dec 1797 (OB)

BEAZLEY, William &
Betsy Powell(d/o
Benjamin Powell); 25
Dec 1797 (OM)

BECK, Morris B. & Sarah
A. Hansen; 5 Mar 1847
(FB)

BECKETT, Richard &
Nancy Thornhill; 26 Dec
1805 (OM)

BECKHAM, Abner &
Frances Thomas (d/o
Elizabeth Thomas); 21
Dec 1791 (OB)

BECKHAM, Abner &
Frances Thomas (d/o
Elizabeth Thomas); 21
Dec 1791 (OM)

BECKHAM, James A. &
Frances J. Alcocke; 23
May 1837 (FB)

BECKLEY, John & Clara
Webb; 11 Oct 1843 (FB)

BECKMAN, John & Rebecca
Hancock (d/o William
Hancock); 25 Jun 1809
(OM)

BECKWITH, A.B. &
Adelade B. Carter; 12
Jul 1830 (FB)

BECKWITH, Barnes &
Elizabeth Cox; 26 Jan
1826 (FB)

BEDFORD, John &
Margaret Golding; 8 Aug
1729 (StM)

BEDINGER, Daniel &
Catharine H. Berry; 23
May 1837 (FB)

BEEDLE, John &
Elizabeth Cassen; 16
Mar 1777 (OB)

BEGOLEY, Jacob &
Elizabeth Boan; 4 Aug
1746 (StM)

BELL, Brockman &
Rebecca Brockman (d/o
John Brockman); 17 Sep
1810 (OB)

BELL, Brockman &
Rebecca Brockman (d/o
John Brockman); 17 Sep
1810 (OM)

BELL, Christopher & Ann
Proudlove; 4 Jun 1726
(StM)

BELL, Francis H. &
Sarah B. Wood; 14 May
1832 (FB)

BELL, George & Anne
Hanson; 15 Apr 1745
(StM)

BELL, Henry & Susanna
Adkins (d/o John &
Nancy Adkins); 19 Sep
1796 (OM)

BELL, Henry & Susanna
Adkins (probably d/o

John & Nancy Adkins
Jr.); 19 Sep 1796 (OB)

BELL, Jacob & Martha H.
Taliaferro (d/o Ann
Taliaferro of Madison
Co., Va.); 4 Jan 1808
(OM)

BELL, John & Fanny
Minton (d/o John
Minton); 4 Dec 1804
(OB)

BELL, John & Judith
Burnley; 3 Jul 1787
(OB)

BELL, Patrick & Polly
Quisenberry; 13 May
1793 (OB)

BELL, Patrick & Polly
Quisenberry; 13 May
1793 (OM)

BELL, Robert & Anne T.
Shenk; 6 Apr 1810 (OM)

BELL, Thomas & Mary
Latham; 25 Jun 1741
(StM)

BELL, Thomas & Sally
Burnley; 28 Dec 1795
(OB)

BELL, Thomas & Sally
Burnley; 28 Dec 1795
(OM)

BELL, Thomas & Sarah
Milburn; 19 Nov 1804
(OM)

BELL, Thomas Jr. & Lucy
Reynolds (d/o Elizabeth
Reynolds); 30 Mar 1799
(OM)

BELL, Thomas Jr. & Lucy
Reynolds (d/o William &
Elizabeth Reynolds); 30
Mar 1799 (OB)

BELL, William &
Elizabeth Cave Johnson
(w/o ? ; d/o Benjamin
Cave); 23 Feb 1786 (OB)

BELL, William & Fanny
Boston (d/o Reubin
Boston); 16 Nov 1803
(OM)

BELL, William & Rhoda
Atkins (d/o John &
Susannah Atkins); 21
Dec 1795 (OB)

BELL, William & Rhoda
Atkins (d/o John &
Susannah Atkins); 24
Dec 1795 (OM)

BELL, William (s/o John
Bell) & Fanny Boston
(d/o Reubin Boston); 16
Nov 1803 (OB)

BENDEN, Jere & Mary
Meredith; 24 Oct 1838
(FB)

BENGER, Elliot &
Dorothea Brayne; 4 Jan
1733 (SpB)

BENNET, Cossom &
Katherine Bunbury; 7
Jan 1742 or 1743 (StM)

BENNET, James &
Elizabeth Hubbud; 10
Dec 1731 (StM)

BENNET, Nicholas &
Elizabeth Knight; 12
Jun 1749 (StM)

BENNETT, Charles & Ann
Dunn; 27 Dec 1782 (FB)

BENNETT, William & Mary
Johnston; 9 Nov 1782
(StM)

BENSON, Enoch & Mary
Doial; 15 Feb 1756
(StM)

BENSON, John & Jane
Lewis (w/o James
Lewis); Oct 1802 (FM)

BENSON, John B. &
Christiana Yates Day; 3
Feb 1813 (FB)

BENTLEY, William & Jane
Bussey; 14 Mar 1765
(StM)

BENTON, William & Sarah
Hyde; 18 Dec 1818 (SpB)

BENTON, William & Sarah
Hyde; 18 Dec 1818 (SpM)

BERKLEY, Edmund & Mary
R. L. Brooke; 3 Oct
1826 (SpM)

BERNARD, Richard &
Elizabeth Storke; 29
Aug 1729 (StM)

BERNARD, William, &
Winifred Thornton; 25
Nov 1750 (StM)

BERNARDO, William &
Sarah Dykes; 15 Aug
1814 (FB)

BERRIS, N.P. & J.H.
Stevenson; 7 Oct 1844
(FB)

BERRY, Enoch &
Dulcebella Bunbury; 12
Dec 1726 (StM)

BERRY, Enoch & Judith
Fowke (of King George
Co.); 23 Nov 1791 (StM)

BERRY, James &
Elizabeth Griffin; 19
Aug 1747 (StM)

BERRY, James & Grace
Powell; 28 May 1723
(StM)

BERRY, John J. & Mary
W. Lucas; 3 Feb 1835
(FB)

BERRY, Lawrence W. &
Ann Scott; 17 Nov 1825
(FB)

BERRY, Nimrod & Sarah
Penn; 2 Mar 1802 (SpM)

BERRY, Thomas &
Elizabeth Washington;
19 Nov 1758 (StM)

BERRY, Thomas & Sarah
Gardiner; 21 Oct 1784
(StM)

BERRY, Thomas J. & Mary
Hill; 29 Dec 1829 (FB)

BERRY, William & Anne
Portch; 26 Jan 1754
(StM)

BERRY, William S. &
Rachel Row (d/o Thomas
Row); 11 Feb 1807 (OM)

BERRYMAN, Newton (of
Port Royal) & A.
Hipkins (d/o Leroy
Hipkins of "Golden
Vale"); 4 Apr 1799 (FM)

BERRYMAN, William &
Rebecca Vowles; 10 Sep
1743 (StM)

BERTON, John & Missouri
Simpson; 1 Feb 1831
(SpM)

BERTON, John & Missouri
Simpson; 31 Jan 1831
(SpB)

BETHANY, Thomas & Mary
Ann Croswell; 21 Dec
1755 (StM)

BETHEL, William & Jean
Hurst; 26 Dec 1739
(StM)

BETTSON, Thomas & Jane
Merringham; 14 Apr 1748
(StM)

BEVERLEY, James G. &
Adriana L. Szymanski;
21 Nov 1850 (SpM)

BIBB, Thomas & Sarah
Brockman (d/o Samuel
Brockman Jr.); 14 Sep
1785 (OB)

BICKERS, George & Nance
Mallory; 25 Nov 1791
(OM)

BICKERS, George & Nancy
Mallory; 22 Nov 1791
(OB)

BICKERS, Joel & Rosanna
Atkins (d/o John
Atkins); 19 Mar 1805
(OB)

BICKERS, Joel & Rosanna
Atkins (d/o John
Atkins); 20 Mar 1805
(OM)

BICKERS, John & Nancy
Landrum; 5 Nov 1788
(OB)

BICKERS, William &
Sally Leathers; 3 Jun
1794 (OB)

BIDDLE, Thomas &
Bridget Amely; 5 Feb
1758 (StM)

BILLINGSLEY, Zachariah
& Amanda M. Furnley; 1
Nov 1821 (SpM)

BINGREY, John & Ruth M. Knight; 4 Jan 1783 (FB)

BINNS, Charles & Anne Alexander; 4 Oct 1759 (StM)

BIRCH, Justinian & Behethland Dade; 30 Jun 1777 (StM)

BISHOP, Joseph & Ann Clark (d/o John & Mary Clark); 28 Mar 1791 (OB)

BISHOP, Joseph & Ann Clark; 31 Mar 1791 (OM)

BISHOP, Joseph & Jane Terrell; 28 Sep 1793 (OB)

BISHOP, Joseph & Jane Terrell; 29 Mar 1793 (OM)

BLACK, Andrew & Elizabeth A.D. Payne; 22 Jan 1839 (SpM)

BLACK, Andrew & Sarah E. Duerson; 25 Jun 1846 (SpM)

BLACK, Michael & Sarah Radford; 3 Dec 1752 (StM)

BLACK, William & Anne Dent; 17 Oct 1745 (StM)

BLACKBURN, Edward & Margaret Harrison; 26 May 1757 (StM)

BLACKBURN, Thomas R. & Mary Ann H. Wright; 5 Apr 1817 (FB)

BLACKERBY, Thaddeus & Jane Marshall (d/o

Merrineau Marshall); 4 Dec 1795 (OM)

BLACKERLY, Thaddeus & Jane Marshall (d/o Merryman Marshall); 4 Dec 1795 (OB)

BLACKERLY, Thomas & Elizabeth Herring (d/o Thomas Harring); 23 Dec 1801 (OB)

BLACKERLY, Thomas & Elizabeth Herring; 24 Dec 1801 (OM)

BLACKFORD, William M. & Mary B. Minor; 12 Oct 1825 (FB)

BLACKWELL, Leland & Nancy Burton (d/o William Burton); 1 Sep 1810 (OB)

BLACKWELL, Leland & Nancy Burton; 11 Oct 1810 (OM)

BLAIR, James & Helen Shepherd (d/o Andrew Shepherd of Orange Co.) May 1791 (FM)

BLAIR, James & Helen Shepherd; 27 Apr 1791 (OB)

BLAIR, John & Elizabeth Smith; 10 Dec 1773 (OB)

BLAKE, John & Elizabeth Thurston; 12 Dec 1741 (SpB)

BLAKE, Robert N. & Mary Ann Anderson; 10 Jul 1848 (FB)

BLAKEY, James & Nancy Branham (d/o Robert Branham); 22 Oct 1807 (OB)

BLAKEY, James & Nancy Branham; 11 Nov 1807 (OM)

BLAKEY, John & Sarah Cowherd (d/o Jonathan Cowherd); 30 Oct 1780 (OB)

BLAKEY, Reubin & Polly Strother; 12 Feb 1807 (OM)

BLAKEY, William & Elizabeth Davis (w/o ?); 18 Jan 1798 (OB)

BLAKEY, William & Elizabeth Davis; 18 Jan 1797 (OM)

BLAKEY, Yelverton C. & Judith Burton (d/o Capt. May Burton); 26 Oct 1803 (OB)

BLAND, Moses & Jane Wiggonton; 14 Jan 1750 (StM)

BLAND, Theodorick & Sarah Fitzhugh; 5 Dec 1772 (StM)

BLANKMAN, Mitchell A. & Jane B. Crawford; 20 Jul 1843 (FB)

BLANTON, John & Mary Grady (d/o Nathaniel Sanders); 29 Mar 1792 (OM)

BLANTON, John & Mary Grady; 9 Mar 1792 (OB)

BLAXTON, ___ & Mary Dade; 10 Oct 1777 (StM)

BLEDSOE, John & Margaret Perry; 1 Mar 1815 (OB)

BLEDSOE, John & Margaret Perry; 1 Mar 1815 (SpM)

BLEDSOE, John & Susanna Pitcher (d/o William Pitcher, Sr.); 14 Dec 1809 (OB)

BLEDSOE, John & Susanna Pitcher (d/o William Pitcher, Sr.); 14 Dec 1809 (OM)

BLEDSOE, John (s/o Aaron Bledsoe) & Polly Dear (d/o Thomas Dear); 5 Jun 1797 (OB)

BLEDSOE, John (s/o Aaron Bledsoe) & Polly Dear (d/o Thomas Dear); 5 Jun 1797 (OM)

BLEDSOE, Moses & Ann Perry; 10 Oct 1777 (OB)

BLEDSOE, William & Sally Morton (d/o Elijah Morton); 21 Jul 1785 (OB)

BLEWER, John & Lucy McCoy; 6 Jan 1808 (SpM)

BLINKENSHOP, George & Jane Butler; 12 Feb 1739 or 1740 (StM)

BLOWS, George (of Augusta Co.) & Catharina Feen; 12 Sep 1773 (OB)

BLOXTON, Robert & Louisa Brown; 12 Dec 1836 (FB)

BLOXTON, Zach. & Arabella Ad; 28 Jun 1837 (FB)

BLUGDES, Hugh F. & Mary
F. Coleman; 15 Aug 1850
(SpM)

BOGGS, Lewis & Mary A.
L. Scott; 16 Feb 1837
(SpM)

BOGGS, Lewis A. & Eliza
Hart; 6 Dec 1831 (SpM)

BOGGS, Lewis Alexander
& Elizabeth Rawlings; 5
May 1841 (SpM)

BOHANNON, Thomas &
Lavinia Marquess (d/o
John Marquess); 31 Mar
1799 (OM)

BOHANNON, Thomas &
Levina Marquess (d/o
John Marquess); 26 Mar
1799 (OB)

BOHANNON, Thomas &
Levina Marquess; 31 Mar
1799 (OM)

BOHANNON, Tom & Sally
Smith; 30 Nov 1815
(SpM)

BOLING, John Jr. &
Cusannah Bell; 19 Apr
1791 (OB)

BOLING, William & Phebe
Hawkins (probably d/o
Phebe Hawkins); 1 Oct
1788 (OB)

BOOTH, Joseph & Polly
Grace (d/o George
Grace); 5 Mar 1792 (OB)

BOOTH, Joseph & Polly
Grace (d/o George
Grace); 5 Mar 1792 (OM)

BOOTH, Thomas &
Behethlem Berryman; 10
Oct 1727 (StM)

BOOTON,(aka BOSTON)
Reubin & Mary Anderson
(d/o Jacob Anderson);
18 Dec 1809 (OB)

BOOTON,(aka BOSTON)
Reubin & Mary Anderson;
21 Dec 1809 (OM)

BOSTON, George &
Elizabeth Vaughn; 11
May 1796 (OB)

BOSTON, George &
Elizabeth Vaughn; 11
May 1796 (OM)

BOSTON, John & Frankey
Petty (d/o George
Petty); 19 Mar 1793
(OB)

BOSTON, John & Sarah
Mosley; 13 Jan 1803
(OM)

BOSTON, Reubin & Sarah
Hawkins; 13 Sep 1783
(OB)

BOSTON, Robert & Lucy
Wright; 30 Jan 1778
(OB)

BOSWEL, James & Mary
Stuart; 6 Apr 1744
(StM)

BOSWELL, Charles & Lucy
Thompson; 31 Mar 1795
(OB)

BOSWELL, Charles & Lucy
Thompson; 31 Mar 1795
(OM)

BOTT, John & Susanna C.
Spotswood; 1 Apr 1802
(OB)

BOTTS, Thomas H. & Ann
C. Willis; 24 Oct 1822
(SpM)

BOTTS, Thomas H. & Mary S. Stone; 10 Oct 1828 (FB)

BOUBER, Peter & Lucinda Bowling; 3 Jan 1828 (SpM)

BOUCHARD, William & Mary Stringfellow; 12 Nov 1751 (StM)

BOURNE, Ambrose & Jane Newman (d/o Frances Newman); 22 Feb 1796 (OB)

BOURNE, Ambrose & Jane Newman (d/o Frances Newman); 5 Mar 1796 (OM)

BOURNE, Francis & Frances Christopher; 2 Jan 1757 (OB)

BOWCOCK, Tandy & Judith Douglass (d/o John Douglass); 25 Nov 1799 (OB)

BOWCOCK, Tandy & Judith Douglass; 26 Nov 1799 (OM)

BOWEN, Francis & Frances Christopher; 2 Jan 1757 (OB)

BOWEN, William & Elizabeth Young; 23 Jun 1825 (FB)

BOWER, P. Alexander & E.M. Rathcock; 10 Dec 1846 (FB)

BOWER, Thomas & Margaret Landrum; 15 Sep 1789 (OB)

BOWIE, James P. & Mary Ann Bradshaw; 16 Sep 1788 (StM)

BOWKOR, Parmonas & Ann Stevens; 29 Dec 1744 (SpB)

BOWLES, Liddall & Sarah Price; 17 Mar 1824 (SpM)

BOWLES, Thomas & Sarah Rawlings; 25 Jan 1825 (SpM)

BOWLIN, James S. & Betsy Newton; 2 Apr 1801 (SpM)

BOWLIN, Simon & Elizabeth Newport; 5 Jun 1728 (StM)

BOWLINE, Benjamin & Mary Lathram; 27 Jul 1725 (StM)

BOWLINE, David & Jane Pilsher; 10 Sep 1741 (StM)

BOWLINE, Samuel & Elizabeth Oxford; 8 Oct 1731 (StM)

BOWLINE, Simon & Ann Newton; 5 Dec 1722 (StM)

BOWLINE, William & Elizabeth Kidwell; 7 Sep 1726 (StM)

BOWLINE, William & Sarah Kirk; 24 Jun 1726 (StM)

BOWLING, Charles & Sarah McKenney (d/o William McKenney); 10 Oct 1791 (OB)

BOWLING, Charles & Sarah McKenney; 13 Oct 1791 (OM)

BOWLING, Daniel &
Elizabeth Scott; 2 Apr
1825 (SpM)

BOWLING, Daniel &
Elizabeth Scott; 4 Apr
1815 (SpB)

BOWLING, Elijah &
Letitia Davis; 23 Dec
1847 (FB)

BOWLING, Francis &
Maria Cooper; 2 Dec
1845 (FB)

BOWLING, Henry & Sarah
Harris; 11 May 1850
(FB)

BOWLING, James & Mary
Overhall; 11 Feb 1750
or 1751 (StM)

BOWLING, Jesse & E.
Harrow; Dec 1802 (FM)

BOWLING, John & Mary
Ballard; 22 Aug 1773
(OB)

BOWLING, Joseph &
Pelatiah Grafford; 15
Jul 1738 (StM)

BOWLING, Lewis & Nancy
Stewart; 31 Jan 1822
(SpM)

BOWLING, Original &
Margaret French; 18 Mar
1752 (StM)

BOWLING, Richard &
Eliza Lewis; 1832 (SpM)

BOWLING, Robert & Sarah
Oliver; 19 Dec 1810
(SpB)

BOWLING, Robert & Sarah
Oliver; 21 Dec 1810
(SpM)

BOWLING, Thomas &
Rachel Colclough; 11
Nov 1729 (StM)

BOWLING, Thornton &
Elizabeth Lewis; 22 Oct
1828 (SpB)

BOWLING, Thornton &
Elizabeth Lewis; 23 Oct
1828 (SpM)

BOWMAN, Henry D. &
Julia M. Magrath; 2 Mar
1837 (FB)

BOWMAN, John &
Elizabeth Elliot; 23
Dec 1750 (StM)

BOXLEY, George &
Drucilla Graves (d/o
Isaac Graves); 16 Jan
1797 (OM)

BOXLEY, George &
Drusilla Graves (d/o
Isaac Graves); 16 Jan
1797 (OB)

BOXLEY, George & Hannah
Jinkins; 11 Mar 1805
(SpB)

BOXLEY, George Jr. &
Hannah Jenkins; 11 Mar
1805 (SpM)

BOXLEY, Thomas &
Elizabeth Cothron; 16
Feb 1815 (SpM)

BOXLEY, Thomas & Martha
Day; 1 Oct 1807 (SpM)

BOYER, Thomas & Martha
Thompson; 6 Mar 1801
(OB)

BOYER, Thomas & Martha
Thompson; 8 Mar 1801
(OM)

BOYLE, George & Mary Whiting; 2 Jun 1778 (StM)

BOZELL, Richard W. & Mary E. Staiars; 10 Sep 1840 (SpM)

BRADEN, Joseph & Polly Neale (d/o Fielding Neale); 18 Mar 1808 (OB)

BRADEN, Joseph & Polly Neale; 22 Mar 1808 (OM)

BRADFORD, Alexander & Hannah Burton (d/o Capt. May Burton); 16 Nov 1802 (OB)

BRADFORD, Alexander & Hannah Burton; 18 Nov 1802 (OM)

BRADFORD, Daniel & Mary E. Morriss; 29 Dec 1837 (FB)

BRADGER, Jesse & Franky Sulavern; 1 Dec 1798 (SpB)

BRADGER, Jesse & Franky Suliven; 5 Dec 1798 (SpM)

BRADLEY, David & Elizabeth Simson; 17 Apr 1755 (StM)

BRADLEY, George & Lucy Rice; 29 Jul 1775 (OB)

BRADLEY, James & Elizabeth Wells; 20 Oct 1803 (OM)

BRADLEY, John & Sally Hancock; 16 May 1801 (OB)

BRADLEY, John & Sally Hancock; 18 May 1801 (OM)

BRADLEY, Thomas & Sarah Carver; 8 Jan 1731 or 1732 (StM)

BRADLEY, William & Margaret Fortick; 26 Mar 1758 (StM)

BRADLEY, William & Polly Marshall; 15 Jan 1802 (OB)

BRADLEY, William & Polly Marshall; 18 Jan 1802 (OM)

BRADSHAW, Uriah & Keziah Bragg; 23 Feb 1791 (StM)

BRADSHAW, Uriah H. & Ellen B. Murray; 11 Sep 1843 (FB)

BRADSHAW, Uriah H. & Jane Wright; 7 Mar 1832 (FB)

BRAGDON, Joseph & Elizabeth Connor; 18 Jul 1825 (FB)

BRAGG, Benjamin & Polly Twentymen; 1 Sep 1785 (OB)

BRAGG, Benjamin & Polly Twentymen; 4 Sep 1785 (OM)

BRAGG, James R. & Sarah Yates; 10 Sep 1835 (SpM)

BRAGG, Moore & Jenny York; 25 Oct 1801 (OB)

BRAGG, Moore & Jenny York; 5 Nov 1801 (OM)

BRANCH, Christopher &
Katharine Stanarch; 10
Dec 1823 (SpM)

BRANHAM, Marmaduke &
Fanny Hughes (d/o
Francis Hughes); 16 Aug
1791 (OB)

BRANHAM, Marmaduke &
Fanny Hughes; 18 Aug
1791 (OM)

BRANHAM, Tavner & Polly
Sisson (d/o Sarah
Sisson); 5 Sep 1792
(OB)

BRANHAM, Tavner & Polly
Sisson (d/o Sarah
Sisson); 5 Sep 1792
(OM)

BRANSAM, Josiah &
Barbara Lindsey; 5 Aug
1742 (StM)

BRATTON, John & Jane
Parish; 20 May 1803
(SpM)

BRAXTIN, Richard F. &
Nancy Calvert; 27 May
1828 (FB)

BRAY, Patrick & Mary
Stocks (d/o Thomas
Stocks); 24 Aug 1786
(OB)

BRAY, Winter & Mary
Frances Dickey; 19 Dec
1843 (FB)

BRAZIER, Zachariah &
Elizabeth Buckner; 12
Nov 1759 (StM)

BREATHETTE, John &
Susan M. Harris; 2 Nov
1825 (SpM)

BREEDING, Ephriam &
Molly Franklin (d/o

Edward Franklin); 7 Dec
1789 (OB)

BREEDING, Richard &
Elizabeth Franklyn (d/o
Edward Franklyn); 31
Jul 1790 (OB)

BREEDLOVE, Armstead &
Mary Grady; 12 Feb 1795
(SpM)

BREEDLOVE, Armstead &
Mary Grady; 6 Feb 1795
(SpB)

BREEDLOVE, Broadus &
Nancy Dovell; 12 Jan
1809 (OM)

BREEDLOVE, Broadus &
Nancy Dovell; 3 Jan
1809 (OB)

BREEDLOVE, Madison &
Juby Buckner; 11 Feb
1784 (OB)

BREEDLOVE, Nathaniel &
Elender Mitchell; 27
Nov 1809 (OM)

BREEDWELL, Thomas (s/o
Thomas Breedwell) &
Anny Blackwell; 10 Aug
1796 (OM)

BREEDWELL, William (s/o
Thomas Breedwell) &
Anky Blackwell (w/o ?);
10 Aug 1796 (OB)

BRENT, George & Harriet
Slater; 5 May 1818 (FB)

BRENT, Kendal C. &
Polly Burton (d/o James
Burton); 30 Oct 1808
(OM)

BREWIN, William &
Catharine Newton; 24
Dec 1817 (SpM)

21

BRIANT, Jesse & Ann
Norman (of King George
Co.,Va.); 1 Jan 1790
(StM)

BRIANT, William &
Elizabeth Simpson; 21
Jun 1779 (StM)

BRIANT, William &
Ursula Burridge; 27 Feb
1782 (StM)

BRICE, John & Ann
Bullock; 24 May 1803
(SpM)

BRIDGES, Matthew & Mary
Row; 30 Dec 1795 (OM)

BRIDGES, William & Ann
Row (d/o Edmund Row); 4
Jul 1788 (OB)

BRIDWELL, ____ & Lucy
Lea; 9 Apr 1758 (StM)

BRIDWELL, Robert &
Elizabeth Jones; 13 Jan
1745 (StM)

BRIEANA, Thomas & Patsy
Harpe; 9 Sep 1819 (FB)

BRIGGS, David & Jane
McDonald; June 1771
(StM)

BRIGHTWELL, Absalom &
Winifred Pines; 24 Feb
1800 (OM)

BRIGHTWELL, Ptolemy &
Frances Todd; 15 Sep
1828 (SpB)

BRIGHTWELL, Ptolemy &
Frances Todd; 17 Sep
1828 (SpM)

BRIGHTWELL, Richard &
Katharine; before 9 Mar
1689 (StM)

BRIGHTWELL, William &
Martha Johnston; 5 Nov
1795 (SpB)

BRIGHTWELL, William &
Martha Johnston; 5 Nov
1795 (SpM)

BRIMMER, Charles &
Mayfield; 19 Aug 1785
(FB)

BRIMMER, Richard M. &
Angelina Portch; 24 Aug
1843 (FB)

BRIMMER, Zacheriah &
Lucy W. Davenport; 29
Sep 1833 (SpM)

BRISSEY, Isaiah E. &
Agnes P. Bibb; 15 Jan
1832 (FB)

BROCK, Archibald &
Sarah Moyers (d/o
Michael Moyers); 15 Mar
1813 (OM)

BROCK, Orvill & Delphia
Gatewood; 23 Nov 1818
(SpB)

BROCK, Orvill & Delphia
Gatewood; 23 Nov 1818
(SpM)

BROCK, Robert & Lucy
Todd; 15 Mar 1805 (SpB)

BROCK, Robert & Lucy
Todd; 28 Mar 1805 (SpM)

BROCK, Winfield & Sarah
Mason Webb; 12 Mar 1824
(OB)

BROCK, Winfield & Sarah
Mason Webb; 12 Mar 1824
(SpM)

BROCKMAN, Andrew &
Amelia Brockman (d/o

William Brockman); 22
Apr 1793 (OB)

BROCKMAN, Andrew &
Amelia Brockman (d/o
William Brockman); 22
Apr 1793 (OM)

BROCKMAN, Asa & Lucy E.
Quisenberry; 15 Jan
1819 (OB)

BROCKMAN, Asa & Lucy E.
Quisenberry; 15 Jan
1819 (SpM)

BROCKMAN, Bledsoe &
Elizabeth Landrum (d/o
Thomas Landrum); 2 Jun
1802 (OB)

BROCKMAN, Bledsoe &
Elizabeth Landrum (d/o
Thomas Landrum); 2 Jun
1802 (OM)

BROCKMAN, Curtis &
Nancy Quisenberry; 28
Oct 1811 (OM)

BROCKMAN, Elijah &
Sally Tomlinson; 9 Jan
1795 (OB)

BROCKMAN, Elijah &
Sally Tomlinson; 9 Jan
1795 (OM)

BROCKMAN, James & Milly
Turner; 18 Jul 1805
(OM)

BROCKMAN, James & Nancy
Bledsoe; 6 Dec 1790
(OB)

BROCKMAN, John & Nancy
Long; 2 Dec 1788 (OM)

BROCKMAN, Major & Mary
Patterson (d/o Turner &
Susannah Patterson); 9
Nov 1779 (OB)

BROCKMAN, Moses & Nelly
Brockman; 25 Apr 1796
(OB)

BROCKMAN, Moses & Nelly
Brockman; 25 Apr 1796
(OM)

BROCKMAN, Samuel Jr. &
Nancy Durrett; 24 Oct
1791 (OB)

BROCKMAN, Samuel Jr. &
Nancy Durrett; 24 Oct
1791 (OM)

BROCKMAN, William &
Mary Smith; 23 Nov 1784
(OB)

BRODERICK, Christopher
& Sarah Hammet; 19 Dec
1744 (StM)

BRONAUGH, Charles &
Mary Daniel; 23 Jan
1805 (OB)

BRONAUGH, Charles B. &
Elizabeth Brockman (d/o
William Brockman); 3
Apr 1810 (OB)

BRONOUGH, Charles B. &
Elizabeth Brockman; 3
Apr 1810 (OM)

BROOK, George & Dorothy
Taylor; 13 Mar 1789
(OM)

BROOKE, Francis T. &
Mary C. Carter; 13 Feb
1804 (FB)

BROOKE, John & Lucy
Thornton; 2 Jul 1777
(StM)

BROOKE, Richard &
Beulah; 4 Jan 1785 (FB)

BROOKE, William & M.
Smith; July 1803 (FM)

BROOKING, Robert &
Patsey Russell; 11 Apr
1788 (OM)

BROOKING, Robert &
Patsey Russell; 8 Apr
1788 (OB)

BROOKING, Samuel & Mary
Taylor; 22 Dec 1785
(OB)

BROOKING, William &
Anne Thompson; 21 Jan
1778 (OB)

BROOKS, Dabney &
Elizabeth Wren; 17 May
1832 (SpM)

BROOKS, George &
Dorothy Taylor; 13 Mar
1789 (OB)

BROOKS, Matthew & Jean
Jack; Feb 1743 (StM)

BROOKS, Matthew & Mary
Box; 23 Aug 1741 (StM)

BROOKS, Thomas &
Elizabeth Bullard; 30
Dec 1823 (SpM)

BROUGHTON, Thomas &
Sarah Kemp; 28 Oct 1786
(OB)

BROWN, Asaph &
Henrietta H. Kendall;
26 Sep 1844 (FB)

BROWN, Bartlett & Peggy
Mahoney; 14 Oct 1835
(FB)

BROWN, Carter & Judy
Evans; 17 Sep 1818 (FB)

BROWN, Charles & Martha
Cary; 5 Feb 1798 (SpM)

BROWN, Charles G. &
Ellen Douglas Ficklin;
28 Feb 1849 (FB)

BROWN, Christopher &
Judith Green; 5 Aug
1786 (FB)

BROWN, Coleman R. &
Emily M. Brown; 19 Dec
1815 (FB)

BROWN, Dr. William &
Margaret Emily Stone;
14 Dec 1814 (FB)

BROWN, Gustavus (of
Charles Co., Md.) &
Frances Fowke (d/o
Gerard Fowke; b. 2 Feb
1691); about 1711 (StM)

BROWN, Hugh & Maria
Hager; 5 May 1808 (SpM)

BROWN, James & Hannah
Mills (w/o ? from King
George Co.); 31 Jan
1786 (StM)

BROWN, James & Nancy
Harrod; 11 Nov 1788
(OB)

BROWN, James & Sarah
Waemark; 11 May 1760
(StM)

BROWN, John & Hannah
Cooke; 28 Nov 1751
(StM)

BROWN, John & Jean
Nowland; 24 Aug 1755
(StM)

BROWN, Joshua & Alice
Lunsford; 21 Jul 1754
(StM)

BROWN, Thomas & Mildred
Smith; 16 Dec 1773
(StM)

BROWN, Thomas & Nancy
Starke; 11 Dec 1804
(SpM)

BROWN, William &
Elizabeth Butler; 2 Aug
1744 (StM)

BROWN, William & Sally
Gibbs; 17 Dec 1810 (FB)

BROWNE, Charles H. &
Sophia Calhoun; 16 Nov
1842 (FB)

BROWNE, Nahum F.D. &
Julia M. Williams; 7
Sep 1844 (FB)

BROWNE, Richard L. &
Ann E. Middleton; 17
Jul 1838 (FB)

BRUCE, James & Mary M.
Bayne; 6 Jan 1825 (SpM)

BRUCE, John & Ann
Bullock; 1803 (SpM)

BRUCE, Loudoun B. &
Milly Estes; 10 Sep
1807 (OM)

BRUCE, Mordecai &
Christiana Aheart; 21
Sep 1777 (OB)

BRUCE, Robert C. & Mary
L. Young; 23 Dec 1823
(FB)

BRUCE, Willaim &
Lucinda Pollard; 20 Dec
1787 (StM)

BRUING, William &
Keziah Simmons; 4 Feb
1753 (StM)

BRUMLEY, William & Ann
Tharley; 18 May 1829
(SpM)

BRUNER, Peter & Catey
Kiblinger; 3 Aug 1801
(OB)

BRUTON, William &
Elizabeth Spiler; 5 Jun
1725 (StM)

BRYAN, Edward & Polly
Hambleton; 15 Mar 1793
(OB)

BRYAN, Richard &
Frances Battaley; 31
Jan 1749 (SpB)

BRYANT, Edward & Polly
Hambleton; 15 Mar 1793
(OM)

BRYANT, George &
Elizabeth Faulkner; 26
May 1832 (FB)

BRYANT, George &
Elizabeth Faulkner; 29
May 1832 (FM)

BRYANT, John & Sarah
Graham; 11 Dec 1768
(StM)

BRYANT, Thomas &
Frankie Thornton; 23
Dec 1775 (OB)

BUCHAMAN, William &
Florinda Brent; 18 Jul
1821 (SpM)

BUCHANAN, Andrew & Anne
Baxter; 16 Jul 1803
(FB)

BUCHANAN, James &
Elizabeth Limmit; 7 Dec
1777 (StM)

BUCK, Anthony & Mary
Shepherd; 15 Dec 1796
(OB)

BUCK, Anthony & Mary
Shepherd; 15 Dec 1796
(OM)

BUCKHANNAN, John & Mary
Smith; 27 Jan 1785 (OB)

BUCKMAN, John H. &
Susanah Day; 24 Aug
1812 (FB)

BUCKNER, Baldwin &
Fanny Burton; 12 Nov
1794 (OB)

BUCKNER, Baldwin &
Fanny Burton; 16 Nov
1794 (OM)

BUCKNER, Dr. Horace &
Mrs. Jones (w/o
Strother Jones of
Culpeper Co.) Aug 1791
(FM)

BUCKNER, George Madison
& Melinda Minor; 25 Apr
1807 (SpB)

BUCKNER, George Madison
& Melinda Minor; 30 Apr
1807 (SpM)

BUCKNER, John &
Elizabeth Washington;
21 Dec 1760 (StM)

BULLOCK, Abner & Martha
Rory Johnson; 22 Jan
1801 (SpM)

BULLOCK, Abner & Martha
Roy Johnston; 20 Jan
1801 (SpB)

BULLOCK, Isaac W. &
Henrietta L. Bullock;
Feb 1839 (SpM)

BULLOCK, James & Amanda
Terrell; Apr 1835 (SpM)

BULLOCK, Slanghton &
Louisa W. Vaughan; 23
Mar 1837 (SpM)

BULLOCK, Thomas & Susan
Swan; 15 Mar 1825 (SpM)

BULLOCK, William &
Shady F. Bullock; 24
Dec 1845 (SpM)

BULLOCK, William S. &
Harriet Stewart; 22 Jan
1847 (FB)

BUMPASS, Joseph & Nancy
Terrill; 24 May 1823
(OB)

BUNBURY, Thomas &
Behethland Massey; 30
Aug 1752 (StM)

BUNBURY, Thomas & Sarah
Broadburn; 15 Oct 1723
(StM)

BUNBURY, William &
Elizabeth Short; 16 Jan
1783 (StM)

BUNDAY, Muscoe & Ann
Maria Jackson; 1 Jul
1841 (FB)

BURBRIDGE, Moses &
Fanny Haney; 24 Dec
1798 (SpM)

BURGES, Garner & Anne
Barby; 19 Feb 1751
(StM)

BURGES, William &
Bathsheba Courtney; 19
Jan 1755 (StM)

BURGESS, Edward & ____
Price; 20 Feb 1765
(StM)

BURGESS, Joseph &
Elizabeth Douglas; 15
Jul 1749 (StM)

BURGESS, Moses &
Elizabeth Price; 30 May
1762 (StM)

BURGESS, Reuben & _____
Stribling; 1 Sep 1765
(StM)

BURK, Edward & Mary
Brightwell; 26 Apr 1810
(SpM)

BURK, John & Elizabeth
Farlow; 31 Aug 1755
(StM)

BURK, Lewis & Eliza
Ferrier; 24 Feb 1848
(FB)

BURKE, George W. &
Eliza F. Taliaferro; 28
Nov 1850 (SpM)

BURKE, Isaac & Jane
Miller; 4 Feb 1809 (OB)

BURKE, Lewis & Mary
Burnley; 30 Dec 1824
(FB)

BURKE, William &
Susanna Sweney; 1 Feb
1778 (StM)

BURKET, John & Mary
Carneby; 27 Sep 1735
(StM)

BURN, James & Catherine
Champ; 14 Oct 1748
(StM)

BURNETT, Charles &
Nancy Young; 23 Feb
1804 (SpM)

BURNETT, Thomas & Alice
Care (of Hanover); 20
Jun 1746 (StM)

BURNLEY, Garland &
Frances Taylor; 8 Nov
1779 (OB)

BURNLEY, James & Nancy
Parsons; 1 Nov 1798
(OB)

BURNLEY, James & Nancy
Parsons; 1 Nov 1798
(OM)

BURNLEY, Richard &
Elizabeth Swan Jones;
26 Jul 1772 (OB)

BURNSPLAT, Jethro &
Sarah Bagjah; 21 Oct
1729 (StM)

BURRELL, Philip & Susan
R. Wellford; 1823 (FB)

BURROUGH, Benjamin &
Mary Stevens; 21 Dec
1802 (SpM)

BURROWS, Thomas O.B. &
Lucy F. Waller; 2 Sep
1847 (FB)

BURRUS, Joseph & Nancy
Terrill; 24 May 1823
(OB)

BURRUS, Joseph & Nancy
Terrill; 24 May 1823
(SpM)

BURRUS, Roger (s/o
Thomas & Frances Tandy
Burrus) & Cynthia Mills
(d/o Nathaniel &
Frances Thompson
Mills); 8 Jan 1790 (OB)

BURRUS, Samuel & Catey
Rucker; 24 Oct 1788
(OM)

BURTON, Doctor May &
Juliette Szymanskie; 7
Dec 1847 (SpM)

BURTON, George W. &
June T. Ellery; 6 Dec
1849 (SpM)

BURTON, James & Betsy
Goodridge; 2 Apr 1799
(OB)

BURTON, James & Betsy
Goodridge; 3 Apr 1799
(OM)

BURTON, James & Mary
White (d/o Jeremiah
White); 19 Jan 1779
(OB)

BURTON, John & Milly
May; 27 Jul 1807 (OM)

BURTON, May & Sarah
Head; 29 Sep 1776 (OB)

BURTON, William & Ann
Goodrich (b.d. 14 Dec
1785); 24 Dec 1806 (OB)

BURTON, William & Ann
Goodrich; 25 Dec 1806
(OM)

BURTON, William & Sarah
Spicer; 14 Dec 1725
(StM)

BURWELL, Lewis & Maria
M. Page; 26 Sep 1808
(FB)

BUSH, Edmund &
Elizabeth Walker; 5 Sep
1798 (OM)

BUSH, Francis & Lucy
Davis; 27 Jul 1773 (OB)

BUSH, George & Mary
Ancrum; 14 Nov 1737
(StM)

BUSH, Thomas & Liddy
Breadwell; 22 Mar 1802
(OB)

BUSH, Thomas & Liddy
Breadwewll; 25 Mar 1802
(OM)

BUSHEL, John &
Elizabeth Mason; 26 Jun
1748 (StM)

BUSHROD, Washington Jr.
& Henrietta Brayne
Spotswood; 4 Aug 1806
(SpM)

BUSKIRK, V.M. & Judith
Curry; 9 Jun 1825 (FB)

BUSSELL, _____ & Sarah
Day; 5 Feb 1758 (StM)

BUSSELL, George &
Catherine Randal; 8 Jan
1754 (StM)

BUSSEY, Cornelius &
Jane Crawford; 23 Jun
1776 (StM)

BUSSEY, Cornelius &
Mary Carver; 14 Oct
1770 (StM)

BUSSEY, Henry & Jane
Jackson; 21 Nov 1758
(StM)

BUSSEY, Henry &
Margaret McCarty; 11
Jul 1741 (StM)

BUTLER, James &
Elizabeth Fleman; 18
Dec 1822 (SpM)

BUTLER, John &
Elizabeth Clement; 19
Feb 1733 or 1734 (StM)

BUTLER, Joseph & Anne
Carter; 28 Nov 1745
(StM)

BUTLER, Thomas & Ann
Baxter; 22 Sep 1742
(StM)

BUTLER, Thomas & Mary
Mason; 7 Apr 1741 (StM)

BUTLER, William & Maria
Vessells; 29 Jun 1824
(FB)

BUTLER, William I. &
Mary A.M. Bullock; 12
Dec 1848 (SpM)

BUTRIDGE, Henry &
Isabel Hodge; 30 Dec
1764 (StM)

BYRAM, Peter & Martha
Horton; 26 Mar 1758
(StM)

BYRAM, Thornton A. &
Mary E.A. Lewis; 10 Aug
1850 (FB)

BYRAM, William & Sarah
Gough; 14 May 1747
(StM)

CABLE, David & Mary
Orr; 7 Sep 1766 (StM)

CALDWELL, James H. &
Maria C. Wormeley; 25
Nov 1819 (FB)

CALDWELL, John C. &
Emily L. Phillips; 19
Mar 1834 (FB)

CALDWELL, Richard &
Caroline H. Verone; 7
Dec 1833 (FB)

CALHOUN, John & Julian
Southard; 27 Dec 1831
(FB)

CALLAHAN, Dennis &
Margaret Atkinson; 22
Dec 1786 (FB)

CALVERT, Joseph & Lucy
Webb; 17 Nov 1739 (SpB)

CAMAKAN, Willis &
Frances Chewning; 22
Oct 1829 (SpM)

CAMMACK, George &
Parshely Cox; 31 Mar
1838 (FB)

CAMMACK, John C. & June
Pendleton; 18 Jan 1844
(SpM)

CAMMACK, William & Caty
Overton; 20 Jan 1800
(SpB)

CAMMACK, William & Caty
Overton; 23 Jan 1800
(SpM)

CAMMEL, William & Mary
Smith; 25 Jul 1742
(StM)

CAMP, James & Mary
Wood; 16 Sep 1803 (OM)

CAMP, William & Frances
Willis; 1 Dec 1772 (OM)

CAMP, William (of
Culpeper Co.) & Frances
Willis; 27 Nov 1772
(OB)

CAMPBELL, Alexander &
Lucy Fitzhugh; 3 Dec
1788 (StM)

CAMPBELL, Archibald &
Rebecca Rallings; 15
Jan 1753 (StM)

CAMPBELL, Archibald &
Susannah Arnold; 1 Nov
1786 (OB)

CAMPBELL, Donald &
Eliza M. Fisher; 30 Nov
1811 (FB)

CAMPBELL, James &
Elizabeth Millener; 27
Sep 1741 (StM)

CAMPBELL, James M. &
Emma N. Gray; 4 Jun
1833 (FB)

CAMPBELL, John & Judith
Pilcher (of Hanover);
20 Aug 1746 (StM)

CAMPBELL, Robert & Ann
Maria Atkins (d/o
Spencer J. Atkins);
(OM)

CAMPBELL, Robert (fpc)
& Jane Ferguson (fpc);
26 Dec 1816 (FB)

CANNADAY, William &
Margaret Lince; 16 Jan
1747 (StM)

CANNADY, Hugh & Mildred
Hutcheson; 6 Nov 1735
(StM)

CANNON, John & Sarah
Broderick; 8 Jul 1745
(StM)

CANNON, William M. Ann
E. Taylor; 11 Sep 1838
(FB)

CARD, Abraham & Ann
Archer; 25 Sep 1773
(OB)

CARLIN, Delphy (of
Louisiana) & Mary J.
Chewning (d/o John
Chewning); 18 Dec 1832
(FB)

CARLTON, Richard &
Elijabeth Powers; 1807
(SpM)

CARMICHAEL, Richard &
Virginia Ann Bernard; 9
Sep 1830 (SpM)

CARMICHAEL, Dr.George &
Mary Carter Welford

(d/o John L. Welford)
19 Jan 1830 (FB)

CARNAHAN, Willis &
Frances Ann Chewning;
21 Oct 1829 (SpM)

CARNAL, John & Sarah
Wharton; 15 Sep 1813
(SpB)

CARNAL, John & Sarah
Wharton; 16 Sep 1813
(SpM)

CARNOCHAN, Basil &
Fanny Humphries; 4 Nov
1813 (SpM)

CARNOHAN, Joseph &
Nancy Gibson; 6 Apr
1803 (SpM)

CARNOHAN, Willis &
Frances Ann Chewning;
21 Oct 1829 (SpB)

CARPENTER, Clayton &
Cornelia A. Woolfolk; 6
Mar 1828 (SpM)

CARPENTER, James &
Rebecca D. Dodd; 29 Nov
1850 (FB)

CARPENTER, James &
Rebecca D. Dodd; 3 Dec
1850 (FM)

CARPENTER, William &
Pheby Michell; 21 Dec
1798 (SpM)

CARR, George R. & Mary
Richardson; 21 Mar 1839
(SpM)

CARR, James & Sarah
May; 6 Jun 1805 (SpM)

CARRICO, Thomas & Jane
McCant; 4 OCt 1744
(StM)

CARROL, Jacob & Tabitha
Reynolds(d/o Rachel
Reynolds); 14 Jan 1783
(OB)

CARTER, Alcock & Louisa
Murphy; 12 Dec 1816
(SpM)

CARTER, Benjamin S. &
Emily Bullock; 22 Dec
1843 (SpM)

CARTER, Bernard Moore &
Lucy Grimes Lee; Dec
1802 (FM)

CARTER, Edwin &
Elizabeth E.P. James;
19 Oct 1830 (FB)

CARTER, James & Mary
Brent; 10 Aug 1724
(StM)

CARTER, John &
Elizabeth Sterling (w/o
Joseph Sterling) 25 Mar
1812 (FM)

CARTER, John & Mary
Butler; 4 Feb 1745
(StM)

CARTER, Joseph &
Lettice Linton; 5 Feb
1755 (StM)

CARTER, Joseph &
Margaret Mason; 27 Nov
1746 (StM)

CARTER, Joseph & Polly
Bell; 23 Apr 1792 (OB)

CARTER, Joseph & Polly
Bell; 23 Apr 1792 (OM)

CARTER, Kingon & Nancy
McWhirt; 4 Sep 1804
(SpM)

CARTER, Nicholas &
Patsey Taylor; 16 Apr
1812 (FB)

CARTER, Rice M. &
Mildred Camalian; 26
Dec 1833 (SpM)

CARTER, Solomon & Mary
Marony; 26 May 1751
(StM)

CARTER, William &
Polley Estes; 23 Dec
1828 (SpM)

CARTER, William & Polly
Estes; 22 Dec 1828
(SpB)

CARUTHERS, John F. &
Mary B. Wilson; 18 May
1827 (FB)

CARVER, John &
Elizabeth Doggett; 31
Aug 1757 (StM)

CARVER, John & Hannah
Clift; 14 Apr 1784
(StM)

CARVER, John & Hannah
Clift; 14 Apr 1784
(StM)

CARVER, John & Mary
Rose; 17 Jul 1768 (StM)

CARVER, Richard & Sarah
Jones; 21 Jan 1722 or
1723 (StM)

CARVER, Thomas & Mary
Clift; 10 Nov 1727
(StM)

CARVER, Thomas &
Rosamund Duncan; 12 Aug
1755 (StM)

CARY, Samuel & Milly M.
Carter (d/o John

Carter); 23 May 1820
(FB)

CARY, Thomas & Julia
Richards; 24 Nov 1841
(FB)

CARY, Thomas & Sarah
Rawlins; 17 Mar 1804
(FB)

CASEY, Robert & Jane
Alsop; 8 Apr 1801 (SpM)

CASEY, William & Agnes
Taylor; 24 Mar 1788
(OB)

CASEY, William & Agnes
Taylor; 6 Apr 1788 (OM)

CASH, James & Sally
Willoughby; 3 Oct 1798
(SpM)

CASH, James A. &
Maatilda Gibson; 17 Feb
1827 (SpM)

CASH, John & Betsy
Stark; 23 Sep 1805
(SpM)

CASH, John & Mildred
Daniel; 21 Nov 1799
(SpB)

CASH, John & Mildred
Daniel; 22 Nov 1799
(SpM)

CASH, Peter & Charity
Bush; 3 Nov 1729 (StM)

CASH, Robert B. &
Elizabeth Kerton; 21
Feb 1828 (SpM)

CASH, Stephen & Jemima
Grining; 26 May 1747
(StM)

CASON, Fendal C. &
Rebecca R. Holladay; 18
Dec 1822 (SpM)

CASON, William & Mary
Thompson (d/o John &
Catherine Thompson); 17
Feb 1795 (OB)

CASON, William & Mary
Thompson (d/o John &
Catherine Thompson); 17
Feb 1795 (OM)

CASON, William J. &
Mary Eleanor Baggett;
19 Aug 1845 (FB)

CATLET, James R. &
Maria Stevens; 18 Nov
1835 (SpM)

CATLETT, George & Mary
Harrison; 23 Nov 1758
(StM)

CATLETT, James R. &
Ruth Stevens; 3 Jun
1824 (SpM)

CATLETT, John & Mary
Grayson; 20 Oct 1726
(SpB)

CATLETT, Thomas & Lucy
Reives (or Raines); 6
Sep 1803 (SpM)

CATLIN, Levi & Nancy
Brown; 30 May 1814
(SpB)

CATLIN, Levi & Nancy
Brown; 30 May 1814
(SpM)

CAVE, Abner (s/o
William Cave Sr.) &
Betsey Sims (d/o
William Sims); 8 Jan
1803 (OM)

CAVE, Bartlett Jr. &
Jenny Snow; 22 Dec 1796
(OM)

CAVE, Benjamin Jr. &
Elizabeth White; 21 Jan
1794 (OB)

CAVE, Benjamin Jr. &
Elizabeth White; 22 Jan
1794 (OM)

CAVE, Richard & Lucy
Shelton; 12 Dec 1806
(OM)

CAVE, Richard & Maria
Porter; 25 Nov 1805
(OM)

CAVE, Robert & Lucy
Bradley; 19 Aug 1806
(OB)

CAVE, Thomas & Nancy
Sims; 4 Nov 1797 (OB)

CAVE, Thomas S. & Ann
Dourrant 18 Dec 1823
(SpM)

CAVE, William & Frances
Christy; 6 Jun 1783
(OB)

CAVE, William & Judy
Jollett (d/o Mary
Jollett); 22 Nov 1791
(OM)

CAVE, William & Judy
Jollett; 22 Nov 1791
(OB)

CAVE, William & Mary
Mallory; 28 Dec 1761
(OB)

CAVE, William & Sarah
Snow; 13 Jul 1810 (OB)

CAVE, William & Sarah
Snow; 16 Jul 1810 (OM)

CAVE, William (s/o John
Cave of Culpeper Co.) &
Frances Christy (d/o
Julius Christy); 6 Jun
1783 (OB)

CAVE, William (s/o John
Cave) & Frances Christy
(d/o Julius Christy);
11 Jun 1783 (OM)

CEAMULE, Thomas B. &
Pamilia Cannon; 31 Jan
1850 (SpM)

CHAMBERS, Abraham &
Mary Dawson (d/o John
Dawson); 17 Nov 1790
(OB)

CHAMBERS, Abraham &
Mary Dawson; 18 Nov
1790 (OM)

CHAMBERS, Thomas &
Milly Robinson (d/o
Artimus Robinson); 15
Jul 1790 (OB)

CHAMPE, John Jr. & Ann
Carter; 17 Apr 1762
(StM)

CHANCELLOR, Sanford &
Fanny L. Pound; 7 Jan
1823 (SpM)

CHANCELLOR, Thomas &
Katherine Cooper; 3 Mar
1723 or 1724 (StM)

CHANDLER, Harvey &
Polly Jones; 21 Aug
1816 (SpM)

CHANDLER, James &
Frances McNeal (d/o
Martha McNeal); 22 Dec
1789 (OB)

CHANDLER, John &
Behethland Rogers; 17
Sep 1767 (StM)

CHANDLER, John &
Elizabeth Terrell (d/o
William Terrell); 26
Dec 1791 (OM)

CHANDLER, John &
Elizabeth Terrell; 26
Dec 1791 (OB)

CHANDLER, Joseph &
Nancy Homes; 15 Jan
1794 (OB)

CHANDLER, Joseph &
Nancy Homs; 15 Jan 1794
(OM)

CHANDLER, Robert &
Suckey Robinson; 24 Feb
1774 (OB)

CHANDLER, Stephen &
Elizabeth Bunbury; 24
Dec 1774 (StM)

CHANDLER, Thomas C. &
Clementine L. Alsop; 20
Sep 1825 (SpM)

CHANDLER, Walker &
Polly Maman; 21 Aug
1813 (SpM)

CHAPMAN, Pearson &
Susannah Alexander; 31
Jul 1766 (StM)

CHAPMAN, Taylor &
Margaret Markham; 13
Sep 1739 (StM)

CHAPMAN, Thomas &
Elizabeth Early (d/o
James Early); 23 Nov
1803 (OB)

CHAPMAN, Thomas &
Elizabeth Early; 29 Nov
1803 (OM)

CHARTERS, William &
Elizabeth Rogers; 22
Dec 1813 (SpB)

CHARTERS, William &
Elizabeth Rogers; 23
Dec 1813 (SpM)

CHESELDINE, Kenelm &
Frances Taliaferro; 9
Aug 1768 (StM)

CHESLEY, George W. &
Frances A. Kent; 28 Feb
1835 (FB)

CHESLEY, Robert & Eliza
Mills; 6 Feb 1837 (FB)

CHESLEY, William S. &
Mary Ann Ferneyhugh; 14
Jan 1840 (FB)

CHESLEY, William S. &
Mary Ann Ferneyhugh; 16
Jan 1840 (FM)

CHEVERAL, James &
Louisa Garner; 21 Jan
1846 (FB)

CHEW, John & Margarett
Beverley; 26 Jun 1729
(SpB)

CHEW, John W. & Ann
Thornton Vass (d/o Mary
Christy); 21 Oct 1819
(FB)

CHEW, Larkin & Mary
Beverly; 30 Sep 1733
(SpB)

CHEW, Richard & Nancy
B. Smith 11 Apr 1826
(SpM)

CHEW, Robert S. & B.
French; Oct 1802 (FM)

CHEWNING, Dr. Francis
B. & Elizabeth H.
Smith; 19 Dec 1843 (FB)

CHEWNING, Dr. Francis
B. & Elizabeth H.Smith

(d/o N.K.Smith) 21 Dec
1843 (FM)

CHEWNING, John & Ann
Percy; 2 Nov 1809 (SpM)

CHEWNING, Oscar L. &
Huldah M. Wiglesworth;
15 May 1832; (SpM)

CHEWNING, Paregrun &
Ellen C. Ann Hopkins; 6
May 1833 (SpB)

CHEWNING, Perigrine &
Helen Ann Hopkins; 1833
(SpM)

CHEWNING, Robert &
Susanna I. Mason; 23
Oct 1823 (SpM)

CHEWNING, Samuel & Ann
Taylor (w/o John
Taylor); May 1799 (FM)

CHEWNING, Samuel &
Susannah Walker; 28 Dec
1809 (FB)

CHEWNION, Will &
Pamilia Henderson; 22
Apr 1813 (SpM)

CHEWS, John James &
Ellen A. Patton; 23 Mar
1825 (FB)

CHIDLEY, Richard &
Sarah Fox; 21 Dec 1722
(StM)

CHILES, James & Jenny
Land; 28 Jan 1779

CHIMP, William &
Catherine Taylor; 31
Jan 1739 (StM)

CHINN, Raleigh & Mary
Haw; 22 Dec 1831 (FB)

CHINN, Rawleigh & Sarah
Lacey; 2 Sep 1748 (StM)

CHISAM, Benjamin &
Elizabeth Beckham (d/o
Henry Beckham); 27 Aug
1796 (OM)

CHISHAM, James &
Catherine Raines; 1 Dec
1789 (OB)

CHISHOLM, Brice &
Martha Carter Haslop;
14 Jul 1809 (SpM)

CHISHOLM, Nimrod & Ann
Swift (of Hanover Co.,
Va.); 23 Apr 1801 (SpM)

CHISHOM, Brice & Martha
Carter Heslop; 14 Jul
1809 (SpB)

CHISIM, Benjamin &
Elizabeth Beckham (d/o
Henry Backman); 27 Aug
1796 (OB)

CHOWNING, Lorimer &
Judith Carter; 11 Dec
1788 (OB)

CHRISMUND, Oswald &
Jane Rose; 27 Jun 1757
(StM)

CHRISMUND, William, &
Anne Tregar; 28 Apr
1779 (StM)

CHRISTIE, Charles & Ann
Smith; 18 Mar 1753
(StM)

CHRISTIE, John &
Elizabeth Griggs; 12
Sep 1751 (StM)

CHRISTIE, John & Sarah
Glover; 28 Aug 1743
(StM)

CHRISTIE, William &
Margaret Thompson; 6
Jun 1775 (StM)

CHRISTY, John &
Elizabeth Gray Dudley;
7 Oct 1785 (StM)

CHRISTY, John & Frances
Johnston; 20 Jan 1771
(StM)

CHRISTY, John & Mary
Rian; 4 May 1749 (StM)

CHRISTY, Joseph & Mary
Vass; 20 Aug 1817 (FB)

CLAIBORNE, Herbert A. &
Mary Anna McGuire; 29
Jan 1845 (FB)

CLANTON, John (of
Hanover) & Ann Spicer;
17 Feb 1731 or 1732
(StM)

CLARK, Ambrose & Mary
Thomas (d/o Joseph
Thomas); 1 Nov 1797
(OB)

CLARK, Benjamin &
Elizabeth McPherson; 9
Jul 1824 (FB)

CLARK, Charles & Phebe
Derrick; 14 Dec 1785
(StM)

CLARK, Henry &
Elizabeth Johnson (w/o
?); 25 Mar 1805 (OB)

CLARK, James &
Elizabeth Graves; 5 Feb
1807 (OM)

CLARK, James & Sally
Payne; 20 Mar 1804 (OM)

CLARK, James & Sally
Payne; 5 Mar 1804 (OB)

CLARK, John & Dillah
Payne; 27 Aug 1804 (OB)

CLARK, John & Winney
Powell (d/o John
Powell); 5 Nov 1794
(OB)

CLARK, Larkin & Rebecca
Bell (d/o Thomas &
Sally Bell); 30 Jan
1797 (OB)

CLARK, Larkin & Rebecca
Bell (d/o Thomas &
Sally Bell); 30 Jan
1797 (OM)

CLARK, Lewis & Sarah
Mitcham (w/o ?); 6 Jan
1825 (FB)

CLARK, Nathaniel &
Nancy Hall; 8 Feb 1804
(OM)

CLARK, Patrick &
Tabitha Kelly; 13 Aug
1764 (StM)

CLARK, Reuben & Lizey
Petty (d/o George
Petty); 31 Jan 1801
(OB)

CLARK, Reubin & Martha
E. Clark (d/o Joseph
Clark); 16 Dec 1801
(OB)

CLARK, Reubin & Martha
E. Clark; 17 Dec 1801
(OM)

CLARK, Robert & Mary
Ann Brown; 20 Mar 1812
(FB)

CLARK, Robert & Sarah
Jones; 23 Mar 1839
(SpM)

CLARK, William & Sarah
Sanders; 5 Aug 1752
(StM)

CLARK, William B. &
Hannah Duerson; 23 Mar
1815 (SpM)

CLARKE, Armstead & Mary
Almand; 2 Mar 1809
(SpM)

CLARKE, Henry & Nanney
Grasty; 28 Dec 1801
(OB)

CLARKE, Henry & Nanney
Grasty; 5 Jan 1802 (OM)

CLARKE, Robert & Martha
Banks; 8 Apr 1826 (SpM)

CLARKE, Walker &
Elizabeth Vawter (d/o
William Vawter); 26 Jan
1802 (OB)

CLARKE, William &
Betsey Cook; 7 Nov 1792
(OB)

CLARKE, William & Betsy
Cook; 7 Nov 1792 (OM)

CLARKSON, Anselm &
Milly Jones; 29 Jan
1789 (OB)

CLAYTON, Henry &
Elizabeth Coyle
(Widow); 30 Oct 1812
(FB)

CLAYTON, Philip &
Elizabeth Hackley
Stubblefield (d/o
George Stubblefield);
17 May 1794 (OB)

CLEMENT, Edward &
Elizabeth Fruyn; 25 Oct
1728 (StM)

CLEMENTS, John & Fanny
Mann; 10 Nov 1831 (FB)

CLIFT, Benjamin &
Frances Peak; 16 Feb
1772 (StM)

CLIFT, Benjamin &
Margaret Sebastian; 6
May 1740 (StM)

CLIFT, Benjamin & Sarah
Rogers; 6 Dec 1772
(StM)

CLIFT, John & Anne
Rogers; 29 Sep 1779
(StM)

CLIFT, John & Jemima
Arnold; 26 Dec 1777
(StM)

CLIFT, John & Margaret
Johns; 2 Mar 1738 or
1739 (StM)

CLIFT, John & Mary
Beach; 2 Jul 1745 (StM)

CLIFT, Robert &
Elizabeth Bolling; 21
Jan 1777 (StM)

CLIFT, Robert & Peggy
Munda (aka Peggy Minor
of King George Co.); 6
Jan 1793 (StM)

CLIFT, William &
Elizabeth Calb; 16 Jan
1764 (StM)

CLIFT, William & Mary
Hill; 19 Jan 1730 or
1731 (StM)

CLIFTON, Burdet &
Frances Hill; 15 Jul
1733 (StM)

CLIFTON, Burdet & Grace
Seaton; 18 May 1745
(StM)

CLOUGH, Robert &
Elizabeth Lewis; 15 Feb
1799 (SpM)

COAD, ____ & Elizabeth
Massey; Dec 1766 (StM)

COAK, William G. &
Catherine Acors; 13 Jul
1848 (FB)

COAKLEY, John &
Elizabeth Thomas; 23
Nov 1836 (FB)

COATES, Jeremiah &
Sally Webster; 15 Feb
1791 (OM)

COATES, John & Sarah
Thompson; 27 Mar 1783
(OB)

COATES, Lewis & Lucy
Duerson; 20 Apr 1805
(SpM)

COATES, William & Betsy
Smith; 6 Oct 1812 (SpM)

COATNEY, Lewis & Hannah
Brennen; 27 Jan 1813
(SpM)

COATS, Jeremiah & Sally
Webster (w/o ?); 15 Feb
1791 (OB)

COBB, Howell & Martha
Jaquelin Rootes; 8 May
1810 (SpB)

COBB, John A. & Sarah
Rooker; 11 Apr 1812
(FB)

COBBS, Nelson & Mary
Hamptons; 23 Dec 1823
(SpM)

COCHLEY, James &
Violett Buttridge; 12
Jan 1786 (StM)

COCKBURN, Robert & Sara
Brown; 23 Jan 1776 (OB)

COCKBURN, Robert &
Sarah Brown; 23 Jan
1776 (OB)

COCKLEY, Robert & Sarah
Sinclair; 21 Sep 1740
(StM)

COCKRANE, Patrick &
Winifred Spencer; 9 Apr
1774 (OB)

COCKRANE, Patrick &
Wintifred Spencer; 9
Apr 1774 (OB)

COGGEN, John & Sophia
Gotley; 22 Feb 1736 or
1737 (StM)

COGGSDALE, James & Mary
Ann Jones (d/o Jane
Jones); 24 Dec 1829
(FB)

COGHILL, Atwell & Phebe
Lindsay; 8 Apr 1801
(SpM)

COGHILL, Reuben & Mary
M. Beasley; 15 Nov 1836
(SpM)

COGWELL, Ralph & Sarah
Reynolds; 1 Feb 1785
(OM)

COGWELL, Ralph & Sarah
Reynolds; 29 Jan 1785
(OB)

COHELEY, William &
Mildred Sullivan; 4 Feb
1781 (StM)

COLBERT, James & Mary
A. Redd; 23 Dec 1830
(SpM)

COLCLOUGH, William &
Mary Rogers; 30 Dec
1741 (StM)

COLE, Councellor &
Sarah E. Carpenter; 1
Nov 1837 (FB)

COLE, Henry H. & Jane
Hummal; 29 Jan 1838
(FB)

COLE, Thomas & Pamela
Nelson 3 Aug 1817 (SpM)

COLEMAN, Ambrose &
Fanny Hilman (d/o
Joseph Hilman); 24 Apr
1810 (OB)

COLEMAN, Francis &
Betty Davis (d/o Joseph
& Elizabeth Davis); 7
Jan 1786 (OB)

COLEMAN, Frank & Sarah
Goodloe; 8 Nov 1810
(SpM)

COLEMAN, Harrison &
Jane F. Wiglesworth; 6
Mar 1848 (SpM)

COLEMAN, James & Betsey
Webber: 18 Dec 1802
(SpM)

COLEMAN, James & Milly
Chew; 18 Dec 1786 (OB)

COLEMAN, James & Molly
Jenny; 15 Sep 1799
(SpM)

COLEMAN, James & Sarah
Taylor; 14 Apr 1780
(OB)

COLEMAN, John &
Elizabeth Bradley; 19
Dec 1794 (OB)

COLEMAN, John &
Elizabeth Bradley; 24
Dec 1794 (OM)

COLEMAN, Ormguin &
_____ Sorrell; 27 Mar
1834 (SpM)

COLEMAN, Richard &
Betsy Coleman; 26 Mar
1816 (SpM)

COLEMAN, Richard (s/o
Nancy Coleman) & Mary
Cunningham; 20 Dec 1821
(FB)

COLEMAN, Richard C. &
Sarah L.C. Harris; 22
Apr 1824 (SpM)

COLEMAN, Robert & Sarah
Coleman (d/o Elizabeth
Coleman); 24 Nov 1800
(OB)

COLEMAN, Robert & Sarah
Coleman (d/o Elizabeth
Coleman); 24 Nov 1800
(OM)

COLEMAN, Thomas & Nancy
Shirley; 27 Oct 1804
(SpM)

COLEMAN, Thomas &
Susannah Hawkins (w/o
?); 28 Jun 1781 (OB)

COLLIE, James & Anne
Cornwall; 21 Feb 1751
(StM)

COLLINS, Albert G. &
Emily P. Bozel (d/o
Richard Bozel); 29 Nov
1837 (FB)

COLLINS, Edward & Ann
Collins; 24 May 1781
(OB)

COLLINS, Francis &
Peggy Dahoney (d/o

Thomas Dehoney); 27 Apr 1794 (OM)

COLLINS, Francis & Peggy Dahoney; 26 Apr 1794 (OB)

COLLINS, George & Elizabeth Mitchell; 10 Feb 1794 (OB)

COLLINS, James & Lucy Burton (d/o Capt. May Burton Jr.); 26 Aug 1793 (OB)

COLLINS, James & Lucy Burton; 26 Aug 1793 (OM)

COLLINS, James & Sarah Harvie (d/o John Harvie); 13 Jan 1792 (OM)

COLLINS, James (s/o George Collins) & Sarah Harvie (d/o John Harvie); 13 Jan 1792 (OB)

COLLINS, James W. & Mary S. McKildoe; 23 Jun 1847 (FB)

COLLINS, John & Betty Yager; 28 Dec 1803 (OB)

COLLINS, John & Betty Yager; 28 Dec 1803 (OM)

COLLINS, John & Elizabeth Kirtley; 4 Jan 1803 (OB)

COLLINS, John & Elizabeth Kirtley; 4 Jan 1803 (OM)

COLLINS, John W.S. & Ann M. Bullock; 13 Sep 1827 (SpM)

COLLINS, Josiah & Isabella Southworth; 6 Mar 1818 (SpM)

COLLINS, Lewis Dillard & Elizabeth Williams; 24 Dec 1792 (OB)

COLLINS, Lewis Dillard & Elizabeth Williams; 24 Dec 1792 (OM)

COLLINS, Reubin & Fanny Riddle (d/o James Riddle); 13 May 1807 (OB)

COLLINS, Reubin & Fanny Riddle; 21 May 1807 (OM)

COLLINS, Tandy & Ann Beazley (d/o James Beazley Sr.); 7 Feb 1809 (OB)

COLLINS, Tandy & Ann Beazley; 9 Feb 1809 (OM)

COLLINS, William & Patty Snell; 16 Sep 1776 (OB)

COLLINS, William & Sally Quisenberry; 18 Oct 1813 (OM)

COLLINS, William W. & Frances Williams (d/o Jacob Williams); 7 Apr 1818 (OM)

COLSON, Charles & Elizabeth Norton; 1 Feb 1739 (StM)

COLYER, Preston & Eliza Hayna; 8 Nov 1804 (OB)

COMBS, John (aka John Fry)(fpc) & Alice Ware (d/o Elsey Ware) (fpc); 11 Dec 1816 (FB)

COMMACK, Robert & Susan
Carter 1 Nov 1838 (SpB)

CONAH, John & Elinor
Ormond; 13 Jun 1725
(StM)

CONAH, John & Helen
Fog; 22 Jun 1724 (StM)

CONNELLY, Patrick & Ann
Irench; 18 Jun 1746
(SpB)

CONNER, John & Lucy
Daniel (d/o Reubin
Daniel); 20 Nov 1776
(OB)

CONNER, John & Mary
Lancaster (d/o Mary
Lancaster); 7 Feb 1785
(OB)

CONNER, William & Sarah
Rogers; 9 Jan 1734
(SpB)

CONNOR, John H. &
Elizabeth Byram; 4 Sep
1849 (FB)

CONWAY, Catlett Jr.
(s/o Catlett & Susanna
(Fitzhugh) Conway of
"Hawfield") & Verlinda
Taliaferro; 26 Sep 1810
(OB)

CONWAY, Edwin H. &
Fanny Scott Gregory; 12
May 1841 (FB)

CONWAY, Francis &
Elizabeth Tapp; 25 Aug
1722 (SpB)

COOK, Elijah & Polly
Turner (d/o Ann
Turner); 16 May 1796
(OM)

COOK, Joseph & Mary
Trenar; 26 Dec 1723
(StM)

COOK, Thomas & Mary
Chiles; 10 Apr 1797
(OB)

COOK, Thomas & Mary
Chiles; 10 Apr 1797
(OM)

COOK, William & Rose
Cogins; 22 Jul 1717
(StM)

COOK, William &
Susannah Garton (d/o
Uriah Garton); 13 Jun
1785 (OB)

COOKE, Elijah & Polly
Turner (d/o Ann
Turner); 16 May 1796
(OB)

COOKE, James & Emily M.
Pearson; 13 Jul 1836
(FB)

COOKE, Travers & Mary
Doniphan; 26 Feb 1754
(StM)

COOPER, Benjamin &
Susannah Lancaster (d/o
John Lancaster); 18 Dec
1804 (OB)

COOPER, Charles &
Susanna Curtis; 26 Dec
1808 (SpM)

COOPER, James & Mildred
Smith (d/o James
Smith); 18 Dec 1798
(OB)

COOPER, James & Mildred
Smith (d/o James
Smith); 18 Dec 1798
(OM)

41

COOPER, William &
Elizabeth Oliford; 5
Jan 1758 (StM)

COOPER, William & Mary
Quisenberry (d/o Moses
Quisenberry); 24 Nov
1787 (OB)

COOTES, John & Sarah
Thompson; 27 Mar 1783
(OB)

COPE, James & Elizabeth
Miflin (of Hanover); 17
Dec 1746 (StM)

COPENHAGEN, John &
Sarah Dobbs; 28 May
1803 (FB)

COPPEDGE, Charles &
Lydia Wayt (d/o James
Wayt); 24 Oct 1803 (OM)

CORBIN, James & Mary
Ann Briscoe; 28 Apr
1829 (FB)

CORBIN, James P. & Jane
Catherine Welford (d/o
John L. Welford); 19
Jan 1830 (FB)

CORBIN, John & Frances
Fant; 7 Dec 1749 (StM)

CORBIN, John & Lettice
Lee; 1 Sep 1737 (StM)

CORBIN, John W. & Jane
M. Todd; 2 Mar 1848
(SpM)

CORBIN, William & Sarah
Jenkins; Jan 1743 (StM)

CORBIN, William & Sarah
Want; 2 Aug 1744 (StM)

CORNELIUS, Augustin &
Sarah Terrell (d/o
Peggy Terrell); 10 Mar
1790 (OB)

CORNISH, Charles &
Elizabeth Smith; 17 Dec
1738 (StM)

CORONO, William &
Elizabeth Hill; 17 Mar
1743 (SpB)

COTNEY, William & Mary
Barbee; 24 Feb 1745
(StM)

COTTOM, Peter & Judith
Robinson Grymes; 25 Jan
1808 (OB)

COTTON, John & Susannah
Smith; 17 Feb 1743
(StM)

COUPAR, Robert & Sophia
Gaines; 23 Sep 1815
(FB)

COURTNEY, William &
Susan Taylor (d/o John
J. Taylor); 20 Oct 1836
(FB)

COWAY, Withers &
Dulcebella Bunbury; 21
Apr 1752 (StM)

COWGILL, Daniel & Betsy
Martin (d/o Ann Bowen);
1 Aug 1785 (OB)

COWGILL, George & Phebe
Wait; 15 Sep 1792 (OB)

COWGILL, Isaac & Sally
Gillock (d/o Elizabeth
Gillock); 3 May 1794
(OB)

COWGILL, Isaac & Sally
Gillock; 15 May 1794
(OM)

COWHERD, Francis & Lucy
Scott (d/o Johnny
Scott); 13 Aug 1787
(OB)

COWHERD, Reuben &
Frances Woolfolk (d/o
Thomas Woolfolk); 28
Jun 1794 (OB)

COWHILL, George &
Phoebe Wait; 15 Sep
1792 (OM)

COWIN, William &
Cathrine Haslope; 1810
(SpM)

COWNE, Boling &
Elizabeth Copenhagen
(his ward); 27 Dec 1821
(FB)

COX, Abraham & Arianna
Cole; 27 Apr 1836 (FB)

COX, George & Elizabeth
Wright; 18 Jan 1830
(FB)

COX, George & Sarah Ann
Fleaman; 1833 (SpM)

COX, George L. &
Elizabeth B. Beckwith
(d/o Barnes Beckwith);
19 Dec 1850 (FB)

COX, Joab & Lucy Estes;
3 Jan 1803 (OB)

COX, John & Mary
Bryson; 6 Feb 1782 (OB)

COX, John G. & Drusilla
Ames; 29 Dec 1829 (FB)

COX, John T. & Ann
Kennedy (d/o Henner &
Mary Kennedy); 2 Jul
1824 (FB)

COX, Mortimer & Frances
Bell; 6 Feb 1845 (SpM)

COX, Obediah &
Elizabeth Penn; 20 Mar
1821 (SpB)

COX, Obediah &
Elizabeth Penn; 21 Mar
1821 (SpM)

COX, Peter & Jane
Finnall (d/o Robert
Finnall of Stafford
Co.); 12 Oct 1831 (FB)

COX, Peter P. &
Margarette Bryan; 14
Apr 1823 (FM)

COX, Peter P. &
Margarette Bryan; 25
Dec 1822 (FB)

COX, Richard & Anne
Crisman; 2 Sep 1750
(StM)

COX, Robert A. & Maria
M. Lane; 8 Dec 1841
(FB)

COX, Thomas & Milley
Olliver (d/o Tabitha
Olliver); 10 Mar 1783
(OB)

COX, William & Betsey
Estes; 29 Jan 1791 (OB)

COX, William & Betsy
Estes; 29 Jan 1791 (OM)

COX, William & Maria B.
King; 1 Jan 1829 (FB)

COX, William & Mary Ann
Funnall (d/o Robert
Funnall); 8 Jan 1827
(FB)

COYLE, Richard &
Elizabeth Hazelgrow
(w/o Bery A.
Hazelgrow); 5 Dec 1811
(FB)

COYLE, Richard & Sally
Day (d/o Sarah Day); 1
Apr 1807 (FB)

CRAFFORD, Peter & Jane
Gladsteans; 7 Aug 1755
(StM)

CRAFFORD, Philip & &
Mary Simmons; 27 Nov
1730 (StM)

CRANK, William, & Sabry
Jones; 8 Feb 1778 (StM)

CRANNIDGE, Samuel &
Elizabeth Dey; 6 May
1741 (StM)

CRAP, James & Joyce
Hinson; 3 Jun 1750
(StM)

CRASK, James & Jane
Collins; 25 Apr 1796
(OB)

CRASK, James & Jane
Hollins; 25 Apr 1796
(OM)

CRAWFORD, Dewitt C.(age
24 "in May next") &
Sarah Embry; 28 Feb
1828 (FB)

CRAWFORD, Innis & Lucy
Haley; 5 Feb 1807 (SpM)

CRAWFORD, Jeremiah &
Janey Crawford (d/o
Archelan Crawford); 31
May 1792 (OM)

CRAWFORD, Jeremiah &
Jany Crawford (d/o
Archelan Crawford); 28
May 1792 (OB)

CRAWFORD, Martin &
Susanna Lamb; 9 Dec
1801 (OM)

CREIGHTON, John & Jane
Barrett; 19 May 1847
(FB)

CREW, Jacob & Martha
Dollins; 2 Feb 1790
(OB)

CREW, Jacob & Martha
Dollins; 2 Feb 1790
(OM)

CRIDLIN, Jacob H. &
Harriet Southard; 1 Aug
1849 (FB)

CRINSHAW, Spotswood &
Winifred Graves (d/o
Isaac Graves Jr.); 18
Jun 1816 (OM)

CRISMAND, Joseph &
Elizabeth Purtle; 16
Feb 1752 (StM)

CROMPSEY, John & Mary
Edds; 1 May 1817 (SpM)

CROOK, Robert & Mary
Gosselen; 15 Apr 1745
(StM)

CROOK, William & Mary
Shepherd; 2 Apr 1801
(SpM)

CROP, William James &
Sally Lindsay Coleman;
9 May 1805 (SpM)

CROPP, Silas F. & Sarah
A.C. Moce; 25 Feb 1824
(SpM)

CROSBY, George & Mary
Hughes; 6 Jan 1744
(StM)

CROSSLEY, William &
Mary Garton; 30 Apr
1818 (FB)

CROSSLY, Thomas &
Dorothea J. Taylor (d/o
Thomas & Dorothy
Taylor); 2 Apr 1807
(FB)

44

CROSTHWAIT, Aaron &
Nelly Brockman (d/o
John Brockman); 17 Aug
1792 (OB)

CROSTHWAIT, Aaron &
Nelly Brockman (d/o
John Brockman); 17 Aug
1792 (OM)

CROUGHTON, Charles &
Betsey Hudson; Jul 1790
(FM)

CROUGHTON, Robert &
Elizabeth Reveley; 18
Feb 1826 (SpM)

CROWLEY, Timothy & Ann
Bloxton; 16 Feb 1826
(FB)

CROXTON, Joseph &
Delphy Turner; 8 Nov
1802 (OB)

CRUMP, Benjamin &
Hannah James; 2 Feb
1749 (StM)

CRUMP, Benjamin & Mary
Barber (Barbour) Price;
12 Apr 1757 (OB)

CRUMP, John & Mary
McDaniel; [No Date]
(SpM)

CRUMP, Reubin & Mary
Green; 8 Feb 1809 (FB)

CRUMP, Robert H. &
Selina M. Ellis; 24 May
1832 (FB)

CRUMP, William & Ann
Eliza Dickey; 11 Jul
1836 (FB)

CRUTCHFIELD, Stapleton
& Sarah Ann Alsop; 13
Jun 1833 (SpM)

CRUTCHFIELD, Thomas &
Ann Pendleton Taylor;
18 Jan 1799 (OM)

CRUTCHFIELD, Thomas &
Ann Pendleton Taylor; 8
Jan 1799 (OB)

CRUTCHFIELD, William &
Jane C. Hicks; 2 Nov
1825 (SpM)

CRYSELL, William &
Frances Rose; 17 Nov
1782 (StM)

CUBBAGE, John & Mary
Jenkins; 10 Jul 1750
(StM)

CULHAM, John & Lettice
Suthard; 17 Feb 1775
(StM)

CULLINGS, James & Sarah
Hutton; 14 Feb 1755
(StM)

CULVY, Peter & Sarah
Sweney; 28 Mar 1758
(StM)

CUMMINGS, John &
Lettice Phillips; 21
Feb 1757 (StM)

CUMMINGS, Thomas &
Sarah Harvey; 1 Dec
1820 (FB)

CUMMINGS, Thomas &
Sarah Harvey; 5 Dec
1820 (FM)

CUNIBERFORD, James &
Elizabeth Holdbroke; 15
Sep 1754 (StM)

CUNNINGHAM, George &
Malvina P. Staiar (d/o
Jacob Staiar); 13 Dec
1819 (FB)

CUNNINGHAM, James &
Behethland Overhall; 21
Jun 1757 (StM)

CUNNINGHAM, James &
Louisa Bowling; 3 Oct
1823 (SpM)

CUNNINGHAM, James &
Mary Ann Hilmsletter;
29 Dec 1819 (FB)

CUNNINGHAM, James Jr. &
Louisa Bowling; 2 Oct
1823 (SpB)

CUNNINGHAM, Morice &
Ann Poplar; 2 Apr 1738
(StM)

CUNNINGHAM, Robert &
Ann Mannan; 6 Jul 1808
(SpM)

CUNNINGHAM, Robert &
Ann Mannon; 6 Jul 1808
(SpB)

CUNNINGHAM, Robert &
Elizabeth Stewart; 13
Apr 1795 (SpM)

CUPPENHAVEN, John &
Catherin; 24 Apr 1837
(FB)

CURLEY, John & Mary
Maddox; 9 May 1767
(StM)

CURRELL, Henry & Nancy
Banett; 28 Jul 1828
(FB)

CURRELL, John B. & Mary
Ann Myers (d/o Sarah
Meyers); 15 Dec 1836
(FB)

CURRIE, James &
Elizabeth Jett (d/o
George Jett); 2 Oct
1819 (FB)

CURRY, John & Anne
Rogers; 25 Dec 1783
(StM)

CURRY, Stephen & Marie
E. Mullen; 8 Apr 1841
(FB)

CURRY, John & Jane
Stribling; 20 Sep 1758
(StM)

CURTES, Christopher &
Mary Frank; 4 May 1804
(SpM)

CURTIS, Christopher &
Mary Frank; 28 Apr 1804
(SpB)

CURTIS, Elijah &
Catherine Myers; 27 Dec
1806 (SpM)

CURTIS, Elijah & Nancy
Daniel; 23 Jan 1801
(OB)

CURTIS, Elijah & Polly
Conune; 28 Oct 1842
(FB)

CURTIS, John & Polly
Baxter; 24 Feb 1814
(SpM)

CURTIS, Rice Jr. & Ann
Brock; 28 Sep 1733
(SpB)

CURTIS, Samuel & Jane
Brown; 7 Sep 1840 (SpM)

CURTIS, Sepe &
Elizabeth Milna; 6 Jul
1826 (FB)

CURTIS, Stiles & Ann B.
Jones (d/o Philadelphia
Jones); 6 May 1820 (FB)

CURTIS, Thomas & Ann
Gray; 19 Jun 1822 (FB)

CURTIS, Thomas &
Elizabeth Baxter; 29
Nov 1816 (SpM)

CURTIS, William &
Elizabeth Coper; 22 Dec
1804 (SpM)

CURTIS, William & Ellen
Jett; 9 Apr 1833 (SpM)

CURTIS, William &
Martha Mastin; 28 Apr
1809 (SpM)

CUSHMAN, John & Nancy
Humphries; 11 Dec 1811
(SpM)

DABNEY, Alexander &
Sally Bell; 25 Aug 1776
(OB)

DABNEY, Augustine L. &
Elizabeth O. Smith; 27
May 1834 (FM)

DABNEY, George & Mary
Waller; 11 Sep 1754
(StM)

DABNEY, John & Sarah
King; 12 Feb 1816 (FB)

DABNEY, Robert C. &
Margarett M. Browne; 12
Nov 1850 (SpM)

DABNEY, William & Lucy
Layton; 24 Jun 1818
(FB)

DADE, Baldwin & Sarah
Alexander; 7 Aug 1736
(StM)

DADE, Caldwallader &
Sarah Berryman; 20 Aug
1752 (StM)

DADE, Francis & Sarah
Taliaferro (d/o
Lawrence Taliaferro);
13 Mar 1782 (OB)

DADE, Henry & Elizabeth
Massey; 7 Jul 1726
(StM)

DADE, Horatio & Frances
Richards; 5 Oct 1749
(StM)

DADE, Horatio & Mary
Massey; 14 Jan 1753
(StM)

DADE, Langhorn &
Mildred Washington; 25
Dec 1742 or 1743 (StM)]

DADE, Robert &
Elizabeth Harrison; 4
Jan 1742 or 1743 (StM)

DADE, Townshend &
Elizabeth Dade; 5 Aug
1782 (StM)

DADE, Townshend & Jane
Stuart(d/o Rev.
William & Sarah
Stuart); 11 Dec 1769
(StM)

DADE, Townshend & Rose
Grigsby; 12 Dec 1745
(StM)

DADE, Townshend Jr. &
Parthenia Massey; 6
May 1736 (StM)

DADE, William & Sarah
Dade; 6 Nov 1792 (OM)

DADE, William (of
Prince William Co.) &
Sarah Dade; 6 Nov 1792
(OB)

DAGG, John & Sarah
Overhall; 14 Nov 1729
(StM)

DAHONEY, Rhodes &
Jinney Chapman (d/o

Joseph Chapman); 19 Oct
1790 (OB)

DAINGERFIELD, Edward &
Adelaide Payne (d/o
Catharine Fulcher
formerly Payne); 14 Mar
1838 (FB)

DAINGERFIELD, John &
Eleanor B. Armistead; 5
Nov 1804 (FB)

DALENY, Edward & Mary
Campbell; 15 Apr 1725
(StM)

DALTON, John & Polly
Earles; 23 Jun 1800
(OB)

DALTON, John & Polly
Earles; 24 Jun 1800
(OM)

DALTON, John & Polly
Earles; 24 Jun 1800
(OM)

DANE, Richard &
Elizabeth Kelly; 30 Jun
1746 (StM)

DANIEL, Beverly & Jane
Hiatt; 28 Feb 1786 (OB)

DANIEL, Cornelius O. &
Peggy Plunkett (w/o ?);
6 Apr 1793 (OB)

DANIEL, Cornelius O. &
Peggy Plunkett (w/o ?);
6 Apr 1793 (OM)

DANIEL, James & Alise
Finnell; 8 Apr 1797
(OB)

DANIEL, James & Alse
Finnell; 8 Apr 1797
(OM)

DANIEL, James & Lucy
Davis; 5 Apr 1772 (OB)

DANIEL, John & Lucy
Marshall; 26 Jul 1776
(OB)

DANIEL, John & Susan
Penny; 22 Dec 1812
(SpB)

DANIEL, John & Susan
Penny; 23 Dec 1812
(SpM)

DANIEL, John T. &
Harriet M. Fitzhugh; 13
Feb 1830 (FB)

DANIEL, Peter & Sarah
Travers; 15 Jul 1736
(StM)

DANIEL, Reuben &
Elizabeth Merry; Nov
1760 (OB)

DANIEL, Robert &
Frances Head Humphries;
23 Nov 1772 (OB)

DANIEL, Samuel G. &
Margaret Lewis; 21 Oct
1833 (SpM)

DANIEL, Thomas & Sarah
Penny; 1 Sep 1807 (SpB)

DANIEL, Thomas & Sarah
Penny; 10 Sep 1807
(SpM)

DANIEL, Thomas N. &
Frances Smith; 27 May
1835 (FB)

DANIEL, Travers &
Frances Moncure; 7 Oct
1762 (StM)

DANIEL, Walter R. &
Eliza Lewis; 7 Nov 1815
(SpM)

DANIEL, William & Mary
Gaines; 3 Feb 1785 (OB)

DARBY, Adam & Catherine Shepherd (d/o Andrew Shepherd); 15 Nov 1796 (OM)

DARLOW, Thomas & Margaret Lynn; 9 Apr 1758 (StM)

DARNABY, Reuben & Elizabeth Fagg; 12 Jan 1827 (SpB)

DARNABY, Reuben & Elizabeth Fagg; 13 Jan 1827 (SpM)

DARRELL, Sampson & _____ Norgrave (d/o John Norgrave); before 1690 (StM)

DAVENPORT, Henry C. & Harriet Dillard; 22 Dec 1834 (SpM)

DAVENPORT, John & Ally Luck; 24 Dec 1807 (SpM)

DAVIS, Absolem & Jerusha Davis; 25 Dec 1796 (OM)

DAVIS, Addison S. & Dorothea Ann Farish (d/o Johnston Farish); 9 Apr 1834 (FB)

DAVIS, Bartlett & Sally Lowry; 31 Jan 1799 (OM)

DAVIS, Edward L. & A. Roe; Sep 1804 (FM)

DAVIS, Gustavis & Mary M. Kelly; 11 Aug 1839 (FM)

DAVIS, Gustavis & Mary M. Kelly; 8 Aug 1839 (FB)

DAVIS, Henry & Margaret Mills; 5 Nov 1758 (StM)

DAVIS, James & Ann Modiset (d/o Mary Modiset); 28 Aug 1785 (OB)

DAVIS, James & Sarah Taylor; 1 Mar 1780 (OB)

DAVIS, Jenkinias & Babby Lowrie; 21 Dec 1794 (OM)

DAVIS, John & Ann Bridwell; 11 Sep 1744 (StM)

DAVIS, John & Elizabeth Pannill (d/o William Panel); 10 Jan 1789 (OB)

DAVIS, John & Mary Brannam; 15 Feb 1745 (StM)

DAVIS, John & Mary Eastin; 27 Jul 1789 (OM)

DAVIS, John & Mary Jones; 25 Feb 1772 (OB)

DAVIS, John & Mary Pendleton; 26 Nov 1808 (SpM)

DAVIS, John & Sarah Haukins; 7 Aug 1750 (StM)

DAVIS, Leonard & Suzanna Burrows; 1 Jan 1776 (OB)

DAVIS, Peter & Frances Hart; 5 Dec 1808 (SpB)

DAVIS, Rev. John LeRoy & Eliza Chew Gordon Wilson (d/o Sam B.

Wilson); 1 May 1833
(FB)

DAVIS, Thomas &
Elizabeth Early (d/o
Theodosia Early); 24
Apr 1783 (OB)

DAVIS, Thomas (of
Spotsylvania Co.) &
Susannah Hiatt; 1 May
1783 (OB)

DAVIS, William &
Catherine Carter; 27
Nov 1755 (StM)

DAVIS, William & Caty
Cammack; 1 Jan 1821
(SpB)

DAVIS, William & Nancy
Easton; 5 Feb 1789 (OB)

DAVIS, William & Sarah
Franklin; 13 May 1752
(StM)

DAVIS, William E. &
Elizabeth Mifflin; 23
Jan 1845 (FB)

DAVIS, William E. &
Elizabeth Mifflin; 23
Jan 1845 (FM)

DAVIS, Wilson & Caty
Cammack; 4 Jan 1821
(SpM)

DAVISON, Andrew & Sarah
McInteer; 5 Nov 1738
(StM)

DAWSON, Christopher &
Jane George; 16 Feb
1750 (StM)

DAWSON, Frederick &
Patsey White; 15 Oct
1832 (FB)

DAWSON, Henry & Betty
Turner; 15 Dec 1754
(StM)

DAWSON, John & Ann
Chism;19 Oct 1775 (OB)

DAWSON, John & Nancy
Pollard; 25 Aug 1795
(OM)

DAWSON, Musgrove & Mary
Waugh; 31 May 1757 (OB)

DAY, Charles M. & Lucy
Ann Lipscomb; 13 Jan
1831 (SpM)

DAY, John & Margaret
Smith; 15 May 1758
(StM)

DAY, John A. & Mary R.
Estes; 30 Sep 1820
(SpM)

DAY, Robert & Mary Gum;
16 Jan 1757 (StM)

DEACON, John & Mary
Sacheveral; 15 May 1785
(StM)

DEAKINS, Ambrose &
Victory Simms; 24 May
1789 (StM)

DEANE, William & Sarah
Boston; 2 Jun 1789 (OM)

DEAR, John & Catherine
Smith; 1 Nov 1774 (OB)

DEAR, Thomas & Lucy
Fennell; 27 Jan 1778
(OB)

DeBAPTIST, Edward &
Henrietta Jordone; 18
Nov 1818 (FB)

DeBAPTIST, William &
Eliza Lewis; 18 Jun
1831 (FB)

DEDMAN, Robert &
Elizabeth J.
Timberlake; 11 Dec 1823
(FB)

DEER, William H. &
Frances Thomas; 29 Apr
1850 (FB)

DEERING, Thomas & Mary
Raursey; 19 Jun 1783
(OB)

DEJAMATTE, James C. &
Lucy Mary Hund; 21 Dec
1843 (SpM)

DELAPLAINE, Daniel L. &
Mary A. Pilcher; 28 Oct
1844 (FB)

DEMPSEY, Daniel & Mary
Fountain; 18 Feb 1825
(FB)

DEMSOE, John & Jane
Knight; 6 Jul 1737
(StM)

DENNET, Thomas & Mary
Horsey; 18 Jun 1758
(StM)

DENORMANDIE, Amos S. &
Elizabeth H. Stone (d/o
William G. Stone); 30
Sep 1814 (FB)

DENT, Thomas & Anne
Cave; 3 Dec 1747 (StM)

DERE, William & Sarah
Head; 16 Sep 1773 (StM)

DEREY, Lavey & Ann Wye;
7 Sep 1785 (OB)

DERRICK, Benjamin &
Katherine Powel; 29 Jul
1737 (StM)

DERRICK, Benjamin &
Margaret Cannaday; 3
Aug 1734 (StM)

DERRICK, Benjamin &
Martha Whiting; 31 Jan
1763 (StM)

DERRICK, Benjamin &
Mary Neal; 30 Sep 1729
(StM)

DERRICK, Edward &
Jemima Powel; 2 Jan
1728 or 1729 (StM)

DESHAZO, Henry L. &
Ellen Taylor; 28 Jun
1849 (SpM)

DEVEAN, John & Mary
Bridges; 4 Aug 1764
(StM)

DEY, John & Behethlem
Bowling; 21 Feb 1747 or
1748 (StM)

DIAL, Mitchell & Mary
Smith; 19 Nov 1752
(StM)

DICK, William & Sarah
Lloyd; 25 Jul 1732
(StM)

DICKENSON, Charles &
Frances Powell; 23 Dec
1814 (SpM)

DICKERSON, Edward &
Sarah Chandler; 19 May
1798 (SpM)

DICKERSON, John & Emily
Hall; 23 Jan 1822 (SpM)

DICKEY, Robert & Eliza
Slater; 19 Jun 1817
(FB)

DICKEY, Robert &
Elizabeth Paull; 17 May
1837 (FB)

DICKINSON, James E. &
Ellen C. Middleton; 26
Oct 1844 (FB)

DICKINSON, Ralph & Ann
Quisenberry (d/o Mary
Quisenberry); 26 Mar
1815 (OM)

DICKINSON, Robert &
Ruth Parish (d/o Joseph
Parish); 10 Feb 1787
(OB)

DICKINSON, Thomas E. &
Annie Harris; 18 Nov
1846 (SpM)

DILLARD, Garland &
Emely Graves; 14 Jan
1813 (SpM)

DILLARD, James & Sally
Collins; 31 Jan 1811
(SpM)

DILLARD, James D. &
Emily Twyman; 8 Jun
1821 (SpM)

DILLARD, Will & Betsey
Mason; 30 Dec 1813
(SpM)

DILLON, James & Anne
Suddeth; 24 Jul 1746
(StM)

DILLON, James &
Margaret Warner; 16 Nov
1742 (StM)

DINT, Arthur &
Elizabeth Manuel; 11
Dec 1742 (StM)

DISHMAN, Churchill &
Mary Noah; 17 Jan 1832
(SpB)

DISHMAN, Churchill &
Mary Noal; 1832 (SpM)

DISKIN, John & Frances
McCarty; 19 Jun 1755
(StM)

DISKINE, John &
Elizabeth Clark; 21 Apr
1724 (StM)

DITMAN, John W. & Grace
Calhoun (Widow); 27 Jun
1810 (FB)

DIXON, John & Lucy
Rumsey; 27 Sep 1813
(OB)

DIXON, John & Lucy
Rumsey; 27 Sep 1813
(SpM)

DIXON, Richard & Ann
Ramsay; 13 Apr 1775
(StM)

DOANE, John & Elizabeth
Mays; 18 Aug 1790 (OB)

DODD, John William &
Susanna Lee; 31 Dec
1792 (OM)

DODD, William & Polly
Johnson; 31 Oct 1799
(SpB)

DODD, Willian & Polly
Johnson; 31 Oct 1799
(SpM)

DODSON, Thomas &
Catherine Webster; 2
Aug 1812 (FB)

DOGGED, Bushrod & Anne
Stribling; 6 Oct 1737
(StM)

DOGGETT, Samuel & Maria
Wilson; 26 Dec 1827
(FB)

DOGGETT, Wishart &
Harriett Courtney; 15
Nov 1828 (FB)

DOHONY, James &
Winifred Vawter; 23 Feb
1775 (OB)

DOICK, William & Esther
Jordon; 20 Dec 1762
(StM)

DOLLINS, Reuben &
Elizabeth Hensley (d/o
William Hensley); 30
Dec 1789 (OB)

DONAHOE, James & Mary
Faulkner; 7 Aug 1837
(FB)

DONAHOE, Joshua &
Lavinia Powel; (FB)

DONAHOE, Joshua &
Margaret W. Adams; 8
Feb 1848 (FB)

DONALDSON, John & Ann
MacMurry; 31 Dec 1741
(StM)

DONAVANT, Archibald M.
& Mary A. Ratcliff; 11
Mar 1841 (SpM)

DONELLE, Isaac (s/o
Andrew Donelle) & Sarah
Shears; 13 Sep 1817
(FB)

DONIPHAN, Alexander &
Mary Waugh (d/o John
Waugh of Belle Plaine &
Mary Crosby); 17 Jun
1740 (StM)

DONIPHAN, George &
Harriet Victor; 1 Nov
1819 (FB)

DONNOLEY, Christopher &
Suckey Moor; 6 Nov 1783
(FB)

DONOHO, Joshua &
Levinia Powell; 25 Jul
1832 (FM)

DONOVER, John & Sally
Gaer (d/o Nathaniel
Gaer); 27 Jan 1790 (OB)

DOODY, Joseph & Rachel
Bowling; 13 Feb 1750 or
1751 (StM)

DOOLING, Thomas &
Elizabeth Finnell; 15
Mar 1791 (OM)

DORBED, Lewis & Nelly
Garner; 21 Dec 1794
(SpB)

DORTON, Lewis & Nelly
Garner; 24 Dec 1794
(SpM)

DOUGLAS, Alexander &
Sarah Martin; 8 Sep
1751 (StM)

DOUGLAS, Alexander &
Keziah Riggins; 21 May
1749 (StM)

DOUGLAS, Charles & Mary
Payne; 25 Apr 1796 (OM)

DOUGLASS, James &
Catherine Brent; 1 Oct
1754 (StM)

DOULING, John & Lettice
Spearman; 1 May 1746
(StM)

DOWLING, Nicholas &
Elizabeth Dunnaway; 30
Jun 1754 (StM)

DOWNER, Larkin & Mary
Foster; 13 Nov 1817
(SpM)

DOWNER, William & Phebe
Goodlos; 20 Oct 1803
(SpM)

DRISCAL, Derby & Jean Noble; 4 Oct 1756 (StM)

DRUMMOND, Andrew & Elizabeth Bussle; 16 Jan 1735 or 1736 (StM)

DUCKETT, John & Elizabeth Skidmore; 6 Aug 1751 (StM)

DUDLEY, Robert & Joyce Gayle; Apr 1745 (SpB)

DUDLEY, William & Eliz. Redd; 9 Mar 1813 (SpB)

DUERSON, Henry & Ann Beasley; 2 Apr 1801 (SpM)

DUERSON, James & Catherine R. Coleman; 25 Nov 1829 (SpM)

DUERSON, John B. & Catharine Beazley; 22 Nov 1825 (SpM)

DUERSON, John F. & Nancy Holladay; 1)ct 1816 (SpM)

DUERSON, Robert C. & Caroline M. Commack (d/o Robert Commack); 15 Oct 1839 (SpB)

DUERSON, Thomas & Hannah Brock; 5 May 1736 (SpB)

DUERSON, William & Mary Noel; Jan 1806 (SpM)

DULANEY, Henry & Fanny A. Carten; (FB)

DUNAWAY, John & Polly Sutherland; 9 Jan 1816 (OB)

DUNAWAY, John & Polly Sutherland; 9 Jan 1816 (SpM)

DUNAWAY, Jordon & Delpha Knight; 9 Jan 1834 (SpM)

DUNAWAY, Thomas & Mary Wright; 3 Jul 1826 (OB)

DUNBAR, John & Elizabeth Elliot; 26 Sep 1752 (StM)

DUNCAN, Alexander Jr. (s/o Alexander Sr.)(fpc) & Fanny Moor (fpc) 13 Mar 1813 (FM)

DUNCAN, Alexander Jr.(s/o Alexander Duncan Sr.) (fpc) & Fanny Moor (mulatto, former property of Edward Moor. emancipated in April 1806 in Stafford Co.); 12 Mar 1813 (FB)

DUNCAN, John & Lettice Woaker; 27 Sep 1735 (StM)

DUNCAN, Joseph & Nancy Stevens; 22 May 1772 (OB)

DUNCAN, William & Caty Lucas; 12 Apr 1805 (SpM)

DUNCUM, Thomas & Sarah Whiting; 2 Jun 1758 (StM)

DUNLOP, William & Jane Bankhead; Aug 1799 (FM)

DUNMAN, Joseph & Honour Bowling; 4 Jan 1726 or 1727 (StM)

DUNN, Godfrey & Polly Morris; 2 Mar 1802 (SpM)

DUNN, Henry (of Tappahannock) & Lucy Julian (d/o Dr. Julian); 27 Jan 1799 (FM)

DUNN, James & Elinor Savage; 13 May 1739 (SpB)

DUNN, William & Mary Bledsoe; 24 Jan 1775 (OB)

DUNNAUANT, Hezekiah & Hilton Breeding; 1813 (SpM)

DUNNAWAY, Daniel & Jean Judd; 1 Mar 1744 (StM)

DUNNAWAY, Edmund & Sarah Ann Knight; 13 Nov 1832 (SpM)

DUNNAWAY, Isaac & Mary Ann Tolson; 25 May 1754 (StM)

DURATT, John & Betsy Roy; 19 Jul 1804 (SpM)

DURRETT, Achilles & Lydia Quisenberry; 25 Sep 1805 (OM)

DURRETT, Albert & Ann Hodges; 22 Feb 1827 (SpM)

DURRETT, Jonathan & Mary Lively; 23 Oct 1804 (SpM)

DURRETT, Jonathan I. & Susan E. Jones; 20 Aug 1848 (SpM)

DURRETT, Richard & Catharine Tyler; 7 Jan 1813 (SpM)

DURRETT, Tarlton & D. Tompkins; Aug 1804 (FM)

DURROOTT, Woodson & Nancy Cammack; 2 Mar 1802 (SpM)

DUVALL, Clabourn & Polly Faulconer; 12 Feb 1812 (OB)

DUVALL, Clabourn & Polly Faulconer; 24 Feb 1812 (SpM)

DUVALL, Robert & Patsey C. Pendleton; 28 Oct 1817 (SpM)

DUVALL, William I. & Jane A. Spooner; 15 Sep 1846 (SpM)

DYAL, Matthew & Jane Wood; 23 Jan 1738 or 1739 (StM)

DYE, George & Rebecca Dye; 10 Mar 1790 (StM)

EAES, I.M. & Ann Kelly; 30 Sep 1839 (FB)

EARLE, Samuel & Elizabeth Holdbrooke (d/o Randall Holdbrook & Jannett Patterson Conyers); 13 Jan 1754 (StM)

EARLY, Joel & Lucy Smith; 23 Jun 1772 (OB)

EASTHAM, Edward & Ann Thornton; 5 Jun 1798 (OM)

EASTIN, John & Sarah Griffith; 28 Apr 1785 (OB)

EASTIN, Philip &
Elizabeth Henderson
(d/o Alexander
Henderson); 23 Mar 1782
(OB)

EATHERTON, James &
Nancy Crawford; 13 Dec
1810 (SpM)

EATHERTON, William &
Frances Pendleton; 30
Jan 1830 (SpM)

EATON, Richard &
Catherine C. Hughlett;
18 Jun 1836 (FB)

EATON, William & Mary
Bowling; 25 Aug 1737
(StM)

EAVES, William & Nancy
Highlander (d/o George
Highlander); 9 Jan 1797
(OM)

ECHOLS, Peregrine &
Sarah Carter; 17 Oct
1825 (SpB)

ECHOLS, Peregrine &
Sarah Carter; 18 Oct
1825 (SpM)

EDDES, John & Nancy
Wiglesworth; 12 Jun
1810 (SpM)

EDDESON, John & Anne
Stratton; 12 Jul 1751
(StM)

EDDINS, Elijah & Nancy
Osborn (d/o William
Osborn); 15 Feb 1797
(OM)

EDDINS, Thomas &
Frances Collins (d/o
William Collins); 26
Dec 1798 (OM)

EDDS, Burkett & Elza
Collins; 27 May 1819
(SpM)

EDDY, Martin &
Elizabeth Collins; 11
Jul 1811 (SpM)

EDENTON, Henry & Polly
Saneley; 4 Jun 1810
(SpM)

EDENTON, Stephen &
Huldah Vass; 27 Dec
1831 (SpM)

EDGE, Benjamin & Polly
Readon; 12 Nov 1802
(SpB)

EDGE, Benjamin & Polly
Readon; 13 Nov 1802
(SpM)

EDGE, Philip & Patsey
Hayden; 21 Dec 1803
(SpM)

EDGE, Philip & Patsy
Haydon; 20 Dec 1802
(SpB)

EDINGTON, Edmund &
Priscilla Gordon; 24
Sep 1798 (OM)

EDINGTON, Gilford &
Lucinda Perry; 15 Jun
1836 (FB)

EDMUND, Vincent N. &
Sarah Franklin Haywood
(d/o Julia Ann
Haywood); 25 Oct 1843
(FB)

EDMUNDSON, Archibald &
Eliza Ann Williams; 19
Apr 1842 (FB)

EDRINGTON, John M. &
Sophia A. Wethers; 11
Mar 1847 (FB)

EDWARDS, ___-her &
Sarah Stacey; 6 May
1757 (StM)

EDWARDS, Andrew & Betty
Brittingham (w/o Hugh
French Jr. & James
Waugh); 1751 (StM)

EDWARDS, Andrew &
Elizabeth Cave Withers
(d/o William Cave; w/o
Keene Withers); 1758
(StM)

EDWARDS, Elisha (s/o
William Edwards) &
Elizabeth Eaton; 28 Aug
1798 (OM)

EDWARDS, Enoch & Ann
Newton; 21 Apr 1818
(FB)

EDWARDS, William & Ann
Payne (d/o Caterine
Fulcher, formerly
Payne); 1 Mar 1837 (FB)

EDWARDS, William &
Eleanor Wheeler; 12 Feb
1756 (StM)

EDWARDS, William & Mary
F. Collis; 6 Sep 1841
(SpB)

EDZAR, James & Eleanor
Grinnan; 22 Nov 1754
(StM)

EGGBORN, Perry A. &
Martha P. Redd (d/o Wm.
Redd); 13 Dec 1842 (FB)

EGGLESTON,_____ &
Matilda H. Maury; 2 Jun
1817 (SpM)

EHART, Abram & Judith
Kirk; 25 Mar 1793 (OM)

ELGIN, Gustavus & Anne
Sutherland; 26 Mar 1793
(StM)

ELIASON, William A. &
Mary L. Carter; 27 Jun
1825 (FB)

ELLEY, Henry & Esther
Thorndow; 23 Dec 1742
(SpB)

ELLIOT, George & Mary
Adams; 26 Apr 1728
(StM)

ELLIOT, Jefferson &
Jane Burton; 1832 (SpM)

ELLIOT, Samuel &
Elizabeth Higgerson; 20
May 1747 (StM)

ELLIOT, Samuel & Esther
Flood; 8 Aug 1742 (StM)

ELLIOT, William & Sarah
Sharpe; 17 Dec 1752
(StM)

ELLIOTT, I.M.W. &
Frances Smith; 10 Aug
1837 (FB)

ELLIOTT, John & Mary
Taylor; 3 May 1818
(SpM)

ELLIS, Benjamin & Ann
Layton; 23 Feb 1807
(SpB)

ELLIS, Benjamin & Ann
Layton; 5 Mar 1807
(SpM)

ELLIS, James H. & Mary
C. Woolfolk (d/o Thomas
Woolfolk); 25 Mar 1816
(OM)

ELLIS, John & Sarah
Berry; 30 Sep 1744
(StM)

ELLIS, John W. &
Harriet H. Wardell; 7
Mar 1827 (FB)

ELLY, Edward & Sarah
Jones (d/o Isaac
Jones); 10 Jul 1815
(FB)

EMBRE,Richard & Judith
Payne; 17 Jan 1785 (OB)

EMBREY, William &
Rachel Davies; 6 Oct
1743 (StM)

EMMERSON, Thomas & Anne
McKey; 17 Apr 1743
(StM)

EMMERSON, William &
Rebecca Armstrong; 4
Oct 1836 (SpM)

ENGLAND, George & Mary
B. Thacker; 10 Aug 1826
(SpM)

ENGLES, John & Lettice
Burges; 15 Feb 1736 or
1737 (StM)

ENGLISH, John A. &
Judith B. Jones; 20 May
1841 (FB)

ENGLISH, Robert &
Jemima Blueford;22 Nov
1756 (StM)

ENGLISH, William &
Eliza Collawn; 5 Nov
1803 (FB)

ESSEX, Benjamin & Ann
Simpson; 24 Dec 1803
(FB)

ESSEX, Benjamin & Ann
Simpson; 25 Dec 1803
(SpM)

ESTES, Samuel & Mary
Jane Chewning; 1833
(SpM)

ESTES, Samuel &
Winifred Holladay; 21
Jul 1776 (OB)

ESTES, Triplett & Sally
Lucas (d/o Zach. Lucas)
21 Nov 1799 (FM)

ESTES, Triplett T. &
Hannah Lee Basye; 9 Jun
1818 (FB)

ESTIS, John & Sarah
Cox; 26 Dec 1799 (OM)

ETHERTON, John & Haty
Wass; 26 Oct 1824 (SpM)

EUBANK, John &
Elizabeth Long; 26 Aug
1840 (FB)

EUSTACE, William C.(of
Lancaster Co.) & Mary
L. Tomlin (d/o
Williamson B. & Ann C.
Tomlin); 21 Nov 1837
(FB)

EVANS, John (fpc) &
Betsy Toombs (d/o
Marietta Lewis) (fpc);
9 Nov 1819 (FB)

EVANS, Robert & Ellen
Lucas; 15 Jun 1841 (FB)

EVANS, Samuel & Jane
Riggin; 29 Jun 1746
(StM)

EVANS, Thomas & Anne
Lucas; 4 Feb 1753 (StM)

EVE, George W. &
Elizabeth Sangers; 25
Nov 1828 (FB)

EVE, Joseph & Polly
Smith (d/o Raif & Patty

Smith); 19 Aug 1799
(OM)

EVERSON, Thomas M. &
Alice Lear; 27 Mar 1816
(FB)

EVES, Thomas & Fanny
Jenkins (d/o William
Atkins); 1 Mar 1805
(OM)

FACKLER, Henry &
Frances Terrill; 25 Jan
1812 (OB)

FACKLER, Henry &
Frances Terrill; 25 Jan
1812 (SpM)

FAGG, James & Nancy
Buckhannon; 22 Dec 1814
(SpM)

FAIRN, Person & Susan
Alsop; 25 Jun 1817
(SpM)

FALLIS, Thomas & Polly
James; 29 May 1797 (OM)

FARISH, Leason & Lucy
Purvis; 17 Feb 1800
(SpM)

FARISH, Richard & Mrs.
Rebecca Stone; Apr 1802
(FB)

FARRISH, George R. &
Sarah A. Landram; 24
Feb 1846 (SpM)

FARRISH, John S. & Jane
Ward (d/o James Ward);
20 Jun 1799 (FM)

FARROW, Alexander & Ann
O'Canion; 5 Oct 1753
(StM)

FAULCONER, Burgess &
Mary Proctor; 10 Dec
1830 (SpM)

FAULCONER, George &
Nancy Coleman (d/o
James Coleman); 8 Jun
1793 (OM)

FAULCONER, James &
Eliza Brightwell; 26
Nov 1835 (SpM)

FAULCONER, John &
Margaret Morrison; 16
Jan 1775 (OB)

FAULCONER, Reuben &
Jenny Faulconer (d/o
Thomas Faulconer); 1
Nov 1796 (OM)

FAULCONER, Richard &
Nancy Sanders (d/o
Nathaniel Sanders); 9
Apr 1792 (OM)

FAULCONER, Samuel &
Sarah Burges; 14 May
1798 (OM)

FAULCONER, Thomas &
Elizabeth Jones; 16 Oct
1811 (OB)

FAULCONER, Thomas &
Elizabeth Jones; 16 Oct
1811 (SpM)

FAULCONER, Thomas &
Harriet Chevis; 7 Sep
1815 (SpM)

FAULCONER, William &
Betsy Chistram; 23 Jan
1797 (OM)

FAULKNER, Amos & Nancy
Sullivan; 15 Jun 1807
(FB)

FAULKNER, Amos & Nancy
Sullivan; 15 Jun 1807
(FM)

FAULKNER, William &
Mary Lewis (d/o Willis
Lewis); 9 May 1821 (FB)

FEARNEY, Thomas & Agy
Lucas; 19 Feb 1776 (OB)

FEARNEY, William &
Sally Morton; 19 Nov
1775 (OB)

FEILD, Thomas & Tabitha
Ware; 19 Feb 1802 (SpM)

FENDALL, John & Sarah
Alexander; 24 Sep 1751
(StM)

FENNEL, Charles & Nancy
Saunders; 9 Nov 1775
(OB)

FENNELL, William Jr. &
Jeany Bourn; 5 Feb 1778
(OB)

FERGUSON, James & Polly
Mann; 14 Nov 1809 (FB)

FERGUSON, Joseph &
Evelina Richards; 21
Nov 1843 (FB)

FERGUSON, Joseph &
Evelina Richards; 22
Nov 1843 (FM)

FERNANDIS, Peter &
Mildred Gooly; 29 Jul
1792 (StM)]

FERNSLEY, James & Sarah
Robinson; 3 Nov 1748
(StM)

FERRELL, George & Polly
Wolf (d/o Lenard Wolf);
13 May 1795 (OM)

FERRELL, Gustavus &
Nancy Chandler; 3 Apr
1830 (FB)

FEWEL, John & Mary
Grigsby; 14 Oct 1726
(StM)

FICKLIN, John F. &
Sarah A. Slaughter; 1
Nov 1847 (FB)

FIELD, Francis &
Tabitha Weir; 9 Feb
1802 (SpM)

FIELDS, Thomas &
Tabitha Ware; 1802
(SpM)

FIFE, James & Margaret
Minor; 16 Sep 1835
(SpM)

FIFE, James & Margaret
Minor; 16 Sep 1835
(SpM)

FIFE, Robert B. & Sarah
L. Banks; 30 Jan 1813
(SpM)

FILLINGER, Henry &
Betsy Ferrell; 1 Jan
1799 (OM)

FINDLESTON, John &
Martha Whiting; 10 Feb
1755 (StM)

FINNALE, Thomas(s/o
Robert Finnalle) & Ann
F. Ballard (d/o Judith
Ballard); 1 Feb 1830
(FB)

FINNALL, Thomas & Ann
F. Bullard; 4 Feb 1830
(FM)

FINNEL, Reuben &
Elizabeth Bowen (d/o
Henry Bowen); 12 Dec
1784 (OB)

FINNELL, Benjamin &
Elizabeth Robinson (d/o
Artemis & Phoebe

Robinson); 28 Dec 1799
(OM)

FINNELL, Benjamin &
Sarah Carter Sleet (w/o
?); 25 Aug 1775 (OB)

FINNELL, George & Sally
Dawson; 27 Jan 1794
(OM)

FINNELL, James &
Rebecca Chambers; 13
Jun 1793 (OM)

FINNELL, James &
Rebecca Chambers; 18
Aug 1791 (OM)

FINNELL, John & Caty
Surry; 2 Feb 1797 (OM)

FINNELL, John &
Elizabeth Chambers; 11
Jan 1797 (OM)

FINNELL, Morgan & Nancy
Almond; 12 Dec 1808
(SpB)

FINNELL, Morgan & Nancy
Almond; 12 Dec 1808
(SpM)

FINNELL, Reubin &
Elizabeth Bourne (d/o
Henry Bourne); 13 Dec
1784 (OM)

FISHER, Silvanus &
Elizabeth Brightwell
(d/o Absolem
Brightwell); 1 Jul 1819
(SpM)

FISHER, William &
Margaret Faulconer; 25
Sep 1815 (SpM)

FISHER, William &
Margarett Faulconer; 25
Sep 1815 (OB)

FITCHETT, Daniel &
Ceraelia Jenkins; 28
Feb 1839 (FB)

FITCHETT, James E. &
Lucinda Perry; 8 Feb
1849 (FB)

FITCHETT, John & Ann
Cayloe (d/o Mary Ann
Cayloe); 9 Jan 1810
(FB)

FITCHETT, John & Martha
Ann Stene; 20 Sep 1847
(FB)

FITCHETT, John & Sally
Downting; 19 Jan 1829
(FB)

FITCHETT, William &
Clarissa Holbrook; 2
Dec 1835 (FB)

FITZGARRELL, Stephen &
Catherine Bruce; 14 Nov
1787 (OM)

FITZGERALD, Jamee &
Elizabeth Thorton; 18
Oct 1810 (SpB)

FITZHUGH, Daniel &
Susanna Potter; 24 Oct
1772 (StM)

FITZHUGH, Henry &
Elizabeth Fitzhugh; 24
Oct 1777 (StM)

FITZHUGH, Henry &
Elizabeth Stith; 28 Oct
1770 (StM)

FITZHUGH, Henry Jr. &
Elizabeth Conway; (May
2 or Apr 17) 1792 (OM)

FITZHUGH, John &
Elizabeth Harrison; 31
Jan 1760 (StM)

FITZHUGH, McCarty &
Lucinda DeBaptist; 15
Sep 1824 (FB)

FITZHUGH, Thomas &
Sarah Stuart; 19 Jun
1750 (StM)

FITZHUGH, William & Ann
Taliaferro (d/o
Lawrence Taliaferro);
24 Feb 1783 (OB)

FITZHUGH, William &
Elizabeth Cason; 30 Oct
1804 (SpM)

FITZHUGH, William &
Elizabeth Lucas; 23 Feb
1847 (FB)

FITZHUGH, William D. &
Martha S. Thorton; 18
Jul 1820 (SpM)

FITZHUGH, William P. &
Martha L. Thornton; 18
Jul 1820 (SpM)

FITZPATRICK, John &
Mary Waters; 12 Feb
1752 (StM)

FITZPATRICK, William &
Mary Wallace; 13 May
1809 (SpM)

FLEAK, Andrew & Frankey
Rhoads (d/o
Epaphroditus Rhoads);
22 Nov 1795 (OM)

FLECK, Henry & Betsy
Smatts; 6 May 1797 (OM)

FLEEK, Andrew & Rachel
Lower; 8 Nov 1793 (OM)

FLEEMAN, Jos. & Eliza
Reynolds; 31 Dec 1815
(SpM)

FLETCHER, Abraham &
Priscilla Grigsby; 28
Nov 1746 (StM)

FLETCHER, Baldwin &
Elizabeth Williams; 14
Feb 1812 (FB)

FLETCHER, Francis &
Lettice Spicer; 8 Nov
1745 (StM)

FLETCHER, George &
Sarah Grigsby; Jan 1743
(StM)

FLETCHER, James &
Rachel Sebastian; 21
Apr 1745 (StM)

FLETCHER, Moses & Sarah
Martin; 10 Jul 1757
(StM)

FLETCHER, Thomas &
Margaret Hogsdale' 29
Mar 1752 (StM)

FLETCHER, Thomas &
Margaret Sharer; 26 Dec
1744 (StM)

FLETCHER, Thomas & Mary
Jones; 28 Dec 1753
(StM)

FLETCHER, Thomas & Mary
Knight; 2 Mar 1742 or
1743 (StM)

FLETCHER, William &
Mary Grigsby; 30 Jun
1764 (StM)

FLICK, John & Barbary
Kiblinger; 9 Jun 1796
(OM)

FLICK, William &
Catherine Lower (d/o
Michael Lower Sr.); 5
Sep 1798 (OM)

FLING, John & Mary
Briand; 31 Dec 1744
(StM)

FLITTER, John & Bridget
Riggins; 16 Mar 1755
(StM)

FLOID, Jasper &
Elizabeth Cupper; 4 Dec
1723 (StM)

FLOYD, James & Margaret
Lee; 20 Feb 1749 or
1750 (StM)

FLOYD, Samuel & Jane
Herring (d/o Thomas
Herring); 16 Apr 1799
(OM)

FOARD, William & Ann
Moore; 12 Dec 1785 (OB)

FOLEY, Henry & Anne
Courtney; 24 Dec 1738
(StM)

FOLEY, John & Sarah
Poole; 11 Dec 1744
(StM)

FOOTE, George & Frances
Berryman; 3 Dec 1731
(StM)

FOOTE, Richard & Jane
Stuart; 16 Dec 1795
(StM)

FOOTE, Richard &
Katharine Fossaker; 6
Oct 1726 (StM)

FORD, Absolem & Molly
Ransdell; 17 Jan 1792
(OM)

FORD, Benjamin & Rhody
Atkins (d/o Annie
Atkins); 29 Dec 1813
(OM)

FORD, John & Elizabeth
Thornton; 27 Jan 1729
or 1730 (StM)

FORD, John Taylor &
Patsy Gregory (d/o
Walter Gregory); 17 Feb
1810 (FB)

FORD, Warrener &
Frances Seaton; 24 Jul
1740 (STM)

FORD, William & Ann
Moore; 14 Dec 1785 (OM)

FORSTER, William &
Nanny Jordan; 15 Jun
1749 (StM)

FORTSON, Benjamin &
Sally Head (d/o James
Head); 6 Dec 1790 (OB)

FORTUNE, Vincent &
Nancy Bullock; Feb 1800
(SpM)

FOSTER, Anthony &
Elizabeth Price; 4 Apr
1776 (OB)

FOSTER, Edmund & Mary
P. Stanard; 1809 (SpM)

FOSTER, Frederick &
Susan F. Foster; 27 Dec
1841 (SpB)

FOSTER, George &
Margaret Grigsby; 22
Dec 1746 (StM)

FOSTER, John & Susannah
Deering (d/o Robert
Deering); 11 Oct 1793
(OM)

FOSTER, Robert &
Frances Brock; 17 Feb
1820 (SpM)

FOSTER, Robert D. &
Elizabeth Mitchell; 27
Dec 1820 (SpM)

FOSTER, Thomas &
Frances Jones; 25 Feb
1777 (OB)

FOSTER, Thomas & Mary
Sawyer; 8 Oct 1774 (OB)

FOSTER, William &
Tabitha Hawkins; 19 Apr
1793 (OM)

FOULKE, Owen I. &
Elizabeth Pusey; 25 Aug
1835 (FB)

FOUSHEE, Thornton &
Nancy Graves (d/o
Richard Graves); 28 Jun
1791 (OM)

FOWKE, Chandler (s/o
Gerard Fowke & Sarah
Burdett) & Mary
Fossaker (d/o Richard
Fossaker & Mary
Withers); before 1723
(StM)

FOWKE, Gerard (s/o
Chandler Fowke) &
Elizabeth Dinwiddie
(d/o John Dinwiddie);
26 Nov 1745 (StM)

FOWKE, Richard & Anne
Bunbury; 16 Mar 1760
(StM)

FOX, John & Lucinda
Lewis; 27 Aug 1818
(SpM)

FOX, Joseph & Susana
Smith; 6 Aug 1730 (SpB)

FOX, Stephen &
Elizabeth Herndon; 7
Mar 1796 (OM)

FOXWORTHY, John & Sarah
Northcut; 29 Sep 1751
(StM)

FOXWORTHY, Nicholas &
Mary Jordan; 26 Jan
1752 (StM)

FOXWORTHY, Thomas &
Sarah Nubal; 25 Dec
1751 (StM)

FRAIR, _____ & Jane
Evans; 1 Dec 1769 (StM)

FRANKAM, William & Mary
Kelly; 22 Jun 1728
(StM)

FRANKLIN, Cesar & Sarah
Kitchen; 28 Aug 1748
(StM)

FRANKLIN, William &
_____ Tenir; 14 Nov 1827
(FB)

FRANKLIN, William &
Mary Turin; 14 Nov 1829
(FM)

FRANKLING, John &
Margaret Bowling; 18
Aug 1716 (StM)

FRANKLYN, John & Mary
Pearson; 11 Mar 1785
(OB)

FRANKLYN, Jonathan &
Susannah Breeding (d/o
Job Breeding); 31 Jul
1790 (OB)

FRANKS, Samuel &
Parthenia Brown; 19 Jan
1786 (StM)

FRAYN, Martin & Mary
Anderson; 9 Jul 1758
(StM)

FRAZER, Edward &
Elizabeth Frazer; 14
Dec 1816 (SpM)

FRAZER, Herndon &
Huldah Herndon; 3 Apr
1817 (SpM)

FRAZER, Thomas & Peggy
Magee; 3 Oct 1815 (SpM)

FRENCH, Janus &
Elizabeth Chew; 22 Mar
1810 (FB)

FRENCH, John & Margaret
Burgess; 15 Jan 1749 or
1750 (StM)

FRENCH, Mason &
Margaret Lacy; 16 Apr
1749 (StM)

FRENCH, Michael &
Philippa Burton (d/o
Charles Burton); 7 Jul
1841 (FB)

FRENCH, William &
Elizabeth Barton (d/o
Seth Barton); 23 Jan
1812 (FB)

FRISTOE, Rev. Daniel
(s/o Richard & Grace
Fristoe Jr.) & Mary
Barker; before 1760
(StM)

FRISTOE, Richard & Mary
Hayes; 24 Nov 1748
(StM)

FRISTOE, Richard &
Virgin Waters; 28 Feb
1757 (StM)

FRISTOE, Robert & Anne
Rhodes; 23 Feb 1752
(StM)

FRITTER, Enoch & Polly
Knight; 10 Mar 1825
(FB)

FRITTER, Moses &
Elizabeth Horton; 1 Dec
1751 (StM)

FROGG, John (of Prince
William, Culpeper,
Augusta & Bath Co., Va)
& Elizabeth Strother
(d/o William Strother &
Margaret Watts of King
George Co., Va,); 9 Nov
1738 (StM)

FRY, George & Sarah
Brown; 18 May 1808
(SpM)

FRY, Hugh W. & Maria
White (d/o Henry
White); 26 Dec 1820
(FB)

FRY, Richard & Margaret
Hudson; 11 Jul 1745
(StM)

FUELL, William &
Johannah Boling; 17 Feb
1750 (StM)

FUGETT, James S. &
Elizabeth T. Clift; 27
Nov 1845 (FB)

FUGETT, James S. &
Rebecca M. Henry; 11
Nov 1847 (FB)

FULCHER, Alexander &
Salley Wisdom; 2 Jan
1812 (SpM)

FULCHER, Philip &
Drusila Wisdom; 25 Jun
1812 (SpM)

FULCHER, William &
Catherine Payne; 13 Sep
1828 (FB)

FULCHER, William H. &
Ann F. Blaydes; 21 Dec
1826 (SpM)

FULCHER, William H. &
Eliza M. Hewlett; 22
Feb 1825 (SpM)

FULLAGER, John & Mary
Dart; 26 Jan 1761 (StM)

FURNIS, Jacob & Mary
Page (d/o John Page); 5
Dec 1782 (OB)

GAER, William & Sally
Ham (granddaughter of
Sam Ham); 21 Aug 1792
(OM)

GAINES, Francis & Betsy
Lewis; 21 Jul 1776 (OM)

GAINES, Francis & Maria
Sales; 2 Apr 1850 (FB)

GAINES, John & Jenny
Gaines; 13 Mar 1793
(OM)

GAINES, John & Joanna
Sanders; 5 Mar 1800
(OM)

GAINES, Richard &
Elizabeth Eastin (d/o
Elizabeth Eastin); 6
Feb 1782 (OM)

GAINES, Richard &
Elizabeth Eastin; 5 Dec
1782 (OB)

GAINES, Thomas & Milly
Row (d/o Thomas Row);
26 Dec 1800 (OM)

GALASBY, John & Betsy
Goodridge; 14 Sep 1795
(OM)

GAMBLE, Mathew & Nancy
Bell; 10 Jan 1796 (OM)

GAMBOE, Samuel &
Catherine Chism (d/o

John Chism); 23 Dec
1796 (OM)

GARDE, William & Mary
Yates; 3 Nov 1795 (OM)

GARNER, Hezekiah &
Eliza Mullen; 27 Feb
1840 (FB)

GARNER, Mason (s/o
Travis Garner) & Louisa
Donaldson (d/o
Priscilla Donaldson); 8
Feb 1843 (FB)

GARNER, Parish &
Margaret Sturdy; 21 Jan
1742 (StM)

GARNER, Robert & Unis
Layton; 9 Jan 1845
(SpM)

GARNER, Robert & Unus
Layton; 9 Jan 1845 (FB)

GARNETT, Andrew & Sally
Bell; 19 Nov 1808 (OM)

GARNETT, George & Fanny
B. Banks (d/o Gerard
Banks); 20 May 1811
(FB)

GARNETT, James &
Frances Chiles (d/o
James Chiles); 23 Dec
1807 (OM)

GARNETT, Philip &
Elizabeth Dudley; 3 Apr
1799 (SpM)

GARNETT, Reubin M. (of
King & Queen County) &
Elizabeth Allen
Williams (d/o James
Williams); 16 Jul 1845
(FB)

GARNETT, Thomas &
Rachel Hawkins; 3 Oct
1756 (OM)

GARNETT, Thomas & Sukey
Brockman (d/o Samuel
Brockman); 15 Nov 1780
(OM)

GARNETT, Thomas H. &
Mary Moseley; 1 May
1814 (SpM)

GARRAT, William & Sarah
Ambry; 4 Feb 1741 or
1742 (StM)

GARREL, James & Sarah
Taylor; 14 Mar 1797
(OM)

GARRELL, Demey & Sally
Stanton (d/o Christy
Stanton); 27 Dec 1788
(OM)

GARRET, Daniel & Mary
Holliday; 4 Sep 1745
(StM)

GARRET, William & Sarah
Ambry; 4 Feb 1741 or
1742 (StM)

GARRETT, John B. &
Elizabeth Ann Walker;
30 Apr 1833 (FB)

GARRETT, William & Ann
Chambers; 28 Jan 1717
or 1718 (StM)

GARRION, Andrew & Ann
Phillips; 1 Dec 1842
(FB)

GARRISON, Aaron &
Elizabeth Bridwell; 18
May 1740 (StM)

GARRIT, John B. &
Elizabeth Ann Walker;
30 Apr 1833 (FM)

GARTON, Spencer & Polly
Hancock (d/o William

Hancock); 15 Feb 1797
(OM)

GASKINS, Hancock & Mary
Rafor; 11 Jul 1817 (FB)

GATES, Charles & Betsey
Loyd; 12 Mar 1810 (OB)

GATEWOOD, B. & Mrs.
Frances Conner; Aug
1805 (FM)

GATEWOOD, Henry & Amy
Quisenberry (d/o Moses
Quisenberry); 10 Aug
1805 (OM)

GATEWOOD, Robert &
Catherine Wiglesworth;
24 Oct 1838 (SpM)

GATTEN, James & Eliza
Bundy; 15 Aug 1833 (FB)

GEAR, Joshua & Jane
Watson (d/o Isaac
Watson); 27 Oct 1800
(OM)

GEAR, William & Polly
Rogers (d/o John
Rogers); 21 Aug 1798
(OM)

GEMISON, William &
Elizabeth Dalbin; 30
Dec 1725 (StM)

GEORGE, Moses & Betsy
Fickett; 27 Jul 1836
(FB)

GEORGE, Nicholas &
Margaret Whitson; 25
Dec 1740 (StM)

GEORGE, William & Flora
McKeen; 28 Jul 1783
(FM)

GEORGE, William & Lucy
Hawkins; 13 Feb 1793
(OM)

GEORGE, William & Mary Whitson; 1 Nov 1745 (StM)

GEYER, Charles & Elizabeth Jackson; 1 Oct 1812 (FB)

GIBBS, James & Ann Johnson (w/o ?); between May 14-17 & between the years 1771 & 1774 (OM)

GIBBS, Julius & Aggy Davis (d/o Joseph Davis); 27 Dec 1779 (OM)

GIBSON, James & Nancy Beazley; 1810 (SpM)

GIBSON, John & Elizabeth Harvey; 7 Aug 1798 (OM)

GIBSON, Jonathan & Elizabeth Carnohan; 7 Apr 1803 (SpM)

GIBSON, Thomas & Elizabeth Willoughby; 11 Dec 1821 (SpM)

GILBERT, Thomas & ---- Tearneaugh (d/o Thomas Tearneaugh); 11 May 1778 (OM)

GILES, James & Nancy Oliver; 24 Mar 1788 (StM)

GILHAUS, John & Mary Riley; 20 Jul 1842 (FB)

GILL, Charles R. & Adeline Towles; 11 Nov 1841 (FB)

GILL, Edward & Lettice Cannaday; 4 Feb 1753 (StM)

GILL, John & Elizabeth Williams; 3 Mar 1754 (StM)

GILLESPIE, James & Mary Harrison Hall; 23 Apr 1838 (FB)

GILLESPY, John & Ann White (d/o John White Sr.); 7 Jul 1796 (OM)

GILLETT, Samuel & Sally Pannill; 3 Jun 1790 (OM)

GILLOCK, John & Hannah Wolfengerger; 7 Jan 1778 (OM)

GILLOCK, Laurence & Betsy Twentymen; 26 May 1789 (OM)

GILLOCK, Thomas & Elizabeth Morgan; 8 Jan 1784 (OB)

GILLOCK, Thomas & Elizabeth Morgan; 8 Jan 1784 (OM)

GILMAN, Granville & Mary Ann Jones (d/o Jane Jones); 30 Dec 1830 (FB)

GIVEN, Benjamin & Sarah Leavel; 13 Apr 1795 (SpM)

GLASCOCK, George G. & Agatha A. G. Moncure (d/o Edwin C. & Elenor Moncure); about 1835 (StM)

GLASCOCK, John & Agnes Davis; 12 Sep 1827 (FB)

GLASSELL, Andrew & Elizabeth Taylor; 21 Oct 1777 (OM)

GLASSETT, Michael &
Mary Ann Burke; 11 Oct
1837 (FB)

GLENDENING, John (s/o
John & Phoebe
Glendening) & Jane
Grant (d/o William
Grant Sr. & Margaret
Glendening); 30 Jan
1746 (StM)

GLOVER, Thomas & Sarah
Kelly; 1 Sep 1737 (StM)

GODEFROY, Augustin &
Elizabeth Williams; 20
Feb 1817 (FB)

GODFREY, William &
Rebecca Robinson; 26
Oct 1746 (StM)

GOFF, William & Mary
Kelly; 8 Sep 1738 (StM)

GOFORTH, Thomas & Milly
Foster; 9 Sep 1788 (OM)

GOING, Peter & Mary
Sullivant; 28 May 1745
(StM)

GOLDEN, Richard & Ann
Walton; 3 May 1798 (OM)

GOLDING, Thomas &
Frances Berry; 28 Jan
1738 or 1739 (StM)

GOLDING, Thomas &
Frances Berry; 28 Jan
1738 or 1739 (StM)

GOLDSBY, David &
Matilda Howard (d/o
William Howard); 4 Sep
1817 (FB)

GOLDSMITH, John &
Martha Powell; 19 Jan
1756 (StM)

GON, John Jr. & Gracey
Grace (d/o George
Grace); 9 Dec 1793 (OM)

GOODALL, David &
Elizabeth Dais (d/o
Joseph Davis); 10 Apr
1793 (OM)

GOODALL, James & Sally
Harvey; 23 Jan 1782
(OB)

GOODALL, James & Sally
Harvey; 23 Jan 1782
(OM)

GOODALL, Jonathan &
Patsy Russell; 23 Dec
1798 (OM)

GOODALL, Parks &
Frankey Cox; 14 Feb
1789 (OM)

GOODALL, William & Lucy
Davis (d/o Jonathan
Davis); 15 Mar 1785
(OB)

GOODALL,William & Lucy
Davis (d/o Jonathan
Davis); 15 Mar 1785
(OM)

GOODLOE, George P. &
Mary E. G. Pendleton;
25 Sep 1845 (SpM)

GOODLOE, Robert &
Louisa Goodloe; 6 Feb
1816 (SpM)

GOODMAN, Christopher &
Nancy Stanley; 4 Aug
1807 (SpM)

GOODRICH, John & Betty
Deer; 14 Mar 1775 (OM)

GOODRICK, William &
Mary Currell; 21 Aug
1850 (FB)

GOODRICK, William &
Mary Currell; 22 Aug
1850 (FM)

GOODWIN, Arthur & Ann
Thom; 16 Oct 1834 (FB)

GOODWIN, Charles &
Jannet G. Carmichael
(d/o James Carmichael);
21 Dec 1819 (FB)

GOODWIN, James & Sarah
Lawyer; 5 Jun 1735
(StM)

GOODWIN, John Thomas &
Ann Elizabeth Goodwin
(d/o W.P. Goodwin); 11
Dec 1838 (FB)

GOODWIN, Joseph G. &
Fanny Graves; 25 Dec
1810 (SpM)

GOODWIN, Loyd & Polly
Graves; 25 Aug 1813
(SpM)

GOODWIN, William P. &
Caroline Heiskell; 26
Sep 1816 (FB)

GOODWIN, William P. &
Mary B. Benlle; 1 May
1827 (SpM)

GOODWIN, William P. &
Mary B. Burke; 24 Apr
1827 (FB)

GORDEN, John & Margaret
Tennins (d/o Dorothy
Tennins); 15 Sep 1739
(SpB)

GORDON, Alexander &
_____; 1717 (StM)

GORDON, Alexander &
Susan F. Gordon (d/o
Samuel Gordon of
Kenmore); 5 Nov 1824
(FB)

GORDON, James & Ann
Hord; 20 Mar 1823 (SpM)

GORDON, James L. & Mary
F. Beale; 16 Oct 1845
(FB)

GORDON, John &
Elizabeth Musten; 24
Nov 1747 (StM)

GORDON, John & Sarah
Raddish; 24 Jan 1722 or
1723 (StM)

GORDON, John Jr. &
Margaret Rogers; 22 Nov
1776 (StM)

GORDON, Nathaniel &
Mary Gordon; 18 Oct
1785 (OB)

GORDON, Nathaniel &
Mary Gordon; 18 Oct
1785 (OM)

GORDON, Reubin S. &
Eliza S. Beale; 5 Mar
1846 (FM)

GORDON, William &
Elizabeth Alders; 1809
(SpM)

GORDON, William &
Rebecca Cooke (d/o John
Cooke); 17 Feb 1808
(FB)

GORE, Charles M. &
Philadelphia Jones; 25
May 1831 (SpM)

GORE, Charles W. &
Elisabeth Pullin; 11
Dec 1833 (FB)

GORE, Jacob & Elizabeth
Hilldrup; 1 Nov 1808
(FB)

GORE, John H. & Jane F. Wood; 30 Mar 1838 (FB)

GORSUCK, Caleb & Mary Virginia Gibbs (d/o Mary H. Gibbs); 13 Jun 1844 (FB)

GOSS, Hamilton & Martha Major (w/o ?); 24 Dec 1798 (OM)

GOSS, Henry & Catharine Steward; 14 Feb 1811 (SpM)

GOSS, Henry & Catherine Steward; 14 Feb 1811 (SpB)

GOSS, Henry & Elizabeth Joy; 8 Aug 1773 (StM)

GOSS, Joseph & Anne Joy; 24 Dec 1747 (StM)

GOSS, Joseph & Lucy Steward; 24 Apr 1804 (SpB)

GOSS, Joseph & Lucy Stewart; 28 Apr 1804 (SpM)

GOUCH, James & Elizabeth Powers (of Caroline Co., Va.); 21 Feb 1762 (StM)

GOUGH, William & Lucy Byram; 19 Oct 1743 (StM)

GOULDMAN, Sansford & Nancy Allen; 1 Sep 1843 (SpM)

GRACE, George & Ann McNeal; 9 Jan 1774 (OM)

GRACE, George & Anne McNeal; 9 Jan 1774 (OB)

GRACEY, Walker & Elizabeth Day; 25 Nov 1824 (SpM)

GRADY, Abraham & Sarah C. Hicks; 22 Dec 1825 (SpM)

GRADY, Benjamin & Catherine Adams; 1 Jan 1800 (OM)

GRADY, John & Sarah Proctor (d/o John Proctor); 18 Dec 1807 (OM)

GRADY, John P. & Eliza T. Ellis; 31 May 1831 (SpM)

GRADY, Reuben & Elizabeth Ford; 2 May 1796 (SpB)

GRADY, Reuben & Elizabeth Ford; 2 May 1796 (SpM)

GRADY, Richmond & Hannah Montague; 24 Oct 1801 (OrB)

GRADY, Richmond & Hannah Montague; 24 Oct 1801 (SpM)

GRADY, William & Mary Adams; 22 Dec 1794 (SpB)

GRADY, William & Mary Adams; 22 Dec 1794 (SpM)

GRAHAM, James S. & Angelina S. Finnalt; 20 May 1845 (FM)

GRAHAM, John & Christian Brown (d/o Gustavus Brown & Frances Fowke); Jul or Aug 1742 (StM)

GRAHAM, Richard & Jane
Brent (of Prince
William Co. ,VA.); 10
Feb 1757 (StM)

GRANT, Andrew & Mary
Matthews; 26 Apr 1770
(StM)

GRANT, Gregory & Sarah
Wharton; 11 Nov 1747
(SpB)

GRANT, James &
Elizabeth Massey; 10
Jan 1793 (StM)

GRANT, John & Hester
Foote; 17 Aug 1727 (StM
?)

GRANT, John & Hester
Foote; 17 Aug 1727
(StM)

GRANT, Samuel & Lidia
Craig; 22 Jul 1784 (OB)

GRANT, Samuel & Lidia
Craig; 22 Jul 1784 (OM)

GRAVAT, George &
Catherine McCartie; 9
May 1756 (StM)

GRAVAT, John &
Behethland Kelly; 27
Dec 1751 (StM)

GRAVATT, George & Mary
S. Long (d/o Joshua
Long); 14 Apr 1836 (FB)

GRAVES, Absolem &
Felicia White (d/o John
White); 19 Dec 1789
(OM)

GRAVES, Benjamin &
Elizabeth Collins (d/o
William Collins); 13
Sep 1796 (OM)

GRAVES, Hermes & Nancy
B. White; 8 Apr 1819
(SpM)

GRAVES, Jacob & Fanny
White; 8 Oct 1800 (OM)

GRAVES, Joel & Sarah
Graves; 20 Dec 1794
(OM)

GRAVES, Jos. & Tammy
Waller; 2 Nov 1815
(SpM)

GRAVES, Paschal &
Elizabeth W. Graves; 25
Aug 1830 (OB)

GRAVES, Roda & Marian
Marquess (d/o John
Marquess); 24 Nov 1800
(OM)

GRAVES, Thomas & Anna
Grady (d/o William
Grady); 18 Jun 1789
(OM)

GRAVES, Thomas &
Mourning Burrus (d/o
Thomas Burrus); 5 Feb
1791 (OM)

GRAVES, William & Betsy
Hilman; 22 Dec 1796
(OM)

GRAVY, James & Amy
Mastin; 27 Jan 1803
(SpM)

GRAY, Aitcheson &
Catharine D. Willis; 16
Oct 1821 (FB)

GRAY, John & Sarah
Thomas; 11 May 1758
(StM)

GRAY, John B. & Jane
Cave; 24 Oct 1829 (FB)

GRAY, Nathaniel &
Elizabeth Fitzhugh; 12
Aug 1734 (StM)

GRAY, Thomas B.W. &
Lucy Y. Wellford; 1 May
1808 (SpM)

GRAY, Thomas M. & Sally
Lucas; 18 Nov 1829 (FB)

GRAY, William F. &
Milly Richards Stone
(d/o W.F. Stone); 24
Sep 1817 (FB)

GREEN, Daniel & Sarah
Foxworthy; 16 Oct 1750
(StM)

GREEN, George &
Elizabeth Whitson; 23
Dec 1744 (StM)

GREEN, James & Lucy
Martin; 4 Oct 1748
(StM)

GREEN, John & Mary
Brown; 24 Dec 1805 (FB)

GREEN, John & Phillis
Smith; 19 Dec 1756
(StM)

GREEN, Jones & Susanna
E.M. Scott; 25 Oct 1821
(FB)

GREEN, Leavell & Delia
Fitchett; 29 Sep 1841
(FB)

GREEN, Nicholas &
Elizabeth Price; 6 Jan
1757 (OM)

GREEN, Robert & Helen
Lowry; 23 Nov 1756
(StM)

GREEN, Thomas & Lydia
Whitridge; 24 Mar 1745
or 1746 (StM)

GREEN, Timothy & Lucy
Carter; 7 Jun 1817 (FB)

GREEN, William & Anne
Robinson; 18 Dec 1743
(StM)

GREEN, William & Judith
Harrel; 21 Jan 1742
(StM)

GREEN, William & Judith
Harrel; 21 Jan 1742
(StM)

GREETEN, Charles &
Elizabeth Richards; 2
Nov 1803 (FB)

GREGG, George & Jane
Vinson; 5 Feb 1734 or
1735 (StM)

GREGG, John & Elizabeth
Waugh; 16 Oct 1737
(SpB)

GREGG, John Ben & Sarah
Smith; 22 Jun 1730
(StM)

GREGG, Matthew & _____
Chinn; 15 Aug 1751
(StM)

GREGORY, Charles &
Sophia P. Hall; 4 Feb
1817 (FB)

GREGORY, Walter &
Alzira Smith (w/o ?);
12 Sep 1819 (FB)

GRIFFEY, Abell &
Catherine Sutton; 13
Sep 1793 (OM)

GRIFFEY, Joseph & Fanny
Wisdom; 15 Oct 1789
(OM)

GRIFFIN, Clinton & Susannah Jones; 14 Jan 1805 (SpM)

GRIFFIN, Lewis & Eliza Grigsby; 19 Mar 1833 (FB)

GRIFFIN, Thomas & Sarah Suddeth; 18 Jul 1745 (StM)

GRIFFIN, William & Margaret Corbin; 6 Apr 1725 (StM)

GRIFFIN, William & Pamelia Lewis; 7 Dec 1837 (FB)

GRIGGS, George & Margaret Humfries; 22 Jun 1749 (StM)

GRIGSBY, Benjamin & Anne Foly; 5 Sep 1725 (StM)

GRIGSBY, Benjamin & Anne Foly; 5 Sep 1727 (StM)

GRIGSBY, Elisha & Elizabeth Porter (d/o Abner Porter); 24 May 1796 (OM)

GRIGSBY, James & Letitia Travers; 18 Jan 1753 (StM)

GRIGSBY, James & Sarah Sudduth; 9 May 1742 (StM)

GRIGSBY, Moses & Katherine Bransom; 1 Dec 1742 (StM)

GRIGSBY, Moses & Mary Matheny; 26 Aug 1753 (StM)

GRIGSBY, Samuel & Anne Grigsby; 25 Dec 1762 (StM)

GRIGSBY, Thomas & Anne Dishman; 25 Nov 1729 (StM)

GRIMES, Uriah & Sarah Hall (d/o Nancy Hall); 11 Mar 1843 (FM)

GRINNAN, Daniel & Eliza Green; 9 Jul 1804 (FB)

GRINNAN, Henry & Jane Gaskins Cropley; 31 Mar 1831 (FB)

GRINNAN, John & Elizabeth Jane Farish; 11 Sep 1835 (FB)

GRINNAN, Robert & Robertina Temple; 17 Jan 1850 (FB)

GRISSET, James & Elizabeth Philips; 19 May 1791 (StM)

GROOM, John & Dise Delaney; 22 Jan 1797 (OM)

GROVES, Edward & Mary Hearne; 15 Sep 1748 (StM)

GROVES, William & Barbara Webster; 2 Feb 1749 (StM)

GRYMES, Benjamin & Betty Fitzhugh; 12 Feb 1746 or 1747 (StM)

GRYMES, Benjamin & Margaret Pratt; 7 Apr 1808 (SpM)

GULLEY, John & Mary Land (d/o John Land); 22 Mar 1781 (OM)

GUNN, John & Martha
Shamlin; 30 Sep 1753
(StM)

GUNTHER, H.D. & Eliza
Ann Rollow; 14 Oct 1835
(FB)

GUTRIDGE, Charles &
Elizabeth Bragdon; 13
Feb 1850 (FB)

GUTRIDGE, Leonard &
Mary E. Cridlin; 26 Dec
1850 (FB)

GUTRIDGE, Thomas &
Sarah Rallings; 16 May
1782 (StM)

GUTTRIDGE, Charles &
Mary King; 17 Dec 1840
(FB)

GWATKIN, James &
Frances Dade; 25 Mar
1774 (StM)

GWIN, James & Elizabeth
Maccaboy; 5 Oct 1755
(StM)

HACHDTT, John W. &
Elizabeth Stevens; 8
Mar 1832 (FB)

HACKER, William & Anne
Dillon; 21 May 1738
(StM)

HACKETT, John &
Elizabeth K. Henslope;
5 Jan 1809 (SpM)

HACKETT, John &
Elizabeth K. Hesslop; 2
Jan 1809 (SpB)

HACKNEY, Robert &
Susanna Keeton; 7 Mar
1816 (SpM)

HACKNEY, Stephen &
Elizabeth Saint John;
15 Dec 1804 (SpM)

HADDOCK, Ignatius &
Winifred Garmony; 20
Oct 1729 (StM)

HADLEY, Alpheus &
Elizabeth Ashley; 11
Nov 1844 (FB)

HAGAN, James &
Catherine Meyers (d/o
Joshua Meyers); 13 Jan
1831 (FB)

HAILSTOCK, John Henry &
Louisa Evans (d/o
Elizabeth Evans); 6 May
1847 (FB)

HALBERT, Elijah & Nancy
Edge; 2 Jan 1798 (SpM)

HALBERT, Elijah & Nancy
Edges; 2 Jan 1798 (SpB)

HALEY, John & Elizabeth
Taylor; 27 Jul 1802
(SpM)

HALL, Charles C. & Mary
Elizabeth Anderson; 23
Nov 1843 (FB)

HALL, Horace B. &
Alverda C. Stuart; 5
Jul 1848 (FB)

HALL, Horace C. & T.
Pierce; 22 Dec 1834
(SpM)

HALL, James & Hardinia
O. Bunnell; 22 Oct 1846
(SpM)

HALL, John & Hannah
Suddath; 6 Nov 1749
(StM)

HALL, John B. & Harriet
Stringfellow; 23 Oct
1817 (FB)

HALL, Joseph & Mary
Barron; 13 Oct 1727
(StM)

HALL, Michael &
Elizabeth Kelly; 29 Dec
1744 (StM)

HALL, Robert P. &
Charlotte Hall; 25 Sep
1845 (FB)

HALL, Thomas &
Elizabeth Davenport; 11
Mar 1802 (SpM)

HALL, William &
Susannha Davis; 2 Jan
1800 (OM)

HALLET, John & Mary
Walker; 1 Aug 1751
(StM)

HALLEY, William &
Catharine Jeffries; 9
Feb 1758 (StM)

HAM, Joseph & Sarah
Hearen (d/o Francis &
Sarah Hearen); 12 Dec
1783 (OM)

HAM, Joseph & Sarah
Hearen; 12 Dec 1783
(OB)

HAMBLETON, Edward &
Elizabeth Rippito (d/o
John Rippito); 9 Aug
1793 (OM)

HAMBLETON, Leroy &
Suckey Blunt (d/o
Michael Blunt); 12 Jan
1800 (OM)

HAMBLETON, Theophilus &
Nutty Powell; 25 Mar
1796 (OM)

HAMET, Daniel & Eleanor
Jones; 22 Dec 1774
(StM)

HAMILTON, Hugh & Janet
H. Scott; 10 May 1829
(FB)

HAMILTON, John &
Frances Richard (d/o
William Richard); 24
Dec 1788 (OM)

HAMILTON, Robert &
Helen Brooke; 1 Jun
1843 (SpM)

HAMILTON, William &
Jenny Olive (d/o
Elizabeth Olive); 24
Dec 1799 (OM)

HAMMAT, Daniel &
Betridge Bowlin; 2 Nov
1728 (StM)

HAMMET, John & Anne
Donahoo; 15 Aug 1757
(StM)

HAMMET, John & Anne
Donahoo; 15 Aug 1757
(StM)

HAMMET, William &
Rosamund Smith; 6 May
1755 (StM)

HAMMIT, Robert & Sythe
Bethel; 7 Feb 1749
(StM)

HAMMIT, Robert & Sythe
Bethel; 7 Feb 1749
(StM)

HAMPTON, Thomas & Sarah
Pattison (aka Conyers);
1 Jun 1749 (StM)

HANCOCK, James &
Elender Hancock (d/o

William Hancock); 11
Oct 1805 (OM)

HANCOCK, Nathaniel J. &
Martha Jane Smith; 19
Dec 1850 (SpM)

HANCOCK, William &
Jemima Brockman; 4 May
1775 (OM)

HANCOCK, William B. &
Mary Bridenheart; 24
Sep 1816 (OM)

HANCOCK, William T. &
Barbara McWhirt (d/o
Richard & Barbara
McWhirt); 31 Dec 1839
(FB)

HANDLEY, Bryan & Sarah
Williams; 28 Dec 1726
(StM)

HANER, William & Ann
Knight; 10 Mar 1837
(FB)

HANER, William & Peggy
Simpson; 30 Nov 1797
(SpB)

HANER, William & Peggy
Simpson; 30 Nov 1797
(SpM)

HANEY James & Nancy
Peters (d/o Mathew
Peters); 1 May 1784
(OB)

HANEY, Benjamin &
Elizabeth Johnson; 15
Nov 1799 (SpM)

HANEY, James & Dorothy
Waller; 7 Dec 1795
(SpM)

HANEY, James & Nance
Petros; 1 May 1784 (OM)

HANEY, Thomas & Mary
McDarmont; 7 Dec 1807
(SpM)

HANSBROUGH, Peter &
Lydia Smith; 27 May
1752 (StM)

HANSBROUGH, Peter &
Margaret French; 26 Feb
1745 (StM)

HANSBURY (aka
Hansbrough), James &
Lettice Sumner; 19 Sep
1741 (StM)

HANSEN, Thomas H. &
Mary C. Parke; 11 May
1842 (FB)

HANSFORD, Stephen (born
in Abbotsbury, Dorset
Co. England) & Margaret
McCarty; 14 Oct 1755
(StM)

HANSFORD, William &
Sarah Doniphan; 12 Feb
1725 or 1725 (StB)

HANSFORD, William &
Sarah Doniphan; 12 Feb
1725 or 1726 (StM)

HANSLEY, Benjamin &
Elizabeth Hikkum; 19
Jan 1730 or 1731 (StM)

HANSON, William &
Susannah Rorh; 19 Nov
1725 (StM)

HARDIN, George & Jane
Bunbury; 3 Dec 1740
(StM)

HARDIN, James E. (s/o
William Hardin) & Ellen
Frances Hogan; 25 Sep
1849 (FB)

HARDIN, William &
Josephine Chismond; 19
Jun 1827 (FB)

HARDING, William &
Patty Green; 28 Jan
1746 (StM)

HARDING, William &
Patty Green; 28 Jan
1746 (StM)

HARDWICK, Haswell &
Mary Northcut; 25 Dec
1750 (StM)

HARDWICK, Solomon &
Anne Peach; 25 Sep 1748
(StM)

HARGES, John &
Elizabeth Luthrel; 1
Oct 1725 (StM)

HARMON, Richard &
Elizabeth Mizing; 28
Mar 1746 (StM)

HAROLINE, Charles Todd
& Matilda Richards; 2
Mar 1824 (SpM)

HARRIS, Edward I. &
Mary F. Core; 10 Jan
1832 (SpM)

HARRIS, George & Mary
Carrol; 14 Jul 1750
(StM)

HARRIS, John & Frances
Rowzie; 17 Nov 1774
(OM)

HARRIS, John & Hannah
Stevens; Apr 1748 (SpB)

HARRIS, John & Milly
Price (w/o ?); 3 Nov
1800 (OM)

HARRIS, John O. & Anne
C.L. Hill; 12 Dec 1820
(SpM)

HARRIS, John W. &
Margaret S. Coleman; 12
Jan 1825 (SpM)

HARRIS, Lewis & Martha
Smith; 17 Nov 1816 (OB)

HARRIS, Lewis & Martha
Smith; 17 Nov 1816
(SpM)

HARRIS, Peter & Mary
Stanfield Estes; 27 Feb
1797 (OM)

HARRIS, Thomas &
Elizabeth Lunnsdary; 19
Jan 1832 (SpM)

HARRISON, Benjamin &
Mary Short; 17 Nov 1770
(StM)

HARRISON, Benjamin Jr.
& Anne March; 14 Oct
1785 (FB)

HARRISON, James & Susan
P. Helmstatlar; 23 May
1834 (FB)

HARRISON, John M. &
Mary Frances Perry (d/o
James T. Perry); 2 May
1850 (FB)

HARRISON, Thomas (s/o
Burr Harrison & Ann
Barnes) & Anne Peyton
(d/o John Peyton); 2
Jul 1747 (StM)

HARRISON, William &
Polly Sims; 4 Oct 1816
(OM)

HARRISON, William (s/o
William Harrison &
Sarah Hawley) &
Isabella Triplett Hore
(d/o William Triplett &
Isabella Miller, w/o
Elias Hore); 1732 (StM)

HARROD, Benjamin &
Betsy Blair; 20 Apr
1796 (OM)

HARROD, John & Mary
Ellis; 4 Aug 1728 (StM)

HART, Archibald & Ann
Charmichael (d/o James
Charmichael); 19 Oct
1815 (FB)

HART, Arthur & Evelina
C.S. Godwin; 26 Oct
1843 (FB)

HART, James & Charlotte
Hogans; Jul 1811 (SpM)

HART, John & Hasich
Green (d/o Timothy
Green); 16 Oct 1815
(FB)

HART, John & Rachel
Oram; 23 Mar 1746 (StM)

HART, John R. Ann M.S.
Goodwin; 21 Oct 1835
(FB)

HART, Robert & Susan
Elizabeth Jenkins; 25
Nov 1829 (SpM)

HART, Robert J. &
Margarett H. Hackett;
19 Dec 1839 (SpM)

HART, Robert W. &
Elizabeth W. Ellis; 20
Nov 1832 (FB)

HART, William &
Elizabeth Tumley; 16
Feb 1819 (SpM)

HART, William T. & Jane
B. Minor; 1 Jun 1848
(SpM)

HARTLY, James & Anne
Walpole; 26 Aug 1778
(StM)

HARTLY, James &
Elizabeth Tilcock; 1
Apr 1768 (StM)

HARTLY, James & Mary
Kelly; 25 Aug 1754
(StM)

HARVEY, Benjamin &
Susanna Harvey; 23 Feb
1775 (OM)

HARVEY, John &
Elizabeth Felix (d/o
William Felix); 22 Jan
1800 (OM)

HARVEY, John & Lucy
Estes; 19 Apr 1778 (OM)

HARVEY, Thomas & Sarah
Hobbs; 19 Apr 1778 (OM)

HARVEY, William & Alley
Wood (d/o Hopeful
Wood); 12 Jul 1800 (OM)

HARVEY, William & Maria
Jones; 26 May 1824 (FB)

HARVISON, Samuel S. &
Ann Eliza Ficklin (d/o
Catharine Ficklin); 13
Nov 1850 (FB)

HARWOOD, Moses &
Elizabeth Sutton; 7 Mar
1791 (OM)

HASEY, Michael &
Elizabeth Leathers; 9
Feb 1823 (OB)

HASEY, Michael &
Elizabeth Leathers; 9
Feb 1823 (SpM)

HAUSE, Conrad &
Susannah Thompson; 2
Apr 1796 (OM)

HAWES, Samuel & Mary
Ann Ralls; 16 Feb 1749
(StM)

HAWKINS, Benjamin &
Sally Scott; 7 Mar 1799
(OM)

HAWKINS, James & Betsy
Coleman (d/o James
Coleman); 3 Sep 1799
(OM)

HAWKINS, James &
Elizabeth Rector; 11
Nov 1799 (OM)

HAWKINS, James &
Frances Pendleton; 2
Oct 1829 (SpM)

HAWKINS, John & Susanna
Haney; 26 Dec 1805
(SpM)

HAWKINS, John B. & Ann
Ford; 2 Oct 1812 (OB)

HAWKINS, Joseph L. &
Nancy Mullin; 10 Jul
1810 (SpM)

HAWKINS, Moses & Joice
Quisenberry; 23 Apr
1803 (OM)

HAWKINS, Moses &
Susanna Strother; 3 Mar
1770 (OM)

HAWKINS, Sebree & Mary
Gaines; 28 Oct 1780
(OM)

HAWKINS, Thomas & Sarah
Ancrum; 13 Jul 1746
(StM)

HAWKINS, William & Rose
Cook; 16 Aug 1723 (StM)

HAY, John & Mary
Garret; 12 Jul 1724
(StM)

HAYDON, Jesse Jr. &
Lucy McCalley; 20 May
1796 (SpB)

HAYDON, Jesse Jr. &
Lucy McCalley; 21 May
1796 (SpM)

HAYDON, John & Susan
Colvert; 20 Feb 1838
(FB)

HAYDON, Patrick &
Martha Jane A. Taylor
(d/o Mary Taylor); 22
Feb 1842 (FB)

HAYES, Moses & Sarah
Petty; 28 Oct 1780 (OM)

HAYNS, John & Margaret
Linsy; 8 Sep 1728 (StM)

HAYWOOD, John & Martha
Mills (d/o Shady
Mills); 1 Jan 1846 (FB)

HAZARD, Henry H. &
Harriett A. Bibb; 5 Dec
1837 (FB)

HAZLEGROVE, Peter &
Jane Reeves (d/o Julia
Reeves); 25 Sep 1838
(FB)

HEAD, Benjamin Jr. &
Margaret Gaar (d/o
Lewis Gaar); 21 Aug
1784 (OB)

HEAD, Benjamin Jr. &
Margaret Garr (d/o
Lewis Garr); 21 Aug
1784 (OM)

HEAD, George Marshall &
Milly Rucker (d/o John
& Mary Rucker); 10 Nov
1789 (OM)

HEAD, Henry & Elizabeth
Sanford (d/o Ann
Sanford); 5 Nov 1794
(OM)

HEAD, James & Elizabeth
Jannet Kirtley; 5 Dec
1775 (OM)

HEAD, John & Nancy
Sanford (d/o Ann
Sanford); 26 Nov 1787
(OM)

HEAD, Tavenah & Jenny
Plunket (d/o Jessy
Plunket); 20 Dec 1798
(OM)

HEADS, Emanuel & Joice
M. Jackson; 10 Feb 1810
(FB)

HEARNE, Mary & Edward
Groves; 15 Sep 1748
(StM)

HEDGEMAN, George &
Hannah Daniel; 27 Nov
1756 (StM)

HEDGEMAN, Peter &
Margaret Mauzy (d/o
John Mauzy); 21 Sep
1721 (StM)

HEFFERNON, James &
Alander Payton; 20 May
1740 (StM)

HEFFERNON, William &
Sarah Martin; 29 Sep
1741 (StM)

HELM, William & Matilda
Taliaferro (d/o Francis
Taliaferro); 31 May
1784 (OM)

HENAGE, George &
Cathrine Jones; 12 Jan
1809 (SpM)

HENDERSON, Alexander &
Eliza Smith; 11 Apr
1815 (FB)

HENDERSON, Francis &
Martha Dillard; 24 Jan
1832 (SpM)

HENDERSON, John &
Frankey Daniel; 2 Jan
1797 (OM)

HENDERSON, John & Sally
Quisenberry; 28 Oct
1811 (OM)

HENDERSON, William &
Nancy Mason; 5 Jan 1826
(SpM)

HENDERSON, William &
Peggy Stears; 4 Mar
1816 (SpM)

HENNEAGE, John & Molly
Sparkes; 22 Oct 1785
(StM)

HENNESSY, Peter &
Winney Routt; 25 Nov
1793 (OM)

HENNINGS, Robert L. &
Mildred Carter; 9 Apr
1838 (FB)

HENRY, Benjamin & Nancy
Roberts (d/o Hugh
Roberts); 17 May 1792
(OM)

HENRY, Hill & Susanna
Jones; 5 Mar 1778 (OB)

HENRY, John S. &
Caroline M. Richardson;
18 Nov 1836 (SpM)

HENRY, Thomas &
Catharine Brewin; 28
May 1818 (SpM)

HENRY, William &
Elizabeth Warren (w/o
?); 22 Apr 1793 (OM)

HENRY, William D. &
Julia A. Hall; 31 May
1842 (FB)

HENSHAW, Edmund & Mary
Newman (d/o James
Newman Sr.); 22 Sep
1785 (OB)

HENSHAW, John &
Elizabeth Newman (d/o
James & Elizabeth
Newman); 20 Aug 1792
(OM)

HENSHAW, John & Patty
Newman (d/o James
Newman); 4 Dec 1780
(OM)

HENSLEY, Lewis & Mary
Foster; 28 Oct 1785
(OB)

HENSLEY, Samuel &
Martha Snell; 3 Mar
1727 (SpB)

HERARD, Jean Baptiste
(born in Seus, France)
& Mary Ralls; 31 Jul
1820 (FB)

HERDON, George & Hildah
Billingsley; 23 Dec
1819 (SpM)

HERNDON, Alexander &
Ann Billingsley; 20 Dec
1821 (SpM)

HERNDON, Benjamin &
Catherine Ehart; 20 Nov
1787 (OM)

HERNDON, Dabney &
Elizabeth Hull; 12 Nov
1806 (SpM)

HERNDON, Edmond Jr. &
Malvina A. Cammack; 24
Oct 1822 (SpM)

HERNDON, Edward &
Elizabeth Lewis; 12 Jul
1809 (SpB)

HERNDON, Edward (of
Spotsylvania Co., Va.)
& Mary Waller (d/o
George Waller &
Elizabeth Allen); 15
Apr 1753 (StM)

HERNDON, James & Ann
Estes (d/o Triplett F.
Estes); 21 Apr 1818
(FB)

HERNDON, John &
Elizabeth Wright (d/o
John Wright); 19 Apr
1781 (OM)

HERNDON, John M. &
Margaretta L. Patton;
18 Apr 1835 (FB)

HERNDON, Thomas D. &
Elizabeth Billingsley;
6 Oct 1814 (SpM)

HERNDON, William &
Sukey Perry; 5 May 1786
(OM)

HERNDON, Zachariah &
Mary Scott; between
1771 & 1774 (OM)

HERRIN, Isaac & Hannah
Montague; 7 Oct 1798
(SpM)

HERRING, James & Judah
Cofer (d/o James
Cofer); 2 Apr 1784 (OM)

HERRING, James & Rachel
Cofer (d/o Judah &
James Cofer); 2 Apr
1784 (OB)

HERRING, William &
Molly Shiflett (d/o
William Shiflett); 7
Feb 1789 (OM)

HERROD, John & Mary
Devane; 21 Aug 1748
(StM)

HESELTON, William &
Hannah Leonard; 7 Jul
1765 (StM)

HESLON, William & Polly
Long; 5 Jan 1814 (SpM)

HESLOP, Edward D. &
Maria Perry; 10 May
1844 (SpB)

HESLOP, Horace & Sally
Hart; 13 Sep 1816 (SpM)

HESLOP, James & Lucy
Ann McCalley; 24 Dec
1850 (SpM)

HESLOP, James & Lucy
Brown; 7 Apr 1817 (SpM)

HESLOP, James & Lucy
Hart; 26 Sep 1816 (SpM)

HESLOP, William A. &
Harriet A. Heslop; 2
Nov 1837 (SpM)

HESTAND, John & Tanlipy
Nowell; 4 Nov 1799 (OM)

HEWITT, James & Eleanor
Swan; 4 Jan 1816 (SpM)

HEWLETT, Thomas B. &
Frances A. Wiglesworth;
9 Jan 1828 (SpM)

HEWLETT, Thomas B. &
Lucy A. Stewart; 18 Sep
1850 (SpM)

HEWLETT, William & Jane
Dixon; 1 Aug 1844 (FB)

HIATT, John & Sarah
Arnold; 30 Dec 1783
(OM)

HIATT, Jonathan & Mary
Conner (d/o Rachel
Conner); 27 May 1784
(OB)

HIATT, Lewis & Barbary
Allen; 24 Dec 1783 (OM)

HIATT, Lewis & Mary
Conner (d/o Rachel
Conner); 27 May 1784
(OM)

HIBBILL, George & Mary
Triplett; 12 Feb 1728
or 1729 (StM)

HICKS, Andrew & Polly
Davenport; 23 Feb 1809
(SpM)

HICKS, Henry & Sarah
Wren; 22 Dec 1831 (SpM)

HICKS, Joseph &
Elizabeth Pendleton; 15
Jan 1807 (SpM)

HICKS, Joseph H. &
Mildred T. Lewis; 4 Apr
1848 (SpM)

HICKS, Martin & Nancy
Pendleton; 11 Dec 1817
(SpM)

HICKS, Richard & Lucy
Wren; 13 Jan 1829 (SpM)

HICKS, Thomas &
Virginia V. Green (d/o
William D. Green); 20
May 1844 (FB)

HICKS, William J. &
Sally Cash; 6 Jan 1845
(SpM)

HIEATT, John & Sarah Arnold; 30 Dec 1783 (OB)

HIEATT, Lewis & Barbary Allen; 24 Dec 1783 (OB)

HIGDON, John & Mary Ross; 3 Jun 1796 (OM)

HIGGERSON, John & Jean Jackson; 20 Jan 1742 (StM)

HIGGINS, William & Sarah Newton 9 Dec 1732 (StM)

HIGHLANDER, Charles & Betsy Brooks; 5 Aug 1805 (SpM)

HILDRUP, James & Jaley Carter; 16 Jan 1816 (FB)

HILES, Samuel & Mary Ann Smith; 2 Apr 1801 (SpM)

HILL Titus H. & Charlotte Matthews; 30 Jan 1820 (FB)

HILL, John & Elizabeth Mehoney; 1 Oct 1716 (StM)

HILL, Moses & Matilda Gaines (fpc); 24 Feb 1849 (FB)

HILL, Richard & Sarah Burnsplat; 22 Dec 1737 or 1757 (StM)

HILL, Robert L. & Maria Tunstall; 2 Aug 1821 (SpM)

HILL, Samuel & Nancy Tate; 24 Dec 1788 (OM)

HILL, Thomas & Elizabeth Grayson; 18 Apr 1731 (SpB)

HILL, Thomas & Sally True; 25 Aug 1795 (SpB)

HILL, Thomas & Sally True; 27 Aug 1795 (SpM)

HILL, William & Catherine Stacy; 17 Sep 1745 (StM)

HILLDRUP, Samual & Elizabeth Taliaferro; 7 Feb 1746 (SpB)

HILLYARD, Nathaniel & June M. Parke; 24 Dec 1833 (FB)

HILMAN, Uriel & Sally Graves; 11 Jul 1797 (OM)

HINSHAW, Edmund & Macy Newman (d/o James Newman); 22 Sep 1785 (OM)

HINSON, George & Margaret Burchell; 29 Dec 1746 (StM)

HINSON, George & Margaret Burchell; 29 Dec 1746 (StM)

HINSON, George & Sarah Sullivan; 4 Feb 1753 (StM)

HITCHCOCK, Samuel J. & Marcipa Whittemore; 23 Dec 1834 (FB)

HITE, Isaac Jr. & Nelly Madison; 3 Dec 1782 (OM)

HITE, Isaac Jr. & Nelly Madison; 31 Dec 1782 (OB)

HOARD, Washington &
Elizabeth Adams; 27 Oct
1810 (SpB)

HOBDAY, John & Mary
Davis; 16 Aug 1790 (OM)

HOCKADAY, Robert &
Caysandra E. Waller; 15
Feb 1844 (SpM)

HOCODY, Thomas & Lucy
Morris; 2 Mar 1802
(SpM)

HODGES, Galen & Mildred
Wibber; 28 Jan 1810
(SpM)

HODGES, Linah M. &
Sarah M. Horn; 25 Feb
1831 (SpB)

HODGES, Lurah & Sarah
M. Horn; 26 Feb 1831
(SpM)

HOGAN, Edward & Martha
Richerson; 6 Jan 1832
(SpM)

HOGDON, Nathaniel &
Margaret Oliver; 2 Mar
1746 or 1747 (StM)

HOGG, John & Eleanor
Savage; 19 Dec 1744
(StM)

HOKINS, Thomas &
Elizabeth Ham; 24 Jul
1716 (StM)

HOLDBROOK, William &
Elizabeth King; 8 Dec
1744 (StM)

HOLDRIDGE, Frederick &
Catharine E. Barton; 16
Oct 1834 (FM)

HOLDRIDGE, Frederick &
Catharine Elizabeth

Burton; 16 Oct 1834
(FB)

HOLLADAY, Alexander R.
& Patsy Q. Poindexter;
6 Sep 1837 (SpM)

HOLLADAY, Benjamin &
Martha W. Dillard; 27
Oct 1847 (SpM)

HOLLADAY, Edward &
Lucinda Pulliam; 24 Dec
1819 (SpM)

HOLLADAY, John &
Elizabeth L. Holladay;
7 Feb 1826 (SpM)

HOLLADAY, Joseph & Jane
Duerson; 18 May 1821
(SpM)

HOLLAND, George & Mary
Coleman; 21 Jan 1757
(OM)

HOLLOWAY, Thomas S. &
Ann M. Crump; 28 Mar
1818 (FB)

HOLMES, William & Anne
Roberts; 28 Feb 1798
(SpM)

HOME, George &
Elizabeth Proctor; 16
Dec 1727 (SpB)

HOMES, James & Sally
Hilman (d/o Joseph
Hilman); 22 Dec 1795
(OM)

HONEY, John & Hannah
Bussel; 2 Feb 1748
(StM)

HONEY, John & Hannah
Bussel; 2 Feb 1748
(StM)

HOOE, Bernard &
Margaret Pratt; 2 Nov
1771 (StM)

HOOE, Henry Dade & Jane
Fitzhugh; 17 Jun 1790
(StM)

HOOE, Howson Jr. & Mary
Dade; 26 Sep 1746 (StM)

HOOE, John & Anne
Alexander; 23 Nov 1726
(StM)

HOOE, John & Anne
Fowke; 14 Mar 1755
(StM)

HOOE, R. & Margaret
Carter; Jun 1804 (FM)

HOOE, Rice Wingfield &
Susanna Fitzhugh; 13
May 1790 (StM)]

HOOE, Rice Wingfield &
Susannah Fitzhugh; 13
May 1790 (StM)

HOOE, Seymour & Sarah
Alexander; 31 Jan 1776
(StM)

HOOE, Seymour & Sarah
Alexander; 9 Mar 1776
(StM)

HOOE, William & Susanna
Pratt; 13 Nov 1782
(StM)

HOOLIDAY, Whorton &
Elizabeth Duwest; 28
Jul 1742 (StM)

HOOMES, Hay B. &
Eleanor E. Johnston; 4
Nov 1840 (FB)

HOOMES, R. & Hannah
Battaile (d/o Hay
Battaile); Apr 1804
(FM)

HOOPER, William & Susan
B. Day; 11 Nov 1829;
(SpM)

HOPKINS, Burton &
Mildred Frances
Chewning; 1833 (SpM)

HOPKINS, Burton &
Mildred Frances
Chewning; 6 May 1833
(SpB)

HOPKINS, Richard &
Betsey Thomas; 23 Nov
1815 (SpM)

HOPKINS, Richard &
Susan P. Lewis; 3 Dec
1836 (SpM)

HORD, Ezekiel & Polly
Parker; 5 Aug 1803
(SpM)

HORD, Peter & Harriet
Benson; 21 Sep 1824
(FB)

HORD, William & Huldah
Parker; 17 Nov 1807
(SpB)

HORD, William & Huldah
Parker; 22 Nov 1807
(SpM)

HORN, Thomas M. & Mary
M. Carter; 23 Sep 1830
(SpB)

HORN, Thomas M. & Mary
M. Carter; 24 Sep 1830
(SpM)

HORNER, Robert & Ann
Brown (d/o Gustavus
Brown & Frances Fowke);
before 1773 (Horner's
death date) (StM)

HORSLEY, James & Jane
Chiles (d/o Robert
Jones); 4 Aug 1809 (OM)

HORTON, Albert & Mary
Jane Rise; 22 Oct 1845
(FB)

HORTON, Anthony &
Rosamund Duncomb; 27
Dec 1745 (StM)

HORTON, Thomas & Hannah
Saunders; 10 Feb 1786
(StM)

HORTON, William &
Harriet E. Martin (w/o
?); 23 Dec 1819 (FB)

HORTON, William &
Margaret Cooke; 21 Dec
1749 (StM)

HORTON, William (of
King George Co., Va.) &
Mary Thornberry; 12 Jan
1741 (StM)

HOUSTEN, John D. &
Martha H. Wilson; 2 Nov
1835 (FB)

HOWARD, Blorcain &
Agnes A. Pendleton; 17
Jan 1030 (SpM)

HOWARD, Charles P. &
Jane Taylor; 11 Mar
1793 (OM)

HOWARD, Joseph H. &
Mary R. Todd; 5 Nov
1849 (SpM)

HOWARD, Richard &
Margaret Sullivan; 28
Dec 1790 (OM)

HOWARD, William & Sally
Mannon; 1 Jul 1811
(SpM)

HOWARD, William Jr. &
Salley Mannon; 30 Jun
1812 (SpB)

HOWARDS, Alexander &
Joana Trippolo; 25 Nov
1727 (SpB)

HUBBARD, Carter & Betsy
Durrett; 16 Jan 1793
(OM)

HUBUD, Moses & Sarah
Lowry; 23 Mar 1726 or
1727 (StM)

HUDGIN, Robert & Sarah
R. Graham; 30 Apr 1828
(FB)

HUDGINS, Westcomb &
Nelly Hardy; 31 Oct
1799 (FM)

HUDSON, John &
Elizabeth Holland; 24
Aug 1780 (StM)

HUDSON, John & Mary
Dedman; 2 Apr 1793 (OM)

HUDSON, William &
Margaret Rallins; 10
Mar 1785 (StM)

HUDSON, William & Nancy
Chiles; 14 Sep 1816
(OB)

HUDSON, William & Nancy
Chiles; 14 Sep 1816
(SpM)

HUFFMAN, Landon & Ann
Proctor (d/o Mary
Proctor); 27 May 1840
(FB)

HUGGINS, Churchill &
Louisa T. Hailey; 15
Nov 1831 (SpM)

HUGHES, Armisted & Sally Chisham; 27 Apr 1800 (OM)

HUGHES, Luke & Behethland Kennedy; 10 Jul 1779 (StM)

HUGHES, Thomas & Mary Davis; 8 Jun 1775 (OM)

HUGHES, Thomas & Tamy Walden; 25 Apr 1811 (SpM)

HUGHES, William & Sophia Dowdall; 6 Jun 1744 (SpB)

HUGHLETT, John & Milly Keaton; 5 Feb 1798 (SpM)

HULL, Aaron R. & Marthy E. Turnley; 23 Apr 1846 (SpM)

HULL, Brodie & Elizabeth Herndon; 20 Nov 1806 (SpM)

HULL, John & Ann Crump; 21 Apr 1845 (FB)

HUMES, James & Margaret Dodd; 30 Dec 1812 (OB)

HUMES, James & Margaret Dodd; 30 Dec 1812 (SpM)

HUMPHREYS, Stephen & Nancy Shackeford; 4 Sep 1804 (SpM)

HUMPHRIES, James & Eliza Davis; 17 Mar 1811 (SpM)

HUMPHRIES, Robert & Susan Fulcher; 11 Oct 1836 (SpM)

HUMPHRIES, Stephen & Polly Dillard; 19 Dec 1826 (SpM)

HUMPHRIES, William & Susannah Webb; 26 Nov 1774 (OM)

HUNDLEY, John & Nancy Loyd; 12 Jul 1794 (OM)

HUNDLEY, Joshua & Betsy Gressom; 9 Feb 1797 (OM)

HUNDLEY, Nehemiah & Elizabeth Cave (d/o Benjamin Cave); 4 Aug 1790 (OM)

HUNGERFORD, Thomas & Anne Washington; 22 Jun 1780 (StM)

HUNLEY, James & Susannah Chiles; 23 Jan 1797 (OM)

HUNT, Conrad H. & Elizabeth Daenvan; 1 Sep 1832 (FB)

HUNT, Gilbert I. & Jane Jones; 12 Dec 1833 (FM)

HUNT, Gilbert J. & Jane Jones; 12 Dec 1833 (FB)

HUNTER, Pleasant & Jane Harris (d/o Lindsay Harris); 25 Oct 1799 (OM)

HUNTER, Taliaferro & Lucy Ann Tennent; 7 Nov 1839 (FB)

HUNTER, William & Martha Taliaferro; 5 Apr 1744 (SpB)

HUTCHEN, William & Siler Robinson (d/o

John Robinson); 23 Mar 1795 (OM)

HUTCHERSON, James & Catherine Dear; 8 Oct 1800 (OM)

HUTCHERSON, Washington & Elizabeth Lancaster; 12 Dec 1816 (OB)

HUTCHERSON, Washington & Elizabeth Lancaster; 13 Dec 1816 (SpM)

HUTCHESON, George & Mildred Wagstaff; 19 Sep 1727 (StM)

HYATT, John & Anne Lloyd; 7 Jan 1717 or 1718 (StM)

HYDE, Benjamin & Mary Young; 26 Aug 1786 (FB)

HYTE, Jacob & Frances Beale; 15 Dec 1756 (OM)

HYTER, William & Anne Hewes; 3 Apr 1743 (StM)

INGLES, Jonathan & Penelope _____; 6 Sep 1686 (StM)

INGRAM, Valentine & Nancy Williams; 13 May 1813 (FB)

ISAAC, George & Caroline Spencer; between May 14-17 & between the years 1771-1774) (OM)

JACKSON, Caesar (fpc) & Rosetta Cole (fpc); 8 Dec 1821 (FB)

JACKSON, James & Elizabeth Sweney; 31 Dec 1767 (StM)

JACKSON, James & Mary Johnston; 3 Sep 1761 (StM)

JACKSON, John & Elizabeth Caldwell; 3 May 1786 (FB)

JACKSON, John & Rachel Rosser; 31 Jan 1731 or 1732 (StM)

JACKSON, Joseph & Mary Howard; 29 Mar 1826 (SpM)

JACKSON, Samuel & Anne Berry; 10 Feb 1739 or 1740 (StM)

JACKSON, Samuel & Maria Lewis (fpc); 8 Nov 1813 (FB)

JACKSON, Samuel & Mary Delander; 21 Feb 1736 or 1737 (StM)

JACKSON, Walter (fpc) & Ann Eliza Lewis (fpc); 29 Feb 1848 (FB)

JACKSON, William & Ann Miller; 20 Dec 1824 (OB)

JACKSON, William & Ann Miller; 20 Dec 1824 (SpM)

JACKSON, William A. & Sarah Ann Hillyard; 6 Feb 1838 (FB)

JACOB, William & Polly Martin (d/o Henry Martin); 24 Aug 1802 (OM)

JACOBS, Benjamin & Sarah Martin (d/o Henry Martin); 30 Dec 1799 (OM)

JAMAR, Richard & Betsy
Soams; 16 Dec 1811
(SpM)

JAMES, Benjamin & Sarah
Scott; 1 Oct 1812 (SpM)

JAMES, Charles P. &
Eliza Cooke; 9 May 1820
(FB)

JAMES, John & Anne
Sebastian; 29 Dec 1737
(StM)

JAMES, John & Anne
Strother; 16 Sep 1763
(StM)

JAMES, John & Nancy
Patterson; 24 Jul 1806
(FB)

JAMES, John & Nancy
Patterson; 28 Jul 1806
(SpM)

JAMES, John H. & Mary
Wilson Crawford (d/o
George Crawford); 30
May 1830 (FB)

JAMES, Richard & Betsey
Soams; 16 Dec 1811 (OB)

JAMES, Spencer &
Frances Davis; 21 Aug
1780 (OM)

JAMESON, Thomas R. &
Polly Samuel; 12 Dec
1792 (OM)

JAMESON, William &
Elizabeth Dalbin; 30
Dec 1725 (StM)

JAMISON, David & Jane
Sebastian; 7 May 1744
(StM)

JARRALD, Jeremiah 7
Lucretia Sims; 2 Oct
1816 (OM)

JARREL, John C. & Mary
E.L.Cropp; 4 Dec 1832
(SpM)

JARRELL, James &
Frances Sirus; 13 Jun
1793 (OM)

JARVIS, Francis D. &
Sarah Lane Ames; 23 May
1831 (FB)

JEFFERSON, Thomas &
Mary Toombs; 8 Mar 1832
(FB)

JEFFERSON, Thomas &
Mary Toombs; 8 Mar 1832
(FM)

JEFFRIES, Alexander &
Lettice Burton; 30 Sep
1741 (StM)

JEFFRIES, George &
Sarah Graves; 8 Feb
1756 (StM)

JEFFRIES, William G. &
Mary E. Tate; 5 Oct
1848 (FB)

JENKINS, Albert G. &
Catherine Wiatt; 12 Apr
1834 (FM)

JENKINS, Alexander G. &
Alice Eliza Courter; 21
Jan 1830 (SpM)

JENKINS, Arthur &
Fenton Garner; 27 Nov
1841 (FB)

JENKINS, James &
Elizabeth Betty; 18 Nov
1840 (FB)

JENKINS, James & Usey
Guthrie; 22 Aug 1849
(FB)

JENKINS, R. & Sally
Hobday; 20 Aug 1813
(SpB)

JENKINS, Robert & Susan
Ann Barnes; 25 Dec 1844
(FB)

JENKINS, Thomas &
Elizabeth Taylor; 14
Jan 1800 (OM)

JENKINS, William & Mary
Ann Lively; 30 Feb 1832
(SpM)

JENKINS, William Smith
& Nancy Carter; 19 Dec
1813 (SpM)

JENNINGS, George &
Susan Portch (d/o
Peishous Portch); 9 Sep
1835 (FB)

JENNINGS, James &
Lucretia Long (d/o
Martha Long); 7 Nov
1850 (FB)

JENNINGS, James & Nancy
Grigsby Grady; 28 Mar
1822 (FB)

JENNINGS, William &
Catharine Curtis; 30
Nov 1848 (FB)

JESSE, William P. &
Emily Lyon; 5 Apr 1838
(FB)

JETT, George & Mary
Rise; 31 Dec 1831 (FB)

JETT, Henry & Susan
Puzey; 30 Apr 1835
(SpM)

JETT, James & Catherine
Southard; 1832 (SpM)

JETT, James & Catherine
Suthard; 7 Nov 1831
(SpB)

JETT, James H, & Mary
Bridewell; 28 Oct 1850
(FB)

JETT, Jefferson & Ellen
Dickinson; 15 Jan 1829
(SpM)

JETT, Thomas & Lucinda
Owens; 12 Jan 1775
(StM)

JETT, Thomas & Susan
Bowling; 2 Nov 1842
(SpM)

JETT, William & Sarah
Jane Dunnevant; 7 Sep
1849 (FB)

JINKINS, David & Jane
Parker; 5 Feb 1801
(SpM)

JOHNS, Griffin &
Elizabeth Gordon; 7 Feb
1731 or 1732 (StM)

JOHNSON, Aquilla &
Dorcus Lewis; 19 Dec
1820 (SpM)

JOHNSON, Benjamin & Ann
Turnby; 4 Jun 1799
(SpM)

JOHNSON, Benjamin (fpc)
& Henrietta Furguson
(d/o James Furguson);
13 May 1843 (FB)

JOHNSON, George & Anne
Cheesman; 9 Jan 1734 or
1735 (StM)

JOHNSON, Isaac & Salley
Pulliam; 17 Mar 1814
(SpB)

JOHNSON, Isaac & Salley Pulliam; 17 Mar 1814 (SpM)

JOHNSON, Isaac Jr. & Elizabeth Terrill; 5 Jun 1795 (OM)

JOHNSON, Jacob & Helenor Delander; 10 Dec 1728 (StM)

JOHNSON, Jacob & Margaret Regan; 13 Oct 1748 (StM)

JOHNSON, James & Lucy Ledwidge; 24 Feb 1808 (SpB)

JOHNSON, James & Lucy Ledwidge; 25 Feb 1808 (SpM)

JOHNSON, John & Betsy Dodd; 8 Mar 1806 (SpB)

JOHNSON, John & Frances Powel; 18 Nov 1731 (StM)

JOHNSON, John & Maria Lewis; 17 Aug 1825 (FB)

JOHNSON, John & Nancy Johnson; 27 Oct 1803 (SpM)

JOHNSON, John & Sarah Rootes; 23 Feb 1807 (SpM)

JOHNSON, Joseph & Elizabeth Bledsoe; 8 Apr 1799 (SpB)

JOHNSON, Joseph & Elizabeth Bledsoe; 8 Apr 1799 (SpM)

JOHNSON, Littleton D. & Jane Cooley; 8 Jul 1819 (FB)

JOHNSON, Patrick & Elinor Chambers; 14 May 1726 (StM)

JOHNSON, Patrick & Sicily Duncan; 17 Nov 1724 (StM)

JOHNSON, Richard & Elizabeth Brightwell; 24 Nov 1801 (SpB)

JOHNSON, Richard & Elizabeth Brightwell; 25 Nov 1801 (SpM)

JOHNSON, Richard L. & Mary Somerville Powell (d/o Elizabeth Powell); 31 Jan 1837 (FB)

JOHNSON, Samuel & Peggy Birch; 28 Jul 1785 (StM)

JOHNSON, Thomas & Diannah Richards (d/o William Richards); 31 Jan 1797 (OM)

JOHNSON, Thomas & Elizabeth Harvey; 19 Oct 1745 (StM)

JOHNSON, William & _____ Goff; 20 Nov 1762 (StM)

JOHNSON, William & _____; 12 Oct 1723 (SpB)

JOHNSON, William & Ann Barnett; 10 Feb 1770 (OM)

JOHNSON, William & Fanny Lewis; 18 Nov 1818 (SpM)

JOHNSON, William & Mary Sebastian; 5 Jan 1743 or 1744 (StM)

JOHNSON, William &
Winifred Gray; 24 Feb
1760 (StM)

JOHNSTON, Charles S. &
Lucy Victor (d/o John
Victor); 28 Apr 1804
(FB)

JOHNSTON, Fayette &
Eliza Pearson (d/o
William Pearson); 28
Mar 1816 (FB)

JOHNSTON, Gabriel &
Adelaide C. Barnett
(d/o Benjamin N.
Barnett); 13 Sep 1830
(FB)

JOHNSTON, James &
Eleanor Evans; 17 May
1806 (FB)

JOHNSTON, James R. &
Mary T. Nicholson; 28
Nov 1831

JOHNSTON, John &
Frances Dounton; 30 Jul
1778 (StM)

JOHNSTON, Larkin &
Frances H. Starke; 31
Mar 1826 (SpM)

JOHNSTON, Larkin &
Julia Pearson (d/o
William Pearson); 28
Mar 1820 (FB)

JOHNSTON, R. Jr. & Mrs.
Ann M. Dare (w/o John
Dare); Aug 1805 (FM)

JOHNSTON, Richard & Ann
M. Dare; 10 Aug 1805
(FB)

JOHNSTON, Richard & Ann
Marie Heiskell; 3 Sep
1811 (FB)

JOHNSTON, Richard &
Mary Dudley; 12 Nov
1812 (SpB)

JOHNSTON, William &
Alice Sterns; 13 Aug
1832 (FM)

JOHNSTON, William &
Alice Stevens; 13 Aug
1832 (FB)

JOHNSTON, William &
Betty Taylor; 6 Jul
1744 (SpB)

JOHNSTON, William &
Patty Wharton; 5 Aug
1778 (StM)

JOHNSTON,Richard &
Nancy Walker (d/o
Thomas Walker); 27 Jun
1799 (FM)

JONATHAN, Valentine &
Nancy Bennett; 31 Jan
1791 (OM)

JONE, Henry & Jane
Jett; 1 Dec 1836 (FB)

JONES, Benjamin &
Elizabeth Foster; 12
May 1774 (OM)

JONES, Benjamin &
Salley Gatewood; 23 Jan
1811 (SpB)

JONES, Benjamin & Sally
Gatewood; 23 Jan 1811
(SpM)

JONES, Burrell &
Matilda Newton; 9 Mar
1820 (SpB)

JONES, Burril & Matilda
Newton; 9 Mar 1820
(SpM)

JONES, C. & Mrs.
Douglas; Jun 1805 (FM)

JONES, Charles F. &
Sophia Stifle; 14 Jul
1827 (FB)

JONES, Churchill &
Keziah Pates; 19 Oct
1837 (SpM)

JONES, David & Amanda
I. Lester; 26 Jun 1848
(SpM)

JONES, David & Mary
Boswell; 18 Feb 1763
(StM)

JONES, Edward & Mary
Ann Wharton; 30 Dec
1818 (SpB)

JONES, Edward & Mary
Ann Whorton; 31 Dec
1828 (SpM)

JONES, Elijah & Mary M.
Horn; 6 Apr 1798 (SpM)

JONES, Evan & ____
Matthews (d/o John
Matthews); before 9 Mar
1689 (StM)

JONES, George &
Elizabeth Green; 3 Apr
1805 (FB)

JONES, James & Agnes H,
Brown; 19 May 1835
(SpM)

JONES, James & Ann
McCalley; 27 Aug 1816
(SpM)

JONES, James & Caty
Robinson (d/o John
Robinson); 7 Sep 1785
(OM)

JONES, James & Caty
Robinson (d/o John
Robinson); 7 Sep 1785
(OB)

JONES, James & Mary
Wilkerson (w/o ? of
King George Co., Va.);
16 Apr 1786 (StM)

JONES, James C. &
Ophelia Layton (d/o
Robert G. Layton); 1
Oct 1849 (FB)

JONES, James R. & Mary
King; 8 Mar 1830 (FB)

JONES, John & Agnes
Durham; 3 Oct 1734
(SpB)

JONES, John & Barbara
Reynolds; 20 Jan 1749
(SpB)

JONES, John & Dorothy
Gatewood; 19 Dec 1804
(SpB)

JONES, John & Dorothy
Gatewood; 20 Dec 1804
(SpM)

JONES, John & Elizabeth
Turner; 20 Dec 1796
(SpB)

JONES, John & Helenor
Moss; 16 Aug 1744 (StM)

JONES, John & Margaret
Abell; 7 Sep 1785 (OB)

JONES, John & Margaret
Abell; 7 Sep 1785 (OM)

JONES, John & Nancy
Mourning; 24 Dec 1812
(SpM)

JONES, John L. & Martha
Short; 5 Jan 1843 (FB)

JONES, John W. & Eliza
Byram; 14 Nov 1849 (FB)

JONES, Joseph & Lucy
Gaines; 26 Mar 1803
(SpB)

JONES, Joseph & Lucy
Ganes; 26 Mar 1803
(SpM)

JONES, Joseph & Mary
Jordan (of King George
Co., Va.); 16 Aug 1774
(StM)

JONES, Lewis & Salley
Edge; 14 Jan 1800 (SpM)

JONES, Matthew & Rose
Cavenoch; 21 Sep 1746
(StM)

JONES, Philemon & Emily
B. Minor; 22 Sep 1824
(SpM)

JONES, Reuben & Patty
Stowers (w/o ?); 3 Aug
1789 (OM)

JONES, Rev. Robert &
Mary Herndon (w/o ?); 3
Jun 1800 (OM)

JONES, Richard & Grace
Leonard; 10 Mar 1756
(OM)

JONES, Rubin & Nancy
Anderson; 8 Apr 1801
(SpM)

JONES, Thomas &
Elizabeth Frye; 24 Mar
1781 (FB)

JONES, Thomas & Sarah
Abbott; 30 Dec 1793
(SpB)

JONES, Thomas & Sarah
Abbott; 30 Dec 1793
(SpM)

JONES, Wharton S. &
Mary A. Alsop; 4 Sep
1834 (SpM)

JONES, William &
Elizabeth Alsop; 9 Feb
1749 or 1750 (StM)

JONES, William & Jane
Reiney; 20 Apr 1752
(StM)

JONES, William &
Lucinda Gordon; 31 Jul
1828 (SpM)

JONES, William & Lucy
Peters; 29 Sep 1810
(FB)

JONES, William & Mary
Baxter; 26 Jul 1744
(StM)

JONES, William & Mary
Baxter; 26 Jul 1745
(StM)

JONES, William &
Rebecca Grady (31 years
old); 10 Aug 1815 (FB)

JONES, William L. &
Lucy Ann Baggott; 29
Mar 1838 (FB)

JONES, William L. &
Mary Eliza Barton; 22
May 1850 (FB)

JONES, William T. &
Frances E. L. Daniel; 4
Sep 1839 (FB)

JONES, Zachariah &
Rebecca Dean; 15 Nov
1787 (OM)

JORDAN, Alexander &
Behethland Gravat; 30
Oct 1758 (StM)

JORDON, Isham & Matilda
Randall; 19 May 1823
(FB)

JOSEPH, Jonathan &
Sarah Deering; 11 Mar
1786 (OM)

JOY, Isaac & Elizabeth
McCant; 23 Mar 1770
(StM)

JOYNER, Daniel & Mary
_____ (age 43 in 1692);
before 8 Sep 1692 (StM)

JULIAN, Charles & Phebe
Wilson, 7 Mar 1749
(SpB)

KAUFFMAN, Christian J.
& Susan A. White; 20
Dec 1842 (FB)

KAY, Robert & Elizabeth
Strother; 13 Dec 1762
(StM)

KEAN, John V. & Mary L.
Hart; 19 Jan 1837 (SpM)

KEEGAN, John & Ann
Long; 3 Apr 1799 (SpM)

KEETON, Abner & Susanna
Starke; 22 Dec 1801
(SpM)

KEETON, William &
Philadelphia Shepherd;
1803 (SpM)

KEITH, John & Amelia
Johnson; 5 Jan 1768
(StM)

KELLEY, William &
Margaret Dew; 24 Apr
1732 (StM)

KELLY, Edmund & Jane
Gregg; 15 Jun 1736
(StM)

KELLY, James & Eleanor
Burnsplat (d/o Jethro &
Sarah Burnsplat); 15
Apr 1757 (StM)

KELLY, James & Eleanor
Burnsplat; 15 Apr 1757
(StM)

KELLY, John & Mary
Garrison; 1 Nov 1745
(StM)

KELLY, John & Mary
Laton; 4 Dec 1725 (StM)

KELLY, John & Selina
Wren (d/o Thomas Wren);
29 Aug 1844 (FB)

KELLY, Perry & Ann
Cunningham; 23 Sep 1824
(FB)

KELLY, Samuel &
Bethlehem White; 25 Aug
1741 (StM)

KELLY, Vincent &
Elizabeth Sharp; 26 Jan
1769 (StM)

KELLY, William & Jane
Minor; 30 Mar 1758
(StM)

KELLY, WIlliam &
Phillis McIntosh; 22
Aug 1751 (StM)

KELLY, Woodford &
Mildred Tunnel; 4 Feb
1769 (StM)

KELTON, Thomas &
Margaret Skerry; 24 Dec
1726 (StM)

KEMEY, William & Ann
F.L. Carmichael; 8 Apr
1846 (FB)

KENDALL, James T. (s/o
Henrietta H. Browne) &

Mary E. Gaskins (d/o
Mary Gaskins); 25 Jan
1848 (FB)

KENDALL, John &
Elizabeth Frank; 24 Apr
1746 (StM)

KENDALL, John & Frances
Sharp; 22 Dec 1737
(StM)

KENDALL, Robert &
Ursula Garnett; 15 Dec
1796 (OM)

KENNEDY, John & Rose
Sudduth; 21 Jun 1736
(StM)

KENNEDY, Thomas &
Frances Lucas; 9 Oct
1763 (StM)

KENNER, Lodham & Judith
Beverley; 1 Mar 1730
(SpB)

KENNY, Michael &
Margaret Bignell; 29
Jul 1750 (StM)

KER, Peter & Sarah
Stribling; 23 Aug 1728
(StM)

KEYS, Thornton &
Christian Razer; 10 Jul
1799 (FM)

KEZTON, William &
Philadelphia Shepherd;
1803 (SpM)

KILGORE, Peter & Mary
Haydon; 1 Nov 1722
(StM)

KIMBALL, Horace L. &
Mahala Ann Wrenn (d/o
Melinda T. Wrenn); 28
Dec 1841 (FB)

KING, Azariah & Mary
Abel; 1780 (OM)

KING, Gabriel & Huldah
Biggers (d/o Macon
Biggers); 6 Dec 1799
(OM)

KING, George H. & May
Jefferson (w/o ?); 18
Oct 1843 (FB)

KING, George P. & Susan
Warren (d/o William
Warren); 19 Aug 1845
(FB)

KING, James & Polly
Burroughes; 4 Aug 1803
(SpM)

KING, James B. & Sarah
Ann Dabney; 20 Jun 1839
(FB)

KING, John & Jinny
Pierce; 7 Jan 1812
(SpM)

KING, John B. Mary L.
Williams; 18 Jul 1840
(FB)

KING, Joseph & Sarah
Carrico; 7 May 1731
(StM)

KING, Robert & Margaret
Sebastian; 26 Apr 1727
(StM)

KING, Sabert & Mary
Wayt (d/o James Wayt);
15 Dec 1785 (OB)

KING, Sadrut & Mary
Wayt; 15 Dec 1785 (OM)

KING, Samuel & Jane
Flagg; 11 Nov 1729
(StM)

KING, Thomas & Jane
Thomas; 19 May 1771
(StM)

KING, William & Eloisa
King; 6 Jan 1833 (FM)

KING, William & Eloise
M. King; 4 Jan 1832
(FB)

KING, William & Mary
Trigger; 2 Aug 1735
(StM)

KIRBY, William & Nancy
Dowles; 14 Sep 1825
(SpM)

KIRK, Charles F. &
Betty M. Byram (d/o
John Byrum); 6 Oct 1849
(FB)

KIRK, Hezekiah &
Behethland Bennet; 10
Feb 1778 (StM)

KIRK, Jeremiah & Ann
Monroe; 18 Aug 1785
(StM)

KIRTLEY, St. Clair &
Ann Panill (William
Pannill); 16 Nov 1800
(OM)

KITCHEN, Anthony & Mary
Overall; 31 Aug 1727
(StM)

KNIGHT John & Ellen
Madison; 7 Apr 1830
(FB)

KNIGHT, Ephriam & Anne
Abbott; 12 Feb 1758
(StM)

KNIGHT, Isaac & Winney
Ann Knight; 25 Dec 1799
(SpM)

KNIGHT, John Ellis &
Agnes Poole (d/o
Francis Poole); 30 Apr
1808 (FB)

KNIGHT, Peter & Rachel
Abbott; 19 Dec 1756
(StM)

KNIGHT, Reuben &
Margaret Wilson; 27 Dec
1827 (SpM)

KNIGHT, Thomas & Mary
Sorrell; 24 Feb 1830
(SpM)

KNIGHT, William &
Delphia Oakes; 23 Feb
1797 (OM)

KNIGHT, William &
Elizabeth Rogers; 29
Jan 1799 (OM)

KNIGHT, William &
Frances Cave; 23 Aug
1791 (OM)

KNIGHT, William & Jane
Butler; 26 Dec 1734
(StM)

KNIGHT, William & Mary
Oaks (d/o Major Oakes)
; 27 Mar 1819 (SpM)

KNOTO, Jordon & Julia
S. Vaughan; 22 Dec 1826
(SpM)

KNOWLAND, Lewis & Mary
Griggs; 26 Mar 1771
(StM)

KNOWLING, John &
Mildred Stribling; 11
Apr 1776 (StM)

KUBE, Brenhard &
Elizabeth Grady; 15 Dec
1836 (SpM)

KUGAN, Patrick & Peggy Humphries; 17 Feb 1800 (SpM)

LACKY, John & Sarah Payn; 6 Jun 1737 (StM)

LACY, James Homer & Betty C. Jones; 17 Oct 1848 (SpB)

LACY, John M. & Maneva P. Cannon; 25 May 1848 (SpM)

LACY, Joseph & Elizabeth Kitchen; 10 Sep 1759 (StM)

LACY, Thomas & Judith Rawlins; 9 Nov 1716 (StM)

LACY, Thomas & Margaret Johnson; 30 Apr 1726 (StM)

LACY, William & Mary Kelly; 4 Dec 1746 (StM)

LACY, William S. & Catharine Flippo; 19 Nov 1849 (SpM)

LAMB, Benjamin & Peggy Lamb (d/o John Lamb); 19 Jan 1797 (OM)

LAMB, James & Ann Watson (d/o Isaac Watson); 20 Oct 1791 (OM)

LAMB, Jeremiah & Ann Jones; 13 Feb 1800 (OM)

LAMB, John & Nelly Lamb (d/o John Lamb); 25 Oct 1784 (OB)

LAMB, John & Nelly Lamb (d/o John Lamb); 25 Oct 1784 (OM)

LAMB, William & Mary Gear; 27 Dec 1798 (OM)

LAMSDEN, Thomas & Cyrinia Peacher; 1 Sep 1836 (SpM)

LANCASTER, Alexander & Milly Webb; 23 Oct 1826 (OB)

LANCASTER, Alexander & Milly Webb; 23 Oct 1826 (SpM)

LANCASTER, Benjamin & Fanny Wright; 28 Oct 1793 (SpB)

LANCASTER, Benjamin & Fanny Wright; 28 Oct 1793 (SpM)

LANCASTER, Edmund & Louisa Tate; 21 Jul 1824 (SpM)

LANCASTER, Henry & Mary Wright; 26 Jul 1794 (OM)

LANCASTER, James & Nancy Lancaster; 16 Jul 1816 (OM)

LANCASTER, Larkin & Nancy Stivers; 25 Nov 1812 (SpM)

LANCASTER, Reuben & Betsy Conner; 2 Jun 1792 (OM)

LANCASTER, Richard & Johanna Singleton; 30 Mar 1777 (OM)

LANCASTER, Robert & Lucy Dear (d/o John Dear); 2 Nov 1780 (OM)

LANCASTER, Thomas & Frances Hailey; 16 Nov 1775 (OM)

LANDRAM, Fontaine &
Huldah Johnson; 6 Aug
1818 (SpM)

LANDRAM, John W. & Mary
L. Gownen; 23 Dec 1847
(SpM)

LANDRAM, Willis & Lucy
P. Ferrell; 22 Jan 1846
(SpM)

LANDRUM, John & Mary
Collins; 7 Feb 1794
(OM)

LANDRUM, Lewis &
Rebecca Atkins (d/o
John & Rebecca Atkins);
24 Dec 1802 (OM)

LANDRUM, Reubin &
Susannah Atkins (d/o
John & Susannah
Atkins); 27 Oct 1802
(OM)

LANDRUM, Willis & Sally
Pendleton; 26 Mar 1817
(SpM)

LANE, John & Tabitha
Crew; 23 Dec 1798 (OM)

LANE, Joseph & Joanna
Kemmet; 22 May 1754
(StM)

LANE, Tandy & Lucy Ann
Day; 16 Mar 1832 (SpM)

LANPHIER, William &
Mary Sexsmith; 2 Feb
1804 (FB)

LANTON, Thomas & Mary
Walker; 28 Aug 1783
(OM)

LANTOR, Jacob & Polly
Webb; 20 Dec 1787 (OM)

LANTOR, Peter & Hannah
Webb; 31 May 1787 (OM)

LAVENDER, Thomas &
Frances L. Bowling; 30
Sep 1828 (SpM)

LAWRENCE, John &
Elizabeth Mead; 20 Aug
1785 (FB)

LAWSON, Boswell & Jane
Lawson; 18 Mar 1807
(SpM)

LAWSON, Catlett & Fanny
Armstrong; 3 Aug 1846
(FB)

LAWSON, Fielding &
Elizabeth Daniel; 16
Jan 1822 (FB)

LAWSON, James & Maria
West; 12 Oct 1832 (FB)

LAWSON, Nathaniel &
Emily Burnett (21 years
old); 30 Oct 1832 (FB)

LAWSON, Nathaniel &
Emily Burnett; 31 Oct
1832 (FM)

LAWYER, Joshua & Sarah
Neal; 24 Jun 1732 (StM)

LAYTHAM, Snowdall &
Sarah Green; 25 Nov
1756 (StM)

LAYTON, Charles &
Georgiana Perry; 15 Feb
1843 (FB)

LAYTON, Charles & Sarah
Foster; 4 Aug 1813
(SpM)

LAYTON, John & Casandra
Porter; 29 Nov 1830
(FM)

LAYTON, John &
Cassandra Porter; 29
Nov 1830 (FB)

LAYTON, John & Susanah
Foster; 27 Dec 1810
(SpM)

LAYTON, Robert & Ann W.
Parker; 2 Oct 1803
(SpM)

LAYTON, Robert & Phebe
Holbrook (sister of
Fanny Holbrook); 17 Jan
1825 (FB)

LAYTON, William &
Rebecca Frances Layton;
26 Dec 1850 (FB)

LEA, Gidieon & Amey
Coffery; 14 Jul 1777
(OM)

LEAGUE, William T. &
Frances Ann Bradshaw;
10 May 1849 (FB)

LEAK, Robert & Susannah
Leak; 21 Dec 1784 (OM)

LEAKE, Robert &
Susannah Leake; 21 Dec
1784 (OB)

LEAR, John & Alice
Doggett; 7 Dec 1808
(FB)

LEARY, William & Nancy
Jones; 21 Nov 1809
(SpM)

LEATHERER, John & Sarah
White; 4 Mar 1777 (OM)

LEATHERS, William &
Nancy Finnell; 18 Apr
1792 (OM)

LEAVEL, Edward & Patsy
Wharton; [No Date]
(SpM)

LEAVELL, Burrell & Mary
Purvis; 13 Apr 1795
(SpM)

LEAVELL, Byrd C. & Lucy
Ann Cammack; 7 May 1835
(FM)

LEAVELL, Edmund S. &
Harriet A. Spindle; 7
Sep 1837 (FM)

LEE, Albert & Eliza
Hooten (age 21, d/o
Margaret Hooten); 5 Feb
1822 (FB)

LEE, Ambrose & Susanna
Hutcherson; 7 Mar 1810
(SpM)

LEE, Ambrose & Susannah
Hutcherson; 5 Mar 1810
(SpB)

LEE, George & Caty
Foster (d/o William
Foster); 10 Nov 1800
(OM)

LEE, Hancock & Mary
Willis; 5 Jan 1734
(SpB)

LEE, Hancock & Susan
Ann Richards; 12 Aug
1819 (FB)

LEE, John & Elizabeth
Bell (d/o Thomas Bell);
18 Dec 1781 (OM)

LEE, John & Fanny
Underwood; 2 Mar 1790
(StM)

LEE, Joseph & Mary
Bethel; 14 Nov 1745
(StM)

LEE, Joseph & Sarah
Fewel; 22 Jul 1792
(StM)

LEE, Kendall & Sarah Gordon; 17 Jun 1785 (OB)

LEE, Kendall & Sarah Gordon; 17 Jun 1785 (OM)

LEE, Lewis & Sally Johnson; 13 Apr 1804 (FB)

LEE, Michael & Mary Steigar; 21 Dec 1804 (FB)

LEE, Richard & Anna Dodd; 24 Feb 1789 (OM)

LEE, RIchard & Elizabeth Johnson; 26 Jan 1727 or 1728 (StM)

LEE, Richard & Margaret Brady; 8 Jul 1723 (StM)

LEE, Richard & Mary Rose; 29 Jun 1744 (StM)

LEE, Richard Henry (s/o Thomas Lee & Hannah Ludwell; b.d. 20 Jan 1732) & Ann Aylett; 3 Dec 1757 (StM)

LEE, Samuel & Mildred Long; 5 Nov 1818 (SpM)

LEE, Thomas Ludwell (s/o Thomas Lee & Hannah Ludwell) & Mary Aylett (d/o William Aylett); (StM)

LEE, William & Polly Limeco; 23 Dec 1799 (OM)

LEE, William & Sally Terrell; 16 May 1812 (OB)

LEE, William & Sally Terrill; 19 May 1812 (SpM)

LEE, Willis (of Fauquier) & Polly Richards (d/o John Richards) (FM)

LEE, Zachariach & Sara Mansfield (d/o Adam & Mary Mansfield); 25 May 1790 (OM)

LEITCH, Ambrose & Lucy Sorrell; 26 Mar 1819 (SpB)

LEITCH, Ambrose & Lucy Sorrell; 27 Mar 1819 (SpM)

LEITCH, William & Nancy Bullock; 11 Jan 1813 (SpB)

LEUBA, Pierre Henry & Claude Victorine Herard; 16 Sep 1820 (FB)

LEUTHERS, George & Sarah Vaughan; 19 Sep 1839 (SpM)

LEVERING, Lamason & Sarah Ann Bernard; 1833 (SpM)

LEVY, Henry & Sarah Leachy (d/o Patsey Leach); 25 Nov 1847 (FB)

LEWIS, Addison M. & Sally Billingsby; 22 Nov 1810 (SpM)

LEWIS, Benjamin & Nancy Ratcliff; 4 Feb 1813 (SpM)

LEWIS, Benjamin & Sarah Handly; 31 Aug 1734 (StM)

LEWIS, Charles & Ellen T. Lemase; 23 Dec 1840 (FB)

LEWIS, Dangerfield & Lucy B. Pratt; 9 Sep 1807 (SpM)

LEWIS, Daniel & Elizabeth Rose; 31 Aug 1762 (StM)

LEWIS, Fleetwood & Jane E. Stewart; 5 Aug 1849 (SpM)

LEWIS, George & Ann Truslow; 27 Nov 1834 (FB)

LEWIS, Henry & Cytha Brown; 11 Dec 1784 (FB)

LEWIS, Henry Byrd & Ellen C. Dickinson; 18 Oct 1849 (SpM)

LEWIS, James & Ann Mecon (aka Micou); 9 May 1840 (FB)

LEWIS, James & Elizabeth Duncan (d/o Alexander Duncan); 14 Sep 1817 (FB)

LEWIS, James & Frances Jane Waller; 13 Nov 1828 (SpM)

LEWIS, James & Maria Butler; 20 May 1836 (FB)

LEWIS, James & Mary Watkins (d/o Isham Watkins); 20 Aug 1794 (OM)

LEWIS, James (fpc) & Milly Webb(fpc); 15 Nov 1820 (FB)

LEWIS, John & Mildred A. B. Mercer; 27 May 1809 (FB)

LEWIS, John E. & Mary Drinan; 15 Sep 1840 (FB)

LEWIS, Joshua & Caroline A. Martin; 8 Oct 1840 (SpM)

LEWIS, Jubiel & Susannah Bounsel; 4 Aug 1801 (SpM)

LEWIS, Richmond & Margaret Richardson; 3 Sep 1830 (SpM)

LEWIS, Robert & Jane McGee; 1 Apr 1841 (SpM)

LEWIS, Robert (of Fauquier Co.) & Lucy Ann Stewart; 29 Sep 1842 (SpM)

LEWIS, Samuel H. & Ann Maria Loman; 14 Sep 1842 (FB)

LEWIS, Stephen & Mary Jane Bowling; 22 Nov 1841 (SpB)

LEWIS, Thomas & Elizabeth Mealy; 5 Oct 1730 (StM)

LEWIS, Walter Morgan & Mary Abram; 27 Aug 1738 (StM)

LEWIS, Washington & Harriet Robey (w/o ?); 17 Dec 1844 (FB)

LEWIS, William &
Henrietta Evans; 9 Sep
1847 (FB)

LEWIS, William &
Lucinda Pendleton; 23
Dec 1824 (SpM)

LEWIS, William & Lydia
Grant; 10 Sep 1811 (FM)

LEWIS, William (fpc) &
Husley Hollinger (fpc);
14 Jun 1820 (FB)

LEWIS, William F. &
Mary Rupel; 11 Jun 1845
(SpM)

LEWIS, William T. &
Elizabeth G.Faulconer;
25 Nov 1829 (SpM)

LEWIS, Willis &
Susannah Penn; 9 Feb
1795 (SpB)

LEWIS, Willis &
Susannah Penris; 12 Feb
1795 (SpM)

LEWIS, Zach &
_____; 3 Jan 1723
(SpB)

LEWIS, Zacharias & Mary
Brent; 24 Aug 1756
(StM)

LEWRIGHT, John & Mary
Kitchen; 8 Aug 1751
(StM)

LEYBURN, John & Mary
Louise Stuart Mercer
(d/o Hugh Mercer); 13
Apr 1841 (FB)

LIGHTFOOT, Philip L. &
Mary Virginia Smith
(d/o Delia Smith); 18
Jun 1838 (FB)

LILLY, Dickinson &
Suckey Jackson (aka
Suckey Chambers); 3 Dec
1838 (FB)

LILLY, London & Emily
Lewis Montague; 18 Nov
1833 (FB)

LILLY, William H. &
Elizabeth Brown (d/o
Charles & Nancy Brown);
13 Mar 1813 (FB)

LIMIT, John & Anne
Bateman; 6 Apr 1751
(StM)

LIMMANDS, Elijah & Lucy
Sandage; 13 Oct 1796
(OM)

LINDCEY, John &
Elizabeth Glass; 15 Jan
1750 (StM)

LINDEN, David & Elener
Emorson; 3 May 1810
(SpM)

LINDLY, Robert & Anne
McLeod; 21 Aug 1744
(StM)

LINDSAY, Cabel & Sally
Stevens (d/o John
Stevens); 3 Mar 1785
(OM)

LINDSAY, Caleb & Aesack
Goodloe; Jan 1806 (SpM)

LINDSAY, John &
Henrietta Daniel; 24
Oct 1825 (OB)

LINDSAY, John &
Henrietta Daniel; 24
Oct 1825 (SpM)

LINDSAY, Robert &
Minerva Daniel; 25 Oct
1824 (OB)

LINDSAY, Robert &
Minerva Daniel; 25 Oct
1824 (SpM)

LINDSAY, William &
Nancy Shepherd; 3 Oct
1781 (OM)

LINDSEY, Caleb & Sally
Stevens (d/o John
Stevens); 9 Mar 1785
(OB)

LINNEY, William & Ann
Burrus (w/o ?); 20 Nov
1780 (OM)

LINSEY, John & Sarah
Clift; 3 Jan 1739 or
1740 (StM)

LINTON, _____ & Susanna
Grayson; 1731 (SpB)

LINTON, Moses & Nancy
Reed; 17 Dec 1800 (OM)

LIPSCOMB, Ambrose &
Winifred Mardus; 23 Dec
1785 (StM)

LIPSCOMB, Granville &
Ellender B. Dueerson;
14 Dec 1825 (SpM)

LIPSCOMB, Ira & Ann
Duerson; 15 Feb 1821
(SpM)

LIPSCOMB, Jesse & Susan
H. Dabney (w/o ?); 14
Apr 1819 (FB)

LIPSCOMB, John Jr. &
Mary Billingsley; 15
Oct 1822 (SpM)

LIPSCOMB, Thomas H. &
Lucinda Duerson; 29 Feb
1816 (SpM)

LIPSCOMB, Willoughby &
Elizabeth Hockaday; 9
Nov 1826 (SpM)

LITRELL, John &
Elizabeth Rose; 15 Apr
1800 (SpM)

LIVERPOOL, Isaac &
Eliza Johnson; 20 Dec
1826 (FB)

LIVERPOOL, John & Ann
Johnston; 29 Sep 1824
(FB)

LIZEN, William &
Pennely Davenport; 16
Jun 1825 (SpM)

LLOYD, Jasper & Anne
Chambers; 7 Jan 1717 or
1718 (StM)

LOCK, Henry & Elizabeth
Blackman; 6 Feb 1724 or
1725 (StM)

LOCK, Henry & Sarah
Ledrim; 17 Sep 1722
(StM)

LOMAX, John Tayloe &
Charlotte Belson
Thornton (d/o Presly
Thornton of New York
State); 22 Jul 1805
(FB)

LOMAX, P. Thornton &
Mildred Henderson
Wellford (d/o John S.
Wellford); 27 May 1844
(FB)

LOMAX, Thomas Lunsford
& Martha Johnston; 10
Feb 1803 (FB)

LONG, Benjamin & Maria
Louisa Kale (d/o
Anthony Kale); 29 Jan
1834 (FB)

LONG, George M. &
Rebecca C. Lucas; 1 Jun
1831 (FB)

LONG, Henry & Lucy
Mansfield; 7 Nov 1785
(OB)

LONG, Henry & Lucy
Manspoil; 7 Nov 1785
(OM)

LONG, James & Amelia H.
Lipscomb; 30 Apr 1825
(SpM)

LONG, James & Elizabeth
Reynolds; 10 Feb 1785
(OM)

LONG, James & Patsy
Clark (d/o Charles
Clark); 21 May 1818
(FB)

LONG, John & Frances
Lanford; 15 Jul 1804
(SpM)

LONG, John Durrett &
Sarah Daniel; 22 Jul
1800 (SpB)

LONG, John Durrett &
Sarah Daniel; 23 Jul
1800 (SpM)

LONG, Lunsford H. & Ann
Lucas (d/o Fielding
Lucas); 17 Dec 1822
(FB)

LONG, Richard & Nancy
Stevinson; 29 dec 1796
(OM)

LONG, Robert & Mary
Stanley; 27 Apr 1846
(SpM)

LONG, Weir & Ann Smith;
20 Nov 1775 (OM)

LONG, William & Eleanor
Bolton; 15 May 1749
(StM)

LONG, William & Joanna
Chivrel; 30 Dec 1790
(StM)

LORD, Thomas Edward &
Anna Stribling (d/o
Samuel Stribling); 29
Dec 1803 (FB)

LORD, William & Anne
Jones; 12 Oct 1748
(StM)

LORD, William & Clary
Mannard; 8 Jan 1741 or
1742 (StM)

LORD, William &
Elizabeth Lewis; 23 Oct
1738 (StM)

LORD, William & Frances
Stratton; 31 Oct 1756
(StM)

LORD, William & Nelly
Wilson; 7 Apr 1780
(StM)

LORRILL, Thomas &
Elizabeth Clee; 10 Jul
1800 (OM)

LOW, Samuel & Hannah
Johnson; 16 Jul 1809
(SpM)

LOWERY, Francis & Susan
Jane Chapman; 14 Nov
1821 (FB)

LOWRY, John & Elizabeth
Seaton; 23 Apr 1726
(StM)

LOYD, John & Nancy
Montague; 12 Nov 1793
(OM)

LOYD, Thomas & Sally
Gusham (w/o ?); 27 Apr
1780 (OM)

LUCAS, Anthony & Sarah Stransford; 4 Nov 1737 (StM)

LUCAS, Elijah & Nancy Brockman (William Brockman); 24 Aug 1801 (OM)

LUCAS, James & Nancy Henderson; 24 Oct 1788 (OM)

LUCAS, James (fpc) & Eliza Vass (fpc); 31 Oct 1848 (FB)

LUCAS, Thomas & Sally Garnett; 9 Mar 1789 (OM)

LUCAS, William & Ann Frazer; 12 Feb 1850 (FB)

LUCAS, William & Jemimah West; 5 Oct 1827 (FB)

LUCAS, Zachariah & Nancy Wood; 31 Jan 1799 (OM)

LUCAS, Zachariah & Polly Harrison Apperson (d/o John Apperson); 19 Apr 1785 (FB)

LUCK, Albert W. & Sally T. Tribble; 9 DEc 1847 (SpM)

LUCK, Ambrose & Lucy Sorrel; 1 May 1819 (SpM)

LUCK, Austin & Lucy Alsop; 3 Aug 1802 (SpM)

LUCK, Diggs & Nancy Henderson; 10 Nov or Dec 1813 (SpM)

LUCK, George & Polly Harris; 18 Apr 1806 (SpM)

LUCK, George A. & Mary Louisa Kendall; 22 Nov 1819 (OB)

LUCK, Richard A. & Letitia Spindle; 23 Mar 1826 (SpM)

LUCK, Walker B. & Elizabeth Holladay; 7 Jan 1819 (SpM)

LUNSFORD, James & Margaret English; 24 Mar 1836 (FB)

LYELL, Samuel & Sarah Wiatt; 7 Oct 1847 (FM)

LYLE, Samuel & Sarah Wiatt; 7 Oct 1847 (SpM)

LYON, J. & Elizabeth Bingy; Nov 1802 (FM)

LYONS, Timothy & Sarah Sebastian; 11 Jan 1746 or 1747 (StM)

MACABOY, Robert & Sucky Magee; 6 Mar 1817 (FB)

MACARTY, Daniel & Mary Mercer; 3 Apr 1764 (StM)

MACCLANIN, John & Elizabeth Barker; 24 Mar 1793 (StM)

MACKAY, Robert & Maria Fisher; 6 Jan 1812 (FB)

MACON, Thomas & Sarah Madison (bondsman was James Madison); 30 Jan 1790 (OM)

MADDOX, John H. &
Frances S. Young; 22
Nov 1831 (FB)

MADDOX, Thomas B. & Ann
Virginia Pollard; 9 Oct
1836 (SpM)

MADDOX, William & Mary
Ann Curtis; 2 Dec 1830
(FB)

MADISON, Francis & Lucy
Smith; 9 Oct 1772 (OB)

MADISON, Francis &
Susanna Bell; 9 Oct
1772 (OM)

MADOWNEY, Francis (fpc)
& Rosa Ann Berry (fpc);
9 Mar 1831 (FB)

MAGEE, Henry & Milley
Bowling; 27 Aug 1818
(SpM)

MAGEE, Henry & Milly
Bowling; 27 Aug 1818
(SpB)

MAGEE, William & Caty
White; 22 Nov 1799
(SpB)

MAGGARD, Henry & Betsy
Lamb; 1 Jan 1792 (OM)

MALLORY, Henry & Ann
Jones; 18 Jan 1795 (OM)

MALLORY, Henry & Lucy
Long; 24 Dec 1781 (OM)

MALLORY, James & Polly
Brockman; 21 Dec 1801
(OM)

MALLORY, John & Sarah
Sawyer; 17 Feb 1778
(OM)

MALLORY, Reuben &
Dorothy Carter; 9 Jun
1789 (OM)

MALLORY, Robert & Nancy
Mallory; 17 Oct 1798
(OM)

MALLORY, Roger & Mary
Payne; 16 May 1797 (OM)

MANAN, William &
Margaret Giles; 11 Feb
1809 (SpB)

MANDORNY, James & Patsy
Jackson; 25 Jun 1834
(FM)

MANDOWNEY, James &
Patsey Jackson; 26 Jun
1834 (FB)

MANN, Henry & Alice
Tascoe; 5 Jul 1838 (FB)

MANNAN, William &
Martha Davis; 13 Aug
1752 (StM)

MANNARD, Robert & Clary
Derrick; 27 May 1723
(StM)

MANNER, William &
Margaret Giles; 12 Feb
1809 (SpM)

MANSELL, John & Mary
Pulliam; 12 May 1820
(SpM)

MANSELL, John & Mary
Pulliam; 29 Apr 1820
(SpB)

MANSFIELD, John & Ann
Waldo Grasty; 21 Oct
1737 (SpB)

MANSPOILE, Johny &
Sally Wood (d/o Katie
Wood); 19 Feb 1796 (OM)

MANUELL, Thomas & Mary Ann Wood (d/o Tomzin Wood); 30 Dec 1839 (FB)

MARCHANT, Levi D. & Henrietta Wroughton; 30 Jul 1850 (FB)

MARDUS, Aaron & Mary Thomas; 12 Mar 1785 (StM)

MARDUS, Moses & Mary Price (of King George); 27 Feb 1791 (StM)

MARKOUS, John & Mary Anne Grigsby; 1 Sep 1763 (StM)

MARR, Alexander & Sarah Rucker; 5 Jan 1756 (OM)

MARRIOTT, Richard W. & Julia B. Smith; 1 Jul 1845 (FM)

MARSHALL, George & Ann Boswell; 30 Sep 1787 (OM)

MARSHALL, Horace & Elizabeth Heiskell; 5 Sep 1805 (FB)

MARSHALL, Hugh R. & Ann Maria Crissey; 15 Feb 1831 (FB)

MARSHALL, Mungo & Lucy Marge; 16 Mar 1748 (SpB)

MARSHALL, Rush & Joanna Pede; 23 Nov 1779 (StM)

MARSHALL, Samuel & Jane Jones; 13 Jun 1782 (StM)

MARSTON, Joseph & Molly Landrum; 2 Apr 1801 (SpM)

MARTIN, Alexander & Sarah McDarmant; 1832 (SpM)

MARTIN, Benjamin & Mary Knight (d/o Ephriam Knight); 6 Jan 1796 (OM)

MARTIN, Brice & Rachel Lucas; 8 Jul 1793 (OM)

MARTIN, Charles & Sarah Ker; 1 Oct 1736 (StM)

MARTIN, Francis & Lucy Ellis; 26 Jul 1820 (SpM)

MARTIN, Francis & Lucy Ellis; 6 Jul 1820 (FB)

MARTIN, George & Elizabeth Jones (d/o Thomas Jones); 14 Jun 1783 (OM)

MARTIN, George & Elizabeth Jones (d/o Thomas Jones); 14 Jun 1783 (OB)

MARTIN, James & Mary Lynes; Jul 1740 (SpB)

MARTIN, James & Sidney Willoughby; 28 May 1818 (SpM)

MARTIN, James H. & Susan W. Olive; 4 Mar 1813 (SpM)

MARTIN, John & Jane T. Lewis; 11 Jun 1834 (SpM)

MARTIN, John & Lucy Todd; 5 Nov 1742 (StM)

MARTIN, Leonard & Elizabeth More; 28 Dec 1764 (StM)

MARTIN, Leonard & Sarah
Lewis; 27 Nov 1736
(StM)

MARTIN, Samuel & Eliza
Herndon; 8 Apr 1825
(SpM)

MARTIN, William &
Fenton Bowlin; 25 Jul
1822 (SpM)

MARTIN, William &
Fenton Bowling; 24 Jul
1822 (SpB)

MARTIN, William & Patsy
Atkins; 3 Dec 1808 (OM)

MARYE, James & Elinor
Porcel Dun; 17 Oct 1739
(SpB)

MARYE, John L. Jr. &
Milly Stone Browne; 29
Oct 1846 (FB)

MASEY, Joseph M & Clara
Pulliam; 2 Aug 1824
(SpM)

MASON, George &
Elizabeth Hooe; 22 Apr
1784 (StM)

MASON, George & Frances
_____; before 19 Jun
1695 (StM)

MASON, Isam B. & Lucy
Sebree; 27 Dec 1797
(OM)

MASON, James & Eliza
Mason; 16 Jan 1816
(SpM)

MASON, James & Mary B.
Brock; 18 Mar 1823
(SpM)

MASON, James & Nancy
Oaks; 26 Aug 1795 (OM)

MASON, John & Elizabeth
Faulconer (d/o Thomas
Faulconer); 16 Aug 1796
(OM)

MASON, John & Lucy
Selbree; 27 Dec 1795
(OM)

MASON, Nehemiah Rodham
& Sarah Dade; 12 Feb
1762 (StM)

MASON, Thomas &
Elizabeth Jones; 29 Dec
1818 (SpM)

MASON, William & Anne
Stuart; 11 Jul 1793
(StM)

MASSEY, Benjamin &
Fanny Overton; 21 Jul
1803 (SpM)

MASSEY, Dade &
Parthenia Alexander; 17
Jan 1731 or 1732 (StM)

MASSEY, John &
Elizabeth Powel; 12 Jun
1736 (StM)

MASSEY, Lovell & Sarah
Whiting; 28 Dec 1786
(StM)

MASSEY, Robert &
Winifred McCarty; 20
Dec 1728 (StM)

MASSEY, Sigismund &
Mary Stuart; 4 Apr 1743
(StM)

MASSEY, Sigismund &
Sarah Short; 16 Jul
1772 (StM)

MASSEY, Thomas &
Elizabeth Daniel; 12
Jun 1800 (SpB)

MASSEY, Thomas &
Elizabeth Daniel; 19
Jun 1800 (SpM)

MASSEY, William &
Hannah Settle; 8 Feb
1784 (StM)

MASSEY, William & Jane
Walker; 8 Jun 1848 (FB)

MASSEY, William & Nancy
J. Redd; 11 May 1820
(SpM)

MASTIN, Benjamin &
Polly Curtis; 4 Oct
1808 (SpM)

MASTIN, Francis & Lucy
Ellis; 26 Jul 1820
(SpM)

MASTIN, Huse & Eleanor
Massey; 1 Jun 1786
(StM)

MASTIN, John &
Elizabeth Smith; 30 Dec
1804 (SpM)

MASTIN, John & Mary
Jones; 27 Oct 1803
(SpB)

MASTIN, John & Mary
Jones; 27 Oct 1803
(SpM)

MASTIN, Mordecai & Lucy
Bennett; 19 Jan 1804
(FB)

MASTIN, Powell & Fanny
Perry; 1832 (SpM)

MASTIN, Powell & Fanny
Perry; 26 Mar 1832
(SpB)

MASTIN, Shadrach & Ruth
Johnson; 6 Jul 1811
(SpM)

MASTIN, Shadrack &
Elizabeth Burke; 24 Sep
1817 (SpM)

MASTIN, William &
Elizabeth McCory (aka
McCoy); 6 Dec 1802
(SpM)

MASTIN, William & Lucy
Jones; 20 Nov 1812
(SpB)

MASTIN, William & Lucy
Jones; 20 Nov 1812
(SpM)

MATHENY, James & Lizzy
Guin; 12 Dec 1751 (StM)

MATTHEWS, John & Anne
Bussey; 21 Jul 1754
(StM)

MATTHEWS, Patrick &
Elizabeth Evans; 17 Aug
1725 (StM)

MATTHEWS, William & Ann
Mary Grant; 5 Dec 1781
(StM)

MAUGEUR, Henry Duval &
Leila Drummond; 30 Apr
1758 (StM)

MAUPIN, Jennings &
Sally Miller; 25 Dec
1797 (OM)

MAURY, Alexander C. &
Mary Goode Thornton; 12
Jan 1834 (FM)

MAURY, John & Patty
Allen; 23 Sep 1812 (FB)

MAURY, Matthew F. & Ann
H. Herndon; 15 Jul 1834
(FM)

MAURY, Richard K. &
Lucy Hurnton; May 1824
(SpM)

MAXWELL, John & Agatha
Henry; 6 Feb 1792 (OM)

MAXWELL, Thomas &
Dulley Henry (d/o
William Henry); 3 Apr
1792 (OM)

MAYER, Philip & Jane
McFarlane; 25 Jun 1803
(FB)

MAYO, Dr. John & Sarah
S. Tennent; 10 Mar 1836
(FB)

MAYS, Robert &
Elizabeth Bolling; 27
Dec 1756 (StM)

MAZEEN, James & Mary
Ann Keeton; 27 Jan 1838
(FB)

MCALISTER, John & Cary
Turner (d/o Ann
Turner); 13 Nov 1798
(OM)

MCCALLAIR, Alexander &
Miriam Belshire; 24 Dec
1751 (StM)

MCCALLEY, Charles &
Mary Head; 24 Sep 1839
(FB)

MCCALLEY, Francis G. &
Hellen W. Anderson (d/o
M. D. Anderson); 17 May
1848 (FB)

McCALLEY, James &
Elizabeth Brinssan; 18
Sep 1806 (SpM)

McCALLEY, James & Mary
B. Beazley; Jan 1806
(SpM)

MCCANT, James &
Elizabeth Walker; 15
Mar 1747 or 1748 (StM)

MCCARTHY, Thomas &
Grisel Matthew; 23 Dec
1728 (StM)

MCCARTY, Daniel & Mary
Mercer; 3 Apr 1764
(StM)

MCCARTY, Daniel &
Winifred Thornton; 13
Jan 1765 (StM)

MCCARTY, Hugh & Helenor
Sulyvan; 22 Apr 1730
(StM)

MCCARTY, Nathaniel &
Frances Southard; 21
Apr 1829 (SpM)

McCARTY, Nathaniel &
Frances Suthard; 21 Apr
1829 (SpB)

MCCLAMOCK, John & Jenny
Estes (d/o Elisha
Estes); 18 Aug 1802
(OM)

MCCLANIN, John &
Elizabeth Barker; 24
Mar 1793 (StM)

MCCLARNEY, Roger &
Sarah Morris; 17 Dec
1795 (OM)

McCLOUD, Charles &
Lucinda Willoughby; 21
Dec 1815 (SpM)

MCCLOUD, Richard &
Frances Pegg; 24 Jul
1817 (SpM)

McCLOUD, Richard &
Frances Pigg; 22 Jul
1817 (SpB)

MCCORMICK, John &
Elizabeth Suttle; 8 Mar
1735 or 1736 (StM)

MCCOY, George & Elizabeth Nickings (d/o Nathaniel Nickings); 11 Mar 1789 (OM)

MCCULLAN, Patrick (s/o John & Theodora Beasley McCullan) & Sarah Walker; 5 Jan 1792 (OM)

MCCULLOH, Rev. Roderick & Elizabeth Weedon; 17 Feb 1734 or 1735 (StM)

MCDAMOTTE William & Ellen Simpson; 5 Oct 1831 (SpM)

MCDAMOTTE, William & Ellen Simpson; 4 Oct 1831 (SpB)

MCDANIEL, Derenzey & Susanna Brooks (d/o Jane Brooks); 25 Sep 1793 (OM)

MCDANIEL, Jeremiah & Rachel Brooks (d/o Jane Brooks); 4 Dec 1799 (OM)

MCDANIEL, John & Mary A. Duvall 29 Dec 1849 (SpM)

MCDANIEL, Stacy & Sally Lamb; 11 Apr 1799 (OM)

MCDANIEL, William & Frances J. Bertier; 17 Nov 1829 (FB)

MCDANIEL, William & Mary Huggins; 9 Oct 1823 (FB)

McDEMEATH, James & Nancy Strutton; 1 Dec 1797 (SpM)

McDERMENT, John & Betsey Tipps; 22 Dec 1815 (SpM)

MCDONALD (or MCDANIEL), Patrick & Elizabeth Miller (d/o Judith Miller); 25 Jul 1792 (OM)

MCDONALD, Edward & Elizabeth Smith; 6 Feb 1735 or 1736 (StM)

MCDONALD, James & Martha Withers; 15 Nov 1732 (StM)

MCDONALD, Rev. Daniel & Ellen Barret; 26 Jul 1740 (StM)

MCDONALD, William & Ursula Gravat; 1 Jul 1767 (StM)

McDORMAN, James & Nancy Young; 16 Dec 1813 (SpM)

McDORMAN, Peter & Tinsy Sullivan; 30 Dec 1813 (SpM)

MCDOUGAL, Mathew & Elizabeth Cavanaugh; 22 Jul 1846 (FB)

MCDOWELL, Edward & Maria Ann Smith; 8 Dec 1828 (FB)

MCDUFF, James & Mary Walker; 3 MAr 1757 (StM)

MCFARLAND, S. & Nancy Brooke (d/o Lawrence Brooke); May 1805 (FM)

MCFARLIN, John & Margaret Swinney; 3 May 1786 (FB)

MCGEE, Alexander & Rebecca Jones; 26 May 1835 (FB)

McGEE, Ebanezar &
Louisa Shelton; 23 Nov
1849 (SpM)

MCGEHU, Samuel &
Evelina Leavell; 20 Sep
1843 (SpB)

MCGILL, Thomas John &
Julia A. Phillips; 6
Dec 1837 (FB)

MCGUIRE, Edward Charles
(Rev.) (b.d. 26 Jul
1793 in Frederick Co.,
Va.) & Judith Carter
Lewis (d/o Robert Lewis
& Judith Brown;
granddaughter of
Fielding Lewis & Betty
Washington,who was
sister of George
Washington); 17 Apr
1816 (FB)

MCGUIRE, James & Jane
Elizabeth Ellis; 11 Nov
1849 (FB)

MCGUIRE, John H, & Ann
F. Fitzhugh; 6 Nov 1833
(FB)

MCHENRY, Thomas & Helen
Virginia Jennings; 19
Jan 1847 (FB)

MCINTOSH, James & Sarah
Howell; 17 Dec 1773
(StM)

MCINTOSH, Malcolm &
Mary Wood; 24 Nov 1743
(StM)

MCKAY, Rev. William
(Rector of Hanover
Parish, King George,
Va.) & Barbara Fitzhugh
(d/o John Fitzhugh); 6
Feb 1738 or 1739 (StM)

MCKEE, Samuel &
Bathsheba Hall; 5 Mar
1744 or 1745 (StM)

MCKENNEY, Gerard &
Elizabeth Whitehead
(w/o ?); 29 May 1816
(FB)

MCKENNEY, Jesse G. &
Mary Ann Ridley; 13 Feb
1823 (FB)

MCKENNEY,Gerard &
Elizabeth Whitehead
(w/o ?); 29 May 1816
(FB)

McKENNY, John & Eliza
Carpenter; 1 Aug 1815
(SpM)

McKENNY, John &
Elizabeth Smith; 15 Mar
1797 (SpB)

McKENNY, John &
Elizabeth Smith; 15 Mar
1797 (SpM)

MCKENNY, William (of
Culpeper Co. Va.) &
Hannah Spenser; 20 Jun
1809 (FB)

McKENT, James & Betsey
Rumsey; 30 Nov 1795
(SpB)

MCKENT, James & Betsey
Rumsey; 30 Nov 1795
(SpM)

McKENT, Joseph & Polly
Williams; 21 Dec 1820
(SpB)

McKENT, Joseph & Polly
Williams; 21 Dec 1820
(SpM)

MCKENZIE, Samuel &
Patsy Wright; 8 Jul
1833 (FB)

MCKINLEY, Hugh & Anna
Reita Finnell; 26 Dec
1796 (OM)

MCKINNEY, John & Lucy
Beazley; 17 Jun 1830
(SpM)

MCLACHLAN, Richard &
Elizabeth Smith; 31 Jan
1760 (StM)

MCLEAN, John & Helenor
Bell; 14 Apr 1745 (StM)

MCLEOD, George & Jane
Meredith; 14 Nov 1840
(FB)

MCLEOD, George & Mary
Ann McFarlane; 15 Nov
1843 (FB)

MCMILLAN, James (s/o
John McMillan) & Edy
Kendall (d/o Henry &
Ruth Kendall); 14 Mar
1796 (OM)

MCSHANE, John & Ann
Elizabeth Newton; 18
Feb 1837 (FB)

McWHIRT, David &
Barbara Stevens; 24 Dec
1813 (SpM)

MCWHIRT, John & Sarah
Scott; 1 Jan 1821 (SpB)

MCWHIRT, John & Sarah
Scott; 25 Jan 1821
(SpM)

MCWHIRT, William &
Elizabeth Ballard; 1
Jun 1827 (SpB)

MCWHIRT, William &
Elizabeth Ballard; 6
Jun 1827 (SpM)

MCWHIRT, William &
Susan Sharp; 18 Jun
1819 (SpM)

MCWHIRT, William &
Susan Sharpe; 18 Jun
1819 (SpB)

MCWILLIAMS, Anderson &
Clary McWilliams (d/o
Joshua McWilliams); 10
Jul 1800 (FM)

MCWILLIAMS, Joshua &
Mary Blythe; 30 Jan
1786 (FB)

MEAD, Henry & Joanniah
Dickerson (of Louisa
Co., Va.); 7 Apr 1798
(SpM)

MEADE, Richard K. &
Rebecca S. Green (d/o
Timothy Green); 19 Dec
1815 (FB)

MEDLEY, Ambrose &
Frankie Burton; 12 Dec
1775 (OM)

MEEZINGS, Joseph &
Polly Clements; 31 Mar
1800 (OM)

MEHANES, Samuel &
Elizabeth Brockman (d/o
William Brockman); 25
Nov 1802 (OM)

MEHONEY, William &
Rebecca Oliver; 15 Sep
1759 (StM)

MEHORNER, Benjamin &
Elizabeth Wiggins (of
King George CO., Va.);
24 Oct 1790 (StM)

MEHORNER, Benjamin &
Margaret Noting; 5 Apr
1778 (StM)

MEHORNER, Dennis & Jane
Carver; 8 Sep 1766
(StM)

MEHORNER, Dennis &
Sarah Thompson; 21 Feb
1781 (StM)

MEHORNER, Henry & Leah
Skinner (of King George
Co., Va.); 13 Sep 1788
(StM)

MEHORNER, James &
Elizabeth Gravat; 7 Feb
1742 or 1743 (StM)

MEHORNER, Thomas &
Bethia Evans; 30 Mar
1786 (StM)

MEHORNEY, Eli & Letty
Owens; 23 Jun 1792
(StM)

MERIWETHER, Francis &
Mary Lewis; 16 Jan 1749
(SpB)

MERRIWETHER, Charles &
Ann Minor; 11 Sep 1800
(OM)

METCALF, John &
Catharine Johnson; 23
Nov 1810 (FB)

METCALFE, John &
Catharine Johnson; 23
Nov 1810 (SpB)

METSTEAD, Joseph &
Catherine Smallwood; 29
Dec 1799 (SpM)

MICAJAH, N. Bailey &
Ann E.H.Shepherd; 7 Dec
1830 (SpM)

MICHI, John & Frances
Early (d/o Theodor
Earley); 23 Jul 1787
(OM)

MICOU, John H. & Ann
Johnson; 18 Nov 1836
(FB)

MIDDLETON, Henry O. &
Mildred E. Crutchfield;
4 Sep 1820 (FB)

MILES, Gibson Z. &
Catharine B. Wood (d/o
Tomzin Wood); 4 Jan
1841 (FB)

MILES, Peter & Ellen
Drynane; Aug 1805 (FM)

MILL, John & Phebe
Stevens; [No Date]
(SpM)

MILL, Killiss & Clary
Stevens; [No Date]
(SpM)

MILLAR, Temple & Peggy
Webber; 18 Jun 1812
(SpM)

MILLER, George & Lucy
A. Parrish; 23 May 1842
(FB)

MILLER, Henry &
Margaret Piglen; 11 Feb
1778 (OM)

MILLER, Henry & Sarah
Peyton; 6 Oct 1840 (FB)

MILLER, James O. &
Judith Hockaday; 6 Nov
1849 (SpM)

MILLER, Jesse & Ann
Stevens (d/o Joseph
Stevens); 11 Feb 1796
(OM)

MILLER, John & Patsy
Williams (d/o Helhy
Williams; Patsy is 36
years old); 29 Sep 1813
(FB)

MILLER, Joseph R. &
Lucy Ellen Graves (d/o
Harriet Graves); 11 Dec
1850 (FB)

MILLER, Thomas & Sarah
Plunkett (d/o Thomas
Plunkett); 13 Jan 1795
(OM)

MILLER, Woodford &
Margaret Butzner; 6 Feb
1849 (SpM)

MILLION, Robert &
Keziah Holliday; 14 Dec
1749 (StM)

MILLS, Benjamin & Amy
Lindsum; 6 Aug 1810
(SpM)

MILLS, Benjamin &
Mildred Johnson; 16 Mar
1813 (SpB)

MILLS, Charles C. &
Catharine A. King; 5
Jul 1837 (FB)

MILLS, Francis &
Margaret Handlee; 6 Apr
1751 (StM)

MILLS, Francis S. &
Catharine White; 22 Feb
1836 (FB)

MILLS, Jackson I. &
Mary Ann Edge; 3 Jan
1832 (SpB)

MILLS, Jackson L. &
Mary Ann Edge; 1832
(SpM)

MILLS, James & Jane
Shelton; 3 Mar 1842
(SpM)

MILLS, James H. &
Harriet O. Shelton; 13
Jul 1847 (FB)

MILLS, James T. &
Elizabeth Mullen (d/o
Charles Mullen); 6 Jan
1840 (FB)

MILLS, Richard &
Elizabeth Bullock; 1
July 1830 (SpM)

MILLS, Robert (s/o
Elizabeth Mills, b.d.
21 Jul 1794) & Eliza
Burden (d/o Archibald
Burden); 13 May 1816
(FB)

MILLS, Robert T. &
Maria Browne; 6 Dec
1838 (FB)

MILLS, Thomas & Mary
Bussey; 2 Jan 1748 or
1749 (StM)

MILLS, Thomas P. &
Joanna Jones; 15 Dec
1819 (FB)

MILLS, Walter M. &
Pamela Perry; 27 Oct
1841 (FB)

MILLS, Willis &
Elizabeth Simpson; [No
Date] (SpD)

MILLS, Willis &
Elizabeth Simpson; 6
Jan 1812 (SpM)

MILLS, Willis & Sarah
M. Perry; 17 Oct 1826
(SpM)

MILUS, William & Shady
Puzey; 17 May 1826 (FB)

MINER, William &
Mildred Lewis (d/o John
Lewis); 28 Jan 1790
(FM)

MINNIS, Callohill & Elizabeth Holman; 16 Nov 1740 (StM)

MINNIS, Wheeler & Lucy Ann Pullen; 12 Sep 1848 (FB)

MINOR James Lawrence (s/o Garrett Minor) & Louisa Smits; 1843 (StM)

MINOR, Andrew Jackson (s/o Garrett Minor) & Mary Baldwin (of St. Louis, Mo.); Oct 1846 (StM ?)

MINOR, Andrew Jackson(s/o Garrett Minor) & Mary A. Massey (of Mossouri); before Oct. 1846 (StM ?)

MINOR, Dabney & Jane H. Hull; 10 Feb 1835 (SpM)

MINOR, Garrett & Eliza McWilliams; 31 Mar 1803 (StM)

MINOR, George & Eliza Chew; 6 Aug 1840 (FB)

MINOR, George (s/o Garrett Minor)& Ann Eliza Chew; Aug 1841 (StM)

MINOR, Henry L. & Margaret W. Herndon; 12 Nov 1829 (SpM)

MINOR, Hubbard L. & Malvina Crutchfield; 17 Jul 1826 (SpM)

MINOR, James & Lucy A. Hicks; 28 Dec 1837 (SpM)

MINOR, James Lawrence (s/o Garrett Minor) &

Sally Goode; before 1843 (StM)

MINOR, John & Margaret Sumner; 3 Feb 1740 or 1741 (StM)

MINOR, Robert Dabney (s/o Garrett Minor) & Landonia Randolph; Dec 1850 (StM ?)

MINOR, Thomas & Alice Thomas; 22 Mar 1741 (SpB)

MINOR, William G. & Ann F. Rootes; 10 Dec 1839 (FB)

MINOR, William Garrett (s/o Garrett Minor) & Anne T. Rootes; 4 Dec 1840 (FM)

MINTOE, Henry & Lurina Ward; 16 Jan 1737 or 1738 (StM)

MISLIN, Anthony & Elizabeth Day; 5 May 1735 (StM)

MITCHEL, William & Behethland Johnston; 4 Sep 1787 (StM)

MITCHEL, William & Rebecca Grinnils; (d/o Sarah Grinnels); 21 Dec 1790 (OM)

MITCHELL, Henry & Molly Lucas (d/o William Lucas Jr.); 8 Mar 1794 (OM)

MITCHELL, Joseph & Willey M. Parker; 26 May 1824 (SpM)

MITCHELL, Samuel & Bridget Berry; 30 Jan 1749 (StM)

MITCHELL, William L. &
Janette Foster; 29 Aug
1822 (SpM)

MOFFATT, Thomas & Anne
Maria Mortimer (d/o Dr.
Charles Mortimer); 7
Mar 1786 (FB)

MOLOM, James & Lucy
Nowton; 8 Apr 1801
(SpM)

MONCURE, John Conway &
Fanny Dulany Tomlin; 8
May 1850 (FB)

MONCURE, Rev. John &
Frances Brown (d/o
Gustavus Brown of
Charles Co., Md. &
Frances Fowke);

MONCURE, Thomas G. &
Clarissa Bernard;
before Sep 1826 (StM)

MONCURE, William Edwin
& Georgiana Bankhead;
about 1850 (StM)

MONDOWNEY, Edward &
Lucy Keyes (d/o Maria
Keyes); 21 Jun 1849
(FB)

MONDOWNEY, James & Jane
Greer; 6 Mar 1848 (FB)

MONHIRT, William &
Elizabeth Ballard; 6
Jun 1827 (SpM)

MONROE, Andrew &
Margaret Washington; 21
Dec 1761 (StM)

MONROE, John & Sarah
Harrison (d/o William
Harrison & Isabella
Triplett); 23 Sep 1756
(StM)

MONROE, Thomas &
Catherine Hore; 16 Apr
1745 (StM)

MONROE, William &
Jemima Smith; 2 Apr
1746 (StM)

MONTAGUE, Clement &
Hannah Lewis (w/o James
Lewis) Sep 1791 (FM)

MONTAGUE, John & Nancy
Grady; 1812 (SpM)

MONTAGUE, John & Nancy
Grady; 19 Sep 1811
(SpB)

MONTAGUE, William &
Sukey Perry; 1 Sep 1812
(OB)

MONTEITH, James & Leah
Owens; 23 Aug 1763
(StM)

MOODY, Richard &
Elizabeth Townly; 5 Feb
1758 (StM)

MOOR, Henry & Lucinda
Duncan; 11 Aug 1824
(FB)

MOORE, Bernard & Catey
Price; 3 Oct 1770 (OM)

MOORE, Edward &
Elizabeth Parke; 3 Oct
1844 (FB)

MOORE, Francis Jr. &
Lucy Hawkins; 9 Nov
1761 (OM)

MOORE, John & Betsey
Magee; 5 Sep 1805 (SpM)

MOORE, John & Betsy
Magee; 4 Sep 1805 (SpB)

MOORE, John & Elizabeth
Smith; 23 Jan 1797 (OM)

MOORE, John & Susan
Jones; 12 Jun 1827 (FB)

MOORE, Nathaniel &
Sally Adams (d/o John
Adams); 1 Jun 1800 (OM)

MOORE, Richard & Mary
Abbott; 16 Nov 1793
(SpB)

MOORE, William & Betty
Johnson Grymes; 10 Apr
1781 (OM)

MOORE, William & Franky
Wheeler; 25 Aug 1799
(SpM)

MORE, William & Mary
Green; 28 Nov 1751
(StM)

MORGAN, Edwin R. &
Eliza Purks; 30 Oct
1838 (FB)

MORGAN, James A. &
Eliza Cudlipp; 31 Oct
1843 (FB)

MORING, Edward &
Catherine Greenleves;
16 Oct 1779 (StM)

MORRIS, Alexander &
Sophia R. Spilman (d/o
Peter Spilman); 20 Sep
1821 (FB)

MORRIS, David & Jemima
Grunter; 18 Feb 1776
(OM)

MORRIS, George & Emily
Hockaday; 17 May 1844
(SpM)

MORRIS, George &
Susannah Graves (d/o
Richard Graves); 7 Apr
1795 (OM)

MORRIS, Gilson & Molly
Knight; 15 Mar 1790
(OM)

MORRIS, James F. & Mary
Ann Elizabeth Wiltshire
(d/o Benjamin
Wiltshire); 25 Mar 1847
(FB)

MORRIS, John & Linny
Brown; 21 Sep 1775 (OM)

MORRIS, John T. & Emily
Ann Scott; 6 Oct 1836
(SpM)

MORRIS, Reubin & Molly
Coleman (d/o James
Coleman); 10 Jun 1793
(OM)

MORRIS, Thomas & Peggy
Reynolds; 1 May 1778
(OM)

MORRIS, William &
Frances Edenton; 8 Jul
1806 (SpM)

MORRIS, William
Anderson & Winifred
Quisenberry; 6 Feb 1802
(OM)

MORRIS, William M. &
Jane McCaill; 26 Nov
1846 (SpM)

MORRISON, Dr. Edwin A.
& Lucia B. Hackley (d/o
M. Hackley); 31 Jul
1849 (FB)

MORRISON, William N. &
Susan Limbrick (w/o ?);
19 Jul 1845 (FB)

MORROW, Patrick & Mary
Delaunder; 6 Oct 1716
(StM)

MORSAN, Alexander & Ann
Carson Alexander (d/o

William Alexander of Snowdon); 26 Jun 1800 (StM)

MORSE, Francis & Lucy Ward; 12 May 1789 (OM)

MORSON, Alexander & Maria M. Berry; 18 Sep 1832 (FB)

MORTIMER, John & Mary French; 5 May 1803 (FB)

MORTON, Allen W. & Jean Mitchell; 8 Nov 1827 (FB)

MORTON, Charles M. & Mary L. Hawkins; 28 Jan 1825 (SpM)

MORTON, Elijah & Elizabeth Hawkins; 3 Jul 1745 (SpB)

MORTON, Elijah & Mary G. Webb; 22 Jun 1812 (OB)

MORTON, John & Mary Tandy (d/o Henry & Ann Mills Tandy; 24 Apr 1789 (OM)

MORTON, William & Milly Taylor; 5 Jan 1775 (OM)

MOSLAY, Samuel & Ann Smallwood; 31 Jul 1808 (SpM)

MOSS, John & Mary Ross; 27 Apr 1724 (StM)

MOSS, Silvester & Elizabeth Reid; 25 Aug 1735 (StM)

MOSS, Silvester & Frances Kelly; 7 Jul 1727 (StM)

MOSS, Thomas & Mary Atwell; 10 Sep 1772 (StM)

MOSS, Thomas & Mary Atwell; 10 Sep 1772 (StM)

MOTHERSHEAD, John & Sukey Burrus; 8 Dec 1789 (OM)

MOTHERSHED, Nathaniel & Mary Minor; 18 Dec 1761 (OM)

MOTHERSHED, Nathaniel & Ruthy Birt; 11 Aug 1781 (OM)

MOUBERRY, Joseph & Amelia Robinson; 11 Oct 1805 (SpB)

MOUBERRY, Joseph & Amelia Robinson; 12 Oct 1805 (SpM)

MOXLEY, Alvin & Anne Hooe; 5 Nov 1772 (StM)

MUFFET, Gabriel & Mary Helms; 25 Jul 1739 (StM)

MUIELER, James A. & Elizabeth Ann Cash; 13 Oct 1834 (SpM)

MUIELER, James B. & Mary Payne; 15 May 1833 (SpM)

MULLEN, Caleb & Sarah Sindall (d/o William & Judey Sindall); 31 Dec 1822 (FB)

MULLEN, Charles & Mary Pitman; 15 Dec 1847 (FB)

MULLEN, James & Olivia Barnes; 18 Oct 1838 (FB)

MULLEN, Ryland & Ann Curtis; 1 Dec 1828 (FB)

MULLEN, Ryland & Susan Burden; 5 Mar 1844 (FB)

MULLIKIN, Moses & Sarah Notes; 19 May 1814 (SpB)

MULLIKIN, Moses & Sarah Notes; 20 May 1804 (SpM)

MULLIN, George & Virginia E. Towles; 17 Dec 1849 (FB)

MULVAY, Nicholas & Betsy Lewis; 20 Aug 1838 (FB)

MUNDAY, Samuel & Milly Crosswhite (d/o John Crosswhite); 5 Sep 1816 (OM)

MUNDILL, John & Jennette McIntosh; 7 Jan 1828 (FB)

MUNDY, Burrus & Elizabeth Crosthwaite (d/o John Croswaite); 14 Feb 1815 (OM)

MURFEY, Osnil & Mary Jenkins; 24 Dec 1818 (SpM)

MURPHES, Alexander & Anne Darbin; 18 Apr 1724 (StM)

MURPHEY, James & Mary Burnett; 5 Oct 1816 (FB)

MURPHEY, William Lewis & Elizabeth Smith; 5 Apr 1768 (StM)

MURPHY, Alexander & Anne Darbin; 8 Apr 1724 (StM)

MURPHY, Isaac & Catherine Ashby; 1 Jan 1756 (StM)

MURPHY, John & Leanah Grady; 3 jun 1811 (FB)

MURPHY, John & Mary G. Murphy; 7 May 1828 (SpM)

MURPHY, Thomas & Jane Starlee; 23 Dec 1813 (SpM)

MURRAY, Alexander & Martha Layton; 20 Nov 1845 (FB)

MURRAY, Anthony & Mary James; 25 Jan 1734 (SpB)

MURRAY, Ebenezer & Elizabeth Saunders; 27 Apr 1811 (FB)

MURRAY, John & Mary Todd; 12 Dec 1727 (StM)

MURRAY, William & Elizabeth Waite (d/o Jesse Wayt); 17 Sep 1839 (FB)

MURREN, William Thompson & Mary McPherson; 19 Jan 1826 (FB)

MUSE, Alexander Alfred & Catharine Mayers; 8 Apr 1830 (FB)

MUSICK, John & Mary Berry; 22 Jul 1776 (OM)

MUSTIN, Thomas & Anne
Martin; 19 Jan 1759
(StM)

MYERS, Aaron &
Catharine Daniel; Nov
1813 (SpM)

MYERS, John & Catharine
Hagan; 23 Dec 1834 (FB)

MYERS, Joshua Jr. (s/o
Joshua Myers of
Spotsylvania Co.) &
Sarah Ann Pope; 30 Apr
1811 (FB)

NALLE, Jesse & Nancy
Botts; 26 Sep 1804 (FB)

NASH, George & Anne
White; 20 Jan 1769
(StM)

NEAL, Charles & Ann
Miller; 23 Aug 1785
(OM)

NEAL, Fielding &
Catherine Beazley (d/o
James Beazley); 12 Nov
1787 (OM)

NEAL, Macajah & Milly
Beasley (d/o James
Beasley); 3 Aug 1782
(OB)

NEAL, Miscajah & Milly
Beazley (d/o James
Beazley); 3 Aug 1782
(OM)

NEALE, Charles & Ann
Miller (d/o Robert
Miller); 22 Aug 1785
(OB)

NEALE, Henry &
Elizabeth Shepherd; Feb
1800 (SpM)

NEEDEMEYER, John M. &
Catharine Fuggett; 10
Aug 1807 (SpM)

NELSON, Alexander &
Margaret Butler; 21 Feb
1745 (StM)

NELSON, Armistead &
Mary Henderson (d/o
David Henderson); 10
Jul 1817 (FB)

NELSON, Henry & Jean
Gwodkin; 18 Oct 1742
(StM)

NELSON, James & Ann
Adams; 11 Jul 1823 (OB)

NELSON, James & Susan
M. Robinson; 12 Oct
1821 (SpB)

NELSON, James & Susan
M. Robinson; 18 Oct
1821 (SpM)

NELSON, Joseph & Ann B.
Horn; 5 Jan 1815 (SpB)

NELSON, Joseph & Ann B.
Horn; 5 Jan 1815 (SpM)

NELSON, Robert A. &
Mary Byram; 7 Sep 1848
(FB)

NELSON, Thomas &
Elizabeth Quisenberry;
25 Jan 1813 (OB)

NELSON, Thomas &
Elizabeth Quisenberry;
28 Jan 1813 (SpM)

NELSON, William
Armistead & Mary
Moncure; about 1839
(StM)

NELSON, William Mead &
Sarah Wilhelmina

Semmes; 16 Jul 1848
(FB)

NEVENS, David & Janet
Patterson; 6 Jun 1759
(StM)

NEVENS, David & Mary
Oard; 28 Jun 1767 (StM)

NEWBLE, Zachariah &
Anne Hamit; 6 Nov 1779
(StM)

NEWBY, James W. & Jane
Phoebe White (d/o Henry
White); 12 Nov 1818
(FB)

NEWMAN, James & Sarah
Griffin; 25 Dec 1759
(StM)

NEWMAN, John & Sidnah
Quisenberry (d/o George
Quisenbery Sr,); 3 Jul
1803 (OM)

NEWMAN, Thomas & Lucy
Barbour; 7 Mar 1798
(OM)

NEWMAN, Thomas & Patsy
Oliver Morris (d/o
George Morris); 22 Oct
1798 (OM)

NEWMAN, William &
Leydia Anderson
Neberker; 11 Jul 1832
(FB)

NEWMAN, William & Lydia
Newbecker; 13 Jul 1832
(FM)

NEWTON, Benjamin &
Elizabeth Nicholson; 6
May 1716 (StM)

NEWTON, Benjamin & Jane
Colclough; 22 Oct 1740
(StM)

NEWTON, Henry & Susanna
Stewart; 3 Feb 1806
(SpB)

NEWTON, Jesse & Nancy
Howard; 30 Jul 1811
(SpM)

NEWTON, John Jr.(s/o
John Newton, brother of
Benney) & Judith
Pollard; 17 Oct 1786
(FB)

NEWTON, Thomas &
Levinia Webster; 5 Aug
1829 (SpM)

NEWTON, Thomas & Mrs.
Levenia Webster; 29 Jul
1829 (SpB)

NICHOLS, Edgar & Lucy
Ann Clarke (d/o Almira
Jenkins); 13 Sep 1843
(FB)

NICHOLSON, George L. &
Bettie B. Wellford; 23
Nov 1850 (FB)

NICHOLSON, J. & Fanny
Baylor; Nov 1802 (FM)

NIPPER, Jacob &
Elizabeth Fleck; 15 Mar
1796 (OM)

NIXON, Richard &
Elizabeth Holmes (w/o
Thomas Holmes); before
14 Nov 1690 (StM)

NOBL, Flavius S. & Anna
Pearson; 25 Apr 1820
(FB)

NOBLE, John & Elizabeth
Griffin; 11 Mar 1812
(FB)

NOLLE, James M. & Mary
Ann Crutchfield; 3 Sep
1834 (SpM)

NOOMES, Joseph & Rachel
Davis; 23 Aug 1776 (OM)

NORFOLK, Thomas & Mary
Burket; 6 Dec 1737
(StM)

NORMAN, Cuthbert &
Sophia Jollett; 2 Aug
1791 (OM)

NORMAN, Thomas &
Elizabeth Duncum; 21
Feb 1736 or 1737 (StM)

NORRIS, John & Sarah
Turner; 29 Aug 1751
(StM)

NORTON Benjamin W. &
Elizabeth Clarke; 24
Sep 1846 (FB)

NORWOOD, George & Mrs.
Ann Ingham (d/o Mrs.
Eleanor Welch); 11 Jan
1806 (FB)

NOSSETT, Peter &
Catharine Aldridge; 20
Jan 1848 (FB)

NOXAL, _____ & Ann
Bruing; 1 Aug 1757
(StM)

NUGENT, Peter & Martha
Sill; 15 Feb 1731 or
1732 (StM)

O'NEAL, Lodowick &
Susanna Procter; 5 Nov
1803 (SpB)

O'NEIL, Lodowich &
Susannah Proctes; 6 Nov
1803 (SpM)

OAKS, John & Belvidena
Howard; 1832 (SpM)

OAKS, John & Belvidera
Howard; 2 Apr 1832
(SpB)

OAKS, Mainyard & Polly
Lancaster (d/o John &
Susannah Lancaster); 22
Sep 1806 (OM)

OAKS, Major & Mildred
Hoard; 11 Jun 1829
(SpB)

OAKS, Major & Mildred
Hoard; 15 Jun 1829
(SpM)

OLIVE, James & Susannah
Minor; 24 Aug 1781 (OM)

OLIVE, Lewis & Nancy
Beazley; 26 Jan 1814
(SpM)

OLIVER, Charles & Nancy
Cooper; 8 Aug 1799
(SpM)

OLIVER, Charles & Polly
Robinson; 25 Dec 1821
(SpM)

OLIVER, Henry & Nancy
Baxter; 6 Nov 1823
(SpM)

OLIVER, John &
Elizabeth True; 29 Mar
1794 (SpB)

OLIVER, Killis & Winney
Riddle (d/o James
Riddle); 26 Jan 1797
(OM)

OLIVER, Presley & Nancy
Abbott; 21 Dec 1794
(SpB)

OLIVER, Presley & Nancy
Abbott; 23 Dec 1794
(SpM)

OLIVER, Robert &
Elizabeth Leavel; 1 Nov
1811 (SpM)

OLIVER, William & Amy
Beasley; 10 Jun 1803
(SpM)

ORANT, John & Peggy
Linton; 11 Dec 1783
(OB)

ORANT, John & Peggy
Linton; 11 Dec 1783
(OM)

ORILL, William &
Elizabeth West (b.d. 11
Feb 1787); 3 Aug 1812
(FB)

OTEY, William & Nancy
Dawbrey; 19 Jan 1810
(SpB)

OTT, Michael &
Catherine Pence; 27 Aug
1798 (OM)

OVERTON, John & Martha
Carleton; 2 Feb 1797
(OM)

OVERTON, Joshua &
Frances Palmer; 15 Jan
1797 (OM)

OWENS, Aaron &
Catherine Wilson; 26
Mar 1785 (StM)

OWENS, John & Susan
Keeton; 13 Aug 1833
(SpM)

OWENS, Sidney H. & Jane
E. Beck; 16 Apr 1831
(FB)

OWENS, Sturd & Caty
Harris; 31 Mar 1795
(OM)

PADGETT, John & Nancy
Beckham; 21 Aug 1799
(OM)

PAGE, Elijah & Nelly
Sisk (d/o Martin Sisk);
25 Dec 1800 (OM)

PAGE, John & Elizabeth
Middlebrook; 7 Oct 1777
(OM)

PAGE, John Jr. (s/o
John & Elizabeth Page
Sr.) & Mary Collins
(d/o Mary Collins); 22
Dec 1783 (OB)

PAGE, John Jr. (s/o
John & Elizabeth Page)
& Mary Collins (d/o
Mary Collins); 22 Dec
1783 (OM)

PAGE, Mann & Mary W.
Lithgow; 24 Apr 1806
(FB)

PAGE, Nelson & Anna
Maria Hamilton; 3 Oct
1850 (SpM)

PAGGETT, James &
Phillis Beecon; 30 Jan
1800 (OM)

PAIN, John & Mrs. Kitty
Robinson; 6 Jan 1832
(SpM)

PAIN, Person W. & Susan
Alsop; 10 May 1817
(SpB)

PAIN, Person W. & Susan
Alsop; 25 Jun 1817
(SpM)

PALMER, Henry & Ann
Burnett; 1 Mar 1731
(SpB)

PARISH, Jeremiah & Mary Ann Clarke (w/o ?); 5 Feb 1817 (FB)

PARISH, John G. & Elizabeth S. Bunberry; 4 Dec 1839 (FB)

PARKER, Edgar & Susan Oliver; 20 May 1849 (SpM)

PARKER, Edward & Sarah Wood; 20 Jun 1844 (FB)

PARKER, George & Hardenia L. Tompkins; 5 Nov 1835 (SpM)

PARKER, Richard & Hannah Cave (d/o William Cave); 17 Apr 1780 (OM)

PARKER, Winslow & Mary Thomas; 4 Aug 1774 (OM)

PARRISH, Lewis & Elizabeth Whiting (ne Scags), (w/o John Whiting, d/o Catharine Boores); 17 Jun 1817 (FB)

PARROT, Thomas Lewis & Hester Stribling; 16 Apr 1744 (StM)

PARROTT, John Jr. & Susan E. Parrott (d/o Robert Parrott); 27 Mar 1833 (FB)

PARROTT, Robert & Ann E. Parrott; 12 Apr 1836 (FB)

PARROTT, Robert & Sally Read; 31 Mar 1799 (FM)

PARSONS, David & Elizabeth Clark; 4 Dec 1800 (OM)

PARTLOW, Elijah & Betsy Cason; 15 Feb 1804 (SpM)

PARTLOW, Elijah & Nancy White; 9 Feb 1813 (SpM)

PARTLOW, John & Milly Darnell; 11 Dec 1804 (SpM)

PARTLOW, John & Milly Darnell; 26 Nov 1801 (SpB)

PARTLOW, Lewis & Susanna Mason; 19 Jan 1826 (SpM)

PARTLOW, Samuel & Ann Peacher; 26 Feb 1835 (SpM)

PATTERSON, John & Page Cudding; 3 Mar 1776 (OM)

PATTON, John & Isbel Smith; 10 Sep 1813 (SpM)

PATTON, John & Martha Payne; 3 Apr 1746 (StM)

PATTON, John M. & Peggy F.S. Williams; 8 Jan 1824 (FB)

PATTON, William Farley & Harriet S. Buck; 31 Aug 1835 (FB)

PAUL, Jacob & Catey Neale (w/o ?); 28 Jul 1793 (OM)

PAXTON, A.M. & Mary L. Ellis (d/o Robert Ellis); 10 Jul 1837 (FB)

PAYNE, Elzey & Catharine Fries; 13 Feb 1850 (FB)

PAYNE, James & Polly
Wheeler; 22 Sep 1830
(SpM)

PAYNE, John & Elizabeth
Bledsoe (w/o ?); 27 Aug
1801 (OM)

PAYNE, John & Jerusha
Balinger; 6 Dec 1836
(SpM)

PAYNE, John & Mildred
Dismukes; 27 Dec 1815
(SpM)

PAYNE, John & Sucky
Lindsay; 6 Aug 1793
(OM)

PAYNE, John M. &
Elizabeth F. Butler; 24
Dec 1846 (SpM)

PAYNE, Joshua A. &
Elizabeth W. Phillips;
16 Jul 1839 (FB)

PAYNE, Robert & Ann
Collins; 24 Jun 1809
(OM)

PAYNE, Thomas & Lucy
Gimber; 24 Dec 1812
(SpM)

PAYNE, Thomas & Sarah
Bowling; 21 Jan 1825
(SpB)

PAYNE, William (s/o
Richard Payne) & Nancy
Foster; 25 Mar 1795
(OM)

PEACHER, Alexander &
Nice Brightwell; 7 Aug
1824 (SpB)

PEACHER, Alexander &
Nice Brightwell; 7 Sep
1824 (SpM)

PEACHER, Uriah & Ann
Louisa Hillman; 3 Aug
1824 (SpM)

PEACHER, Washington &
Sarah Partlow; 2 Nov
1826 (SpM)

PEACHER, Washinton H. &
Sarah Partlow; 31 Oct
1826 (SpB)

PEAK, James B. & Louisa
L. Jenkins; 15 Nov 1832
(SpM)

PECILLE, William B. &
Frances M. Parker; 26
May 1826 (SpM)

PECK, Jacob & Polly
Coursey; 24 Feb 1778
(OM)

PENCE, John & Elizabeth
Lucas; 13 Apr 1795 (OM)

PENDLETON, Benjamin &
Elizabeth Quisenberry
(d/o William
Quisenberry); 2 Jun
1796 (OM)

PENDLETON, Benjamin &
Mary Mason; 27 Sep 1750
(SpB)

PENDLETON, Benjamin &
Rebecca Arnold; 6 Mar
1815 (SpM)

PENDLETON, Edmund &
Lucy Elen Lewis; 12 Jan
1837 (SpM)

PENDLETON, Hugh G. &
Mary Ann Swan; 5 Jan
1830 (SpM)

PENDLETON, Jackson &
Maria E. Duerson; 24
Dec 1835 (SpM)

PENDLETON, John &
Elizabeth Taylor; 8 Nov
1785 (OB)

PENDLETON, John &
Elizabeth Taylor; 8 Nov
1785 (OM)

PENDLETON, John F. &
Hulday Lewis; 10 Feb
1831 (SpM)

PENDLETON, Rice & Agnes
Robbins; 24 Apr 1817
(SpM)

PENDLETON, Robert &
Elizabeth Burrus; 31
Jan 1797 (OM)

PENDLETON, Robert &
Martha A.E.Kelsoe; 7
Dec 1847 (SpM)

PENN, Edmund & Jane
Johnson; 28 Oct 1806
(SpM)

PENN, Reuben & Eliza A.
Leitch; 27 Jul 1841
(SpM)

PENN, Thomas & Mary
Mastin; 26 Feb 1811
(SpM)

PENNOCK, William & Ann
Tucker; 30 Sep 1782
(FB)

PERCY, Charles &
Elizabeth Lower (d/o
Mical Lower); 2 Jan
1798 (OM)

PERKINS, Abner &
Asinath Merrill; 6 Oct
1841 (FB)

PERRY, Abraham & Polly
Wharton (d/o George
Wharton); 18 Jul 1797
(OM)

PERRY, Austin & Emily
Milna; 20 Oct 1819 (FB)

PERRY, Elijah & Ann
Webb (d/o Richard
Crittendon Webb); 12
Jan 1797 (OM)

PERRY, Elisha & Gracey
Waugh; 30 Jan 1783
(StM)

PERRY, Elisha & Juliet
Ann Jenkins; 13 Mar
1839 (FB)

PERRY, Elr. P. & Sarah
Young; 24 May 1809
(SpM)

PERRY, Francis & Milly
Mullin; 22 Nov 1815
(SpM)

PERRY, George &
Elizabeth Fagg; 25 Feb
1800 (SpM)

PERRY, George &
Susannah Sanaram; 28
Nov 1815 (SpM)

PERRY, Henry T. & Anna
Tandy; 16 Mar 1815
(SpM)

PERRY, Hiram & Mary
Southard; 9 Dec 1834
(FB)

PERRY, Hugh N. & Lucy
Ann Ballard; 21 Sep
1848 (SpM)

PERRY, James & Jane
Perry; 12 Sep 1814 (OB)

PERRY, James L. & Ann
Perry; 8 May 1827 (SpM)

PERRY, James L. & Jane
Perry; 13 Sep 1814
(SpM)

PERRY, Jesse & Ann M.
Turnley; 16 Mar 1815
(SpM)

PERRY, John & Mary
Carnal; 8 Dec 1812
(SpB)

PERRY, Joseph & Susanna
Hart; Jan 1806 (SpM)

PERRY, Joseph W. &
Margaret Ingram; 4 Nov
1847 (FB)

PERRY, Moses & Betsy
Turnby; 15 Dec 1799
(SpM)

PERRY, Moses & Susan
Brockman; 23 mar 1786
(OM)

PERRY, Pierce & Nancy
Long; 10 Jun 1803 (SpM)

PERRY, William & Mary
Wood; 11 Dec 1834 (OB)

PETTIGREW, James &
Polly Taylor; Mar 1790
(FM)

PETTUS, Stephen Jr. &
Ann Dillard; 26 Jan
1748 (SpB)

PETTY, Jesse & Harriott
Lindsay; 22 Dec 1814
(SpM)

PEYTON, Alexander &
Elizabeth Davis; 4 May
1850 (FB)

PEYTON, Alexander &
Mary Snipe; 5 Mar 1829
(FB)

PEYTON, Charles C. &
Mary Ann Gutridge; 23
Nov 1843 (FB)

PEYTON, George & Aletha
P. Cason; 3 Feb 1824
(SpM)

PEYTON, George Henry
(s/o V. Peyton & Ann
Sacrey)& Lucy Barrett;
31 Mar 1847 (FB)

PEYTON, John G. &
Catharine Goodloe; 30
Nov 1825 (SpM)

PHILEUM, Henry &
Isabella McIntosh; 6
Jul 1816 (FB)

PHILIPS, David & Mary
Davis; 2 Mar 1778 (OB)

PHILLIPS, George P. &
Eliza Fox White; 24 Dec
1835 (SpM)

PHILLIPS, John &
Lucinda Reeves (d/o
Mary Reeves) 7 Feb 1810
(FB)

PHILLIPS, John T. &
Lucinda Reeves (d/o
Mary Reeves); 3 Jan
1811 (FB)

PHILLIPS, Richard &
Katherine Smith; 5 Aug
1727 (SpB)

PHILLIPS, Richard H. &
Eleanor Thom; 11 Nov
1835 (FB)

PHILLIPS, Shelton &
Ellen Massey; 20 Dec
1838 (FB)

PHITS, Thomas & Polly
Montague; 18 Oct 1799
(OM)

PICKETT, George W. &
Mary Jane True (d/o
Adolphus True); 17 Oct
1849 (FB)

PICKETT, Jeremiah &
Elizabeth Solivan; 26
Jul 1833 (FB)

PIER, George & Betsy W.
Gregory; 12 Dec (SpM)

PIERCE, Edward & Molly
Month; 8 Mar 1802 (SpB)

PIERCE, Edward & Molly
Mouth; 12 Mar 1802
(SpM)

PIERCE, James M. &
Elizabeth C. Templin;
30 Sep 1819 (SpM)

PIERCE, John & Hannah
Gimboe; 14 May 1794
(SpB)

PIERCE, William & Ann
Pierce; 12 Dec 1832
(SpM)

PILCHER, Hiram & Mary
Beck (d/o Elizabeth
Beck); 23 Oct 1828 (FB)

PIME, John & Becca
Fluman; 4 Jan 1803
(SpM)

PINN, Robert &
Elizabeth Jackson; 17
Apr 1839 (FB)

PIPER, William Henry &
Sarah West; 20 Mar 1849
(FB)

PITMAN, David & Nancy
Grotz (d/o John Grotz);
5 Jun 1844 (FB)

PITTMAN, John F.
Caroline M. Muse; 13
Jun 1850 (FB)

PITTMAN, John W. &
Betty Grotz; 30 Jan
1838 (FB)

POINDEXTER, Thomas &
Frances R. Schooler; 7
Oct 1817 (SpM)

POLLARD, Edmund & Sally
Herndon; 26 Dec 1794
(OM)

POLLARD, Henry &
Elizabeth Williams; 22
Dec 1803 (SpB)

POLLARD, Henry W. &
Mildred Ann Peyton; 24
Dec 1850 (SpM)

POLLARD, Joseph &
Susannah Peacock (d/o
Richard Peacock); 7 Dec
1803 (FB)

POLLETT, George &
Mildred Daingerfield;
20 Aug 1849 (FB)

POPE, Thomas S. & Sarah
Flack; 29 Oct 1803 (FB)

PORTER, Charles Jr. &
Betsy Proctor (d/o
George Proctor); 11 Nov
1782 (OM)

PORTER, Charles Jr. &
Betsy Proctor (d/o
George Proctor); 11 Nov
1782 (OB)

PORTER, John & Casandra
Thompson; 31 Jul 1823
(FB)

PORTER, John &
Catherine Carter; 24
Dec 1793 (OM)

PORTER, William & Polly
McCauley; 22 Aug 1796
(OM)

PORTER, William A. &
Malissa A. Buckman; 11
Jan 1844 (SpM)

PORTS, Lewis L. &
Elizabeth M. Breedon; 2
Oct 1818 (SpM)

POTTER, Peter F. & Mary
Crawford; 8 Apr 1817
(SpM)

POTTS, Timothy &
Catharine Curran; 13
Nov 1807 (FB)

POULTER, John & Patty
Ransdell; 24 Jan 1786
(OM)

POWEL, Joseph & Sarah
Overhall; 21 Sep 1750
(StM)

POWEL, Thomas &
Elizabeth Lewis; 14 Jun
1815 (SpM)

POWELL, Ambrose & Sally
Gritt (d/o Mary Gritt);
8 Sep 1783 (OM)

POWELL, Ambrose (s/o
Thomas Powell) & Sally
Britt (d/o Mary Britt;
8 Sep 1783 (OB)

POWELL, James & Letty
Simpson; 26 Jun 1816
(SpB)

POWELL, James & Lilly
Simpson; 27 Jun 1816
(SpM)

POWELL, James & Polly
Magee; 27 Dec 1808
(SpM)

POWELL, Lewis & Lucy
McMillan (d/o John
McMillan); 22 Sep 1796
(OM)

POWELL, Ptolemy &
Sidney Lavit (w/o ?);
23 Dec 1793 (OM)

POWELL, Reuben &
Elizabeth Ballard (d/o
Moreman & Martha
Ballard); 21 Dec 1800
(OM)

POWELL, Richard & Ellen
Elkins; 11 Oct 1848
(FB)

POWELL, Richard W. &
Nancy C. Mason; 5 Jan
1830 (SpM)

POWELL, William & Ann
Duerson; 16 Sep 1813
(SpM)

POWELL, William &
Betsey Lavender; 12 Dec
1804 (SpM)

POWELL, William &
Betsey Lavinder; 10 Dec
1804 (SpB)

POWELL, William &
Elizabeth Dunneusant;
13 Jun 1850 (SpM)

POWELL, William &
Elizabeth Regan; 2 Apr
1747 (StM)

PREBLE, John & Nancy
Bancroft; 10 Feb 1826
(FB)

PREVOST, Lewis M. &
Laura E. McCarty; 7 Feb
1844 (FB)

PRICE, Anthony &
Elizabeth Stribling; 17
Jan 1768 (StM)

PRICE, Patrick H. &
Ellen L. Crutchfield; 1
Dec 1829 (SpM)

PRICE, William & Sarah
Allenthorp; 5 Aug 1748
(StM)

PRITCHARD, Edward &
Mary Brown (d/o James
Brown); 7 Nov 1806 (FB)

PRITCHARD, John &
Harriet S. Barnett; 15
Aug 1839 (FB)

PRITCHETT, Benjamin &
Polly Herndon; 7 Apr
1798 (OM)

PRITCHETT, Pamienus B.
& Sarah Goodloe; 1813
(SpM)

PRITCHETT, William A.
Sarah I. Pritchett; 4
Mar 1847 (SpM)

PRITCHETT, William W. &
Matilda Luck; 24 Dec
1822 (SpM)

PROCKEY, George W. &
Martha I. Jones; 6 Feb
1845 (SpM)

PROCTOR, Austin &
Marthanne Hillman; 29
Oct 1850 (SpM)

PROCTOR, Charles &
Maria Trainer; 19 Jul
1833 (FB)

PROCTOR, Hezikiah &
Nancy Young (d/o John
Young); 20 Mar 1783
(OM)

PROCTOR, Hezikiah &
Nancy Young (d/o John
Young); 25 Mar 1783
(OB)

PROCTOR, John & Eliza
Hoard; 14 Oct 1816
(SpB)

PROCTOR, John & Eliza
Hoard; 14 Oct 1816
(SpM)

PROCTOR, John & Eliza
Leitch; 8 Jun 1837
(SpM)

PROCTOR, Lewis & Susan
A. Stephens; 29 Sep
1836 (SpM)

PROCTOR, Thomas &
Charlott Brent; 14 Nov
1817 (SpM)

PROCTOR, Thomas &
Charlotte Brent; 13 Nov
1817 (SpB)

PROCTOR, Thomas &
Christiana Keys (w/o
?); 26 Dec 1815 (FB)

PROCTOR, Thomas &
Eleanor Snellings (d/o
Elizabeth Snellings);
14 Mar 1844 (FB)

PROCTOR, Thomas &
Frances Peacher; 24 Dec
1824 (SpB)

PROCTOR, Thomas &
Frances Peacher; 29 Dec
1824 (SpM)

PROCTOR, Thomas & Sarah
Heslep; 5 Apr 1847 (FB)

PROCTOR, Uriah & Martha
Singleton (of
Fredericksburg); 22 Aug
1776 (OM)

PROCTOR, William &
Elizabeth Haynes; 2 Feb
1804 (SpB)

PROCTOR, William &
Elizabeth Haynes; 8 Feb
1804 (SpM)

PROCTOR, William &
Elizabeth Hiatt; 8 May
1777 (OM)

PROUDLOVE, Pemberton & Alse Ware; 10 Feb 1717 or 1718 (StM)

PRUETT, William & Elizabeth E. Taylor; 4 Mar 1834 (SpM)

PUCKETT, John & Susanah Edthnton; 8 Jan 1807 (SpM)

PUCKETT, Peter & Nancy Payne; 23 Aug 1807 (SpM)

PUCKETT, William & Martha Long; 12 Jul 1810 (SpM)

PULLAM, David & Mary Jane Brightwell; 1833 (SpM)

PULLEN, Edwin R. & Elizabeth Sibley; 14 Mar 1850 (FB)

PULLEN, Jesse & Eliza Shepherd (d/o Lucy Shepherd); 2 May 1828 (FB)

PULLEN, Jesse & Lucy M. Ames; 5 Mar 1834 (FB)

PULLER, James & Mary Duerson; 11 Dec 1816 (SpB)

PULLER, James & Mary Duerson; 12 Dec 1816 (SpM)

PULLER, John G. & Catharine Puller; 31 Oct 1816 (SpM)

PULLER, John G. & Catherine Puller; 31 Oct 1816 (SpB)

PULLIAM, David & Mary Brightwell; 26 Feb 1833 (SpB)

PULLIAM, Rich. & Elizabeth Jarrell; 19 Dec 1796 (SpB)

PULLIAM, Richard & Rebecca K. Duson; 3 Dec 1829 (SpM)

PURTON, May & Sara Head; 29 Sep 1776 (OM)

PURVIS, George & Amanda M. Fox; 17 Jun 1845 (SpM)

PURVIS, George & Elizabeth Jarrell; 11 Dec 1823 (SpM)

QUARLES, John & _____; 3 Oct 1722 (SpB)

QUARLES, John & Sarah Daniel; 21 Dec 1831 (FB)

QUARLES, William & Frances Vivion (d/o John Vivion); 3 Sep 1779 (OM)

QUESENBERRY, William & Frances Davis (w/o?); 1 May 1821 (FB)

QUINN, Richard & Ann Wood; 27 Mar 1783 (OB)

QUINN, Richard & Ann Wood; 27 Mar 1783 (OM)

QUISENBERRY, Aaron & Henrietta Reynolds; 17 Nov 1805 (OM)

QUISENBERRY, Albert & Sarah Reynolds; 18 Apr 1831 (OB)

QUISENBERRY, Albert &
Sarah Reynolds; 21 Apr
1831 (SpM)

QUISENBERRY, Benjamin &
Sally B. Groom; 11 Jan
1816 (OB)

QUISENBERRY, Benjamin &
Sally B. Groom; 14 Jan
1816 (SpM)

QUISENBERRY, Benjamin &
Sally Groom; 14 Jan
1815 (SpM)

QUISENBERRY, George &
Jane Daniel; 22 May
1783 (OB)

QUISENBERRY, George &
Jane Daniel; 22 May
1783 (OM)

QUISENBERRY, George &
Margaret Reynolds (d/o
William Reynolds); 22
Jun 1802 (OM)

QUISENBERRY, George &
Polly Wallace; 18 Feb
1835 (SpM)

QUISENBERRY, James &
Jane Burrows; 2 Dec
1776 (OM)

QUISENBERRY, James M. &
Francis M. Spindle; 9
Jun 1840 (SpM)

QUISENBERRY, Moses &
Sarah Burnley; 10 Aug
1805 (OM)

QUISENBERRY, Vivian &
Sally Wright; 28 Oct
1811 (OM)

RAINES, Libern P. &
Caroline H. Kersey; 21
Dec 1848 (FB)

RAINES, Merry & Annie
Floyd; 21 Mar 1799 (OM)

RAINES, Richard &
Theodosia Eastridge; 22
May 1783 (OM)

RALLINGS, James &
Margaret Stribling; 5
Jan 1778 (StM)

RANALDSON, James &
Lydia A.M. Barton; 16
Aug 1814 (FB)

RANDOLPH, Charles C. &
Ann L. Mortimer; 25 Jul
1825 (SpM)

RANDOLPH, Charles C. &
Mary Ann F. Mortimer;
25 Jun 1825 (SpM)

RANDOLPH, Edward &
Elizabeth Beverley; 7
Jan 1825 (SpM)

RANDOLPH, Nicholas &
Margaret Raddish; 21
Feb 1733 or 1734 (StM)

RANY, James & Amy
Miller; 22 Jan 1801
(SpM)

RAWLINGS, James B. &
Ann E. Cason; Dec 1833
(SpM)

RAWLINGS, Richard &
Katherine Rice; 11 Apr
1746 (StM)

RAWLINS, John & Mildred
Triger; 1809 (SpM)

RAYMOND, Garret V.W. &
Margaret White (d/o
Henry White); 16 Mar
1816 (FB)

RAYMOND, John &
Margaret Robertson; 27
Feb 1746 or 1747 (StM)

REA, James & Honour
Poates; 2 Jul 1738
(StM)

READ, John & Margaret
Allenthorp; 5 Mar 1754
(StM)

READER, Michael &
Elizabeth Day (d/o
Sarah Day); 13 Dec 1804
(FB)

READY, William &
Rebecca Jones; 10 Aug
1820 (SpM)

REAMEY, Octavius &
Elizabeth Turner; 26
Jan 1843 (SpM)

REAT, William & Ann
Minor; 11 Oct 1785 (FB)

REAVES, William & Mary
Parker; 15 May 1850
(FB)

REED, Benjamin & Sarah
Payne; 11 May 1826 (OB)

REED, Benjamin & Sarah
Payne; 11 May 1826
(SpM)

REEDER, Hezekiah &
Jemima Suthard; 3 Jan
1816 (FB)

REES, Philip & Sarah
Beech (d/o Ann
Williams); 4 Jul 1844
(FB)

REEVES, Aaron & Fanny
Lewis (d/o Adam &
Matilda Lewis); 10 Dec
1834 (FB)

REEVES, Peter & Jane
West; 20 Jul 1836 (FB)

REISKELL, T. & Fanny
Badger; Jul 1804 (FM)

RELINS, Thomas & Mary
Rigby; 16 Jul 1742
(StM)

REVEER, George & Judah
Hughlett; 17 Jul 1817
(FB)

REVELEY, Thomas &
Elizabeth Stubblefield;
30 Dec 1813 (SpM)

REVES, William & Amanda
Lee; 28 Dec 1849 (FB)

REYNOLDS, Aaron & Caty
Chambers; 13 Aug 1784
(OB)

REYNOLDS, Aaron & Caty
Chambers; 13 Aug 1784
(OM)

REYNOLDS, John & Anna
Darnell; 23 Jan 1774
(OM)

REYNOLDS, John & Anna
Darnell; 23 Jan 1774
(OM)

REYNOLDS, Johnson & Ann
Drinnan; 6 Aug 1842
(FB)

REYNOLDS, Joseph &
Susanna Wright; 10 Feb
1774 (OM)

REYNOLDS, Joseph &
Susanna Wright; 11 Feb
1774 (OM)

REYNOLDS, Philip S. &
Elizabeth Reynolds; 18
Apr 1831 (OB)

REYNOLDS, Philip S. &
Elizabeth Reynolds; 21
Apr 1831 (SpM)

REYNOLDS, Richard & Ann Roach (w/o ?); 24 Aug 1778 (OM)

REYNOLDS, Richard & Catherine_____; 15 Aug 1775 (OM)

REYNOLDS, Richard & Lucy Finnel (d/o Simon Finnel); 24 Dec 1800 (OM)

REYNOLDS, Robert & Frances Martin; 20 Nov 1819 (SpM)

REYNOLDS, William & Joice Quisenberry; 27 Nov 1809 (OM)

REYNOLDS, William & Nancy Nixon; 22 May 1777 (OM)

RHODES, Robert & Lissa Delaney (of Albemarle Co.); 27 May 1782 (OM)

RIADER, Isaac & Susannah McKelamy; 26 Dec 1796 (OM)

RIADON, George & Sally Owen; 3 Apr 1799 (SpM)

RICH, James & Mary Taliaferro; 15 Jan 1845 (FB)

RICHARDS, George B. & Catharine Graham; 22 Dec 1818 (FB)

RICHARDS, John & Judy Parker; 26 Jan 1842 (FB)

RICHARDS, John & Milly Watts; 3 Apr 1776 (OM)

RICHARDS, Philemon & Susannah Woods; 3 Feb 1778 (OM)

RICHARDS, Robert (b.d. 23 Jun 1789) & Martha H. Jones (d/o Letitia Jones); 20 Feb 1811 (FB)

RICHARDSON, Henry & Maria Backhouse; 19 Nov 1814 (FB)

RICHARDSON, James & Susanna McKenna; 5 Feb 1798 (SpM)

RICHARDSON, John M. & Virginia Ann Underwood (d/o John Underwood); 17 Dec 1819 (FB)

RICHARDSON, William & Harriet Robinson; 25 Feb 1808 (SpM)

RIDDLE, Fielding & Milly Waits; 17 Feb 1795 (OM)

RIDDLE, William & Joyce Riddle; 25 Dec 1783 (OM)

RIDDLE, William & Martha Pipman; 17 Feb 1800 (SpM)

RIDDLE, William (s/o Lewis Riddle) & Joyce Reddel; 25 Dec 1783 (OB)

RIDGAWAY, Robert O. & Sarah Jane Daingerfield; 31 Oct 1850 (FB)

RIGHT, James & Sarah Rawson; 3 Mar 1785 (OM)

RINE, Abraham & Ann Hart; 1813 (SpM)

RINE, Abraham & Melinda
Smith; 12 Jan 1826
(SpM)

RIPPITO, William &
Betsy Stow (d/o Zanny
Aranzy); 12 Apr 1797
(OM)

ROACH, Benjamin & Sally
Price; 22 Dec 1786
(StM)

ROACH, James & Mary
Duerson; 28 Dec 1815
(SpM)

ROANE, Reuben T. & Lucy
A.E. Masey; 9 May 1839
(SpM)

ROBB, Patrick C. &
Maria Pratt; Nov 1820
(SpM)

ROBBINS, John &
Elizabeth Taylor; 26
Nov 1806 (SpM)

ROBBINS, Thomas & Mary
Foster; 24 Dec 1775
(OM)

ROBERSON, Charles C. &
Angelina W. Vaughan;
1832 (SpM)

ROBERTS, Hugh &
Elizabeth Silk; 2 Jan
1799 (OM)

ROBERTS, John & Agnes
Knight (d/o Mathew
Knight); 8 Jan 1796
(OM)

ROBERTS, John & Mary
White; 27 Jan 1794 (OM)

ROBERTS, Lorenso & Mary
Ann Donaldson (d/o
Persilla Donaldson); 8
Feb 1838 (FB)

ROBERTS, Samuel &
Elizabeth Bryant; 18
Nov 1834 (FB)

ROBERTS, William J. &
Martha Lomax; 26 Jun
1817 (FB)

ROBERTSON, John &
Frances Porter; 5 Mar
1787 (OM)

ROBERTSON, Richard &
Elizabeth Collins; 23
Sep 1799 (OM)

ROBERTSON, Richard &
Elizabeth Collins; 23
Sep 1799 (OM)

ROBEY, Henry R. &
Clarissa T. Brooks; 3
Jun 1834 (FB)

ROBEY, Henry T. & Susan
Frances Brownlow; 4 Nov
1844 (FB)

ROBINS, Elijah & Sally
Lewis; 27 Jul 1809
(SpM)

ROBINS, John &
Elizabeth Taylor; 20
Nov 1806 (SpB)

ROBINSON, Achilles D. &
Sally B. Bell (d/o
Roger Bell); 1817? (OM)

ROBINSON, Charles H. &
Maria Turner (d/o
Alexander Turner); 24
Dec 1844 (FB)

ROBINSON, George & Mary
Herndon; 20 Jun 1814
(SpB)

ROBINSON, George & Mary
Herndon; 20 Jun 1814
(SpM)

ROBINSON, Henry & Sarah
Anne Faulconer; 17 Nov
1831 (SpM)

ROBINSON, Henry &
Winifred Barlis; 1 Aug
1750 (StM)

ROBINSON, James & Judy
Embree; 16 Jan 1760
(OB)

ROBINSON, James & Judy
Embry; 16 Jan 1760 (OM)

ROBINSON, John & Lucy
Smith; 24 Nov 1757 (OB)

ROBINSON, John & Lucy
Smith; 24 Nov 1757 (OB)

ROBINSON, John & Lucy
Smith; 24 Nov 1757 (OM)

ROBINSON, John & Nancy
Brown (w/o Charles
Brown); 23 Feb 1809
(FB)

ROBINSON, John &
Susanna Suffrense; 21
Aug 1807 (SpM)

ROBINSON, Joseph &
Margaret C. Grotz; 18
Nov 1847 (FB)

ROBINSON, Michael &
Polly Williams; 20 Dec
1799 (OM)

ROBINSON, Thomas & Lucy
Robinson; 25 Apr 1777
(OB)

ROBINSON, Thomas &
Nancy Roach; 11 Feb
1813 (OB)

ROBINSON, Thomas &
Nancy Roach; 14 Feb
1813 (SpM)

ROBINSON, William &
Agatha Beverly; 17 Feb
1736 (SpB)

ROBINSON, William &
Agnes Smith; 27 Jan
1757 (OM)

ROBINSON, William &
Agnes Smith; 27 Jan
1758 (OB)

ROBINSON, William &
Agness Smith; 27 Jan
1757 (OB)

ROBINSON, William &
Joanna Embry; 25 Jan
1754 (OB)

ROBINSON, William &
Margaret Collins (d/o
Richard Collins); 26
Nov 1794 (OM)

ROBINSON, William P. &
Eleanor Pearson (d/o
William Pearson); 20
Dec 1821 (FB)

ROBUKS, Hugh &
Elizabeth Sisk; 26 Dec
1798 (OM)

ROCKFELLER, Jacob F.M.
& Frances M. Whaling;
19 Nov 1840 (FB)

RODES, Robert (of
Albemarle Co., Va.) &
Liza Delaney; 27 May
1782 (OB)

RODGERS, Daniel & Anna
G. Barefoot; 9 May 1824
(FB)

ROGERS, Henry W. &
Helen Shape; 5 Apr 1813
(SpB)

ROGERS, Henry W. &
Helen Snape; 20 Apr
1813 (SpM)

ROGERS, John &
bElizabeth Knight; 27
Dec 1798 (OM)

ROGERS, John & Lucy
Darnell (d/o Mary Ann
Darnell); 28 Feb 1803
(OM)

ROGERS, Samuel & Sally
Davis; 10 Dec 1796 (OM)

ROGERS, William & Sarah
Branham; 10 Jan 1798
(SpB)

ROGERS, William & Sarah
Branham; 17 Jan 1798
(SpM)

ROLLINS, Enoch & Lydia
Ann Layton; 26 Jan 1836
(FB)

ROLLINS, Henry & Susan
Rose (d/o Margaret Rose
of Stafford County); 19
May 1835 (FB)

ROLLOW, John J. &
Malvira Long (d/o
Joshua Long); 20 Mar
1834 (FB)

ROLLOW, William & Eliza
Ann Shuletice (d/o John
L. Shuletice); 17 Jan
1825 (FB)

ROOTES, George F. &
Sarah A. White; 27 Dec
1836 (FB)

ROOTES, Thomas R. Jr. &
Ann French (d/o George
French); 22 Apr 1807
(FB)

RORRE, Absalom & Nancy
Estes; 2 Nov 1825 (SpM)

ROSE, Abram & Ann
Perry; 12 Sep 1810
(SpM)

ROSE, Elias & Sarah
Sweeney; 2 Sep 1758
(StM)

ROSE, Francis & Hester
Stribling; 31 May 1756
(StM)

ROSE, John & Anne
Swillakeen; 4 Jan 1776
(StM)

ROSE, Robert & Sarah
True (d/o Fanny True);
2 Jun 1842 (FB)

ROSE, Thomas &
Elizabeth Hammond; 27
Sep 1806 (SpM)

ROSE, William & Jane
Abbott; 21 Apr 1800
(SpM)

ROSE, Zachariah & Sarah
Taylor; 19 Mar 1778
(StM)

ROSS, Daniel & Jean
Lindsay; 8 Jun 1786
(FB)

ROSS, John & Mary
Brumfield; 9 Nov 1819
(FB)

ROSSON, Archelaus &
Haney Ritter Warren
(d/o Elizabeth Warren);
23 jan 1797 (OM)

ROTHROCK, George &
Elizabeth Pollock (d/o
William Pollock); 30
Oct 1793 (OM)

ROTHROCK, George W. &
Louisanna, Johnston; 14
Mar 1827 (FB)

ROUTT, William &
Winifred Byram; 27 Nov
1753 (StM)

ROWE, Absalom & Almidin
F. Gale; 2 Jun 1845
(SpM)

ROWE, John G. (Rev.) &
Margaret A.L. Purcell
(d/o Sarah S. Blackey);
4 Nov 1850 (FB)

ROWLINGS, Bez. S. &
Annie F. Leach; 20 Jun
1845 (SpB)

ROWZIE, Edward T. &
Dorothy Waller; 20 Sep
1798 (SpM)

ROY, John & Eliza
Alexander; Apr 1824
(FB)

ROY, William H. & Ann
Seddon; 3 May 1825 (FB)

RUCKER, Ephriam &
Elizabeth Randall; 25
Jun 1775 (OM)

RUCKER, Joel & Nancy
Olliver (d/o Tabitha
Olliver); 20 Dec 1786
(OM)

RUCKER, John & Betty
Tinsley (d/o John
Tinsley); 27 Apr 1780
(OM)

RUCKER, William & Caty
T. Taliaferro; 25 Dec
1794 (OM)

RUMAGE, James & Ann
Snow (d/o John Snow,
b.d.28 Dec 1801); 7 Jan
1823 (FB)

RUMBOLTZ, Gottleb &
Susan G. Tompkins; 7
Sep 1837 (SpM)

RUMMAGE, James & Lynia
Ann White (previously
married); 26 Sep 1823
(FB)

RUMSEY, Thomas & Patty
Cope; 15 Mar 1777 (OM)

RUNNELS, John H. Eliza
B. Dade; 14 Sep 1819
(FB)

RUNNELS, Robert &
Frances Martin; 29 Oct
1819 (SpB)

RUPEL, Bartlett & Nancy
Middlebrook; 19 MAy
1816 (SpM)

RUSSELL, Nehemiah &
Sally Collins; 11 Aug
1775 (OM)

RUST, Benjamin &
Frances Davis; 6 Apr
1824 (FB)

RYAN, James J. & Susan
F. Gordon; 24 May 1843
(FB)

RYAN, Thomas &
Elizabeth West, 21 Jul
1836 (SpM)

RYE, Archibald &
Elizabeth Condiffe; 24
Oct 1818 (FB)

RYE, Rawleigh &
Parthenia Posey; 7 MAy
1790 (StM)

SACHEVEREL, William &
Elizabeth Trunnel; 26
Feb 1784 (StM)

SACRA, Charles & Sally
Crawford; 15 Dec 1802
(SpM)

SACREY, Benjamin &
Sarah G. Godfrey; 17
Mar 1845 (FB)

SAERA, Charles & June
Humphries; 1 Dec 1813
(SpM)

SALE, George & Betsy
Puller; 31 Oct 1816
(SpM)

SALE, Robert & Anne
Puller; 15 Oct 1818
(SpM)

SALE, Samuel &
Catherine Dudley; 22
Oct 1828 (SpM)

SALE, William & Rebecca
A. Hicks; Dec 1835
(SpM)

SAMPSON, Elijah & Amy
Rogers (d/o John
Rogers); 6 Jun 1804
(OM)

SAMPSON, James & Anney
James; 27 Jun 1800 (OM)

SAMS, John & Mary
Bledsoe; 22 Sep 1785
(OB)

SAMS, John & Mary
Bledsoe; 22 Sep 1785
(OM)

SAMUEL, John & Mary
Faulkner; 7 Jan 1830
(FB)

SAMUEL, Philemon &
Maria Pitts; 12 Oct
1815 (FB)

SANDRUM, Peter & Suckuy
Sampson; Jan 1806 (SpM)

SANDS, John & Pina
Donaldson (d/o

Prissilla Donaldson);
12 Sep 1839 (FB)

SANDY, Henry &
Charlotte Hill (w/o ?);
26 Apr 1825 (FB)

SANFORD, Charles H. &
Judith Ellis Bibb; 12
Nov 1839 (FB)

SANFORD, Joseph & Agnes
J.M. Crawford; 26 Aug
1835 (SpM)

SANFORD, Reuben & Nancy
Wallace (d/o James
Wallace Sr.); 24 Dec
1800 (OM)

SANGER, Henry &
Elizabeth Whaley; 20
Jan 1825 (FB)

SAVAGE, Thomas S. &
Susan A. Metcalf; 19
Sep 1838 (FB)

SAWYER, William &
Elizabeth Wright; 21
Feb 1775 (OM)

SCAPLEHORN, William &
Mary Stoward; 21 Feb
1754 (StM)

SCHALDEFORD, Thomas &
Mildred Ana Fagg; 3 Nov
1806 (SpM)

SCHAUT, Jacob & Mary
Jane Long (d/o Martha
Long); 18 Jul 1844 (FB)

SCHOFIELD, Thomas T. &
Catherine Coleman; 21
Jul 1817 (FB)

SCHOLLER, Richard &
Rachel Mastin; 15 Sep
1822 (SpM)

SCHOOLER, Garritt &
Elizabeth Johnson; 15
Jun 1806 (FB)

SCHOOLER, Joseph H. &
Dolly Quisenberry; 13
Mar 1810 (SpM)

SCHOOLER, Joseph H. &
Dolly Quisenberry; 8
Mar 1810 (OB)

SCHOOLER, Landon J. &
Sophie L. Holladay 26
Feb 1818 (SpM)

SCHOOLER, Richard &
Rachel Mastin; 12 Sep
1822 (SpB)

SCHRICKEL, John F. &
MAry M. King; 30 May
1837 (FB)

SCOFIELD, Samuel &
Elizabeth Rennolds (d/o
Elizabeth Rennolds); 2
Jan 1849 (FB)

SCOTT, Day & Sarah K.
Carter; 24 Feb 1813
(SpB)

SCOTT, Day & Sarah K.
Carter; 25 Feb 1813
(SpM)

SCOTT, Francis W. & Ann
M. Miner; 1 Oct 1838
(FB)

SCOTT, George & Miss
Ann Lee; 22 Sep 1825
(OB)

SCOTT, James & Sarah
Lewis; 13 Dec 1832
(SpM)

SCOTT, James M. Mary S.
Leferre; 5 Mar 1834
(FB)

SCOTT, John T. & Huldah
Lewis; 5 Jan 1832 (SpM)

SCOTT, Mortimer & Mary
L. Duerson; Oct 1832
(SpM)

SCOTT, Reuben &
Margaret Cope; 7 Feb
1781 (OM)

SCOTT, Robert E. & Ann
Morson; 18 Oct 1838
(FB)

SCOTT, Thomas C. & Mary
L. Seddon; 5 Dec 1815
(FB)

SEA, Carr & Jane
Dillard; 26 Dec 1815
(SpM)

SEAY, John & Sarah
Etherton; 6 Aug 1835
(SpM)

SEBASTIAN, Isaac &
Rachel Spicer; 11 May
1727 (StM)

SEBREE, William &
Hannah Kavanaugh; 31
May 1774 (OM)

SEDREB, William & Mary
Strother; 27 jun 1775
(OM)

SEDDON, John & Mary A.
Little; 25 Apr 1848
(FB)

SELDON, James & Eliza
Simpson; 1832 (SpM)

SELDON, James H. &
Eliza J. Simpson; 11
Jan 1832 (SpB)

SELDON, Robert T. &
Sarah Agnes Day; 7 Dec
1830 (SpM)

143

SELVIE, John &
Elizabeth Thomson; 29
Jun 1727 (StM)

SENOR, Joseph M. & Mary
Ann Raines; 1 Jun 1836
(FB)

SERLE, George D. &
Betsey Pullen; 31 Oct
1816 (SpB)

SETTLE, Reuben & Mary
Taylor; 15 Jun 1792
(StM)

SETTLE, Thomas &
Elizabeth Wharton; 26
Feb 1778 (StM)

SETTLE, Thomas &
Elizabeth Wharton; 26
Feb 1778 (StM)

SEWARD, William B. &
Mary McWilliams (d/o
Clara McWilliams); 23
Sep 1834 (FB)

SEWELL,James & Eliza
Seysmith; 11 Jan 1820
(FB)

SEWERS, Christopher &
Sarah Pierce; 18 Jul
1796 (OM)

SEYSMITH, John &
Mildred Summers; 17 May
1815 (FB)

SHACKELFORD, John & Ann
Dillard; 12 Jun 1811
(SpM)

SHACKELFORD, Richard &
Sarah D. Johnson; 18
Dec 1807 (SpB)

SHACKELFORD, Richard &
Sarah Johnson; 8 Oct
1808 (SpM)

SHACKLEFORD, Benjamin &
Betsy (or Betty)
Thomas; 26 Jan 1848
(SpM)

SHADLER, Abraham &
Elizabeth Kennedy (d/o
Mary Kennedy); 11 Aug
1835 (FB)

SHADRACK, Thomas &
Sarah Sanders (d/o
Nathaniel Sanders); 21
Jul 1795 (OM)

SHAFER, William &
Pamela Stewart; 1833
(SpM)

SHAKELFORD, Richard &
Mary Lewis; 27 Dec 1747
(SpB)

SHARMARARD, Elisha &
Elisha Powell; 11 Jul
1783 (OM)

SHAY, Dennis & Mary
Feomer; 29 Jul 1785
(FB)

SHEETS, John & Virginia
Quisenberry; 7 Dec 1841
(FB)

SHELTON, John Nancy
Bates; 8 Oct 1850 (FB)

SHELTON, Thomas H. &
Sarah Hoard; 24 Dec
1812 (SpM)

SHELTON, Wallace &
Susan Ann Briscoe (d/o
Mary Briscoe); 10 Jan
1832 (FB)

SHELTON, Yelvington &
Ann Cunningham; 21 Mar
1829 (SpB)

SHELTON, Yelvington &
Ann Cunningham; 22 Mar
1829 (SpM)

SHEPHERD, George & Ann
Porter; 18 Nov 1793
(OM)

SHEPHERD, James & Cary
Keaton; Feb 1800 (SpM)

SHEPHERD, John M. &
Judith Benson (d/o G.
Benson); 28 May

SHEPHERD, William &
Rebecca Moxley; 3 April
1799 (SpM)

SHER, Robert & Jean
Addison; 31 Jun 1796
(OM)

SHIFFLET, John & Rhoda
Shifflet; 29 Dec 1798
(OM)

SHIFFLET, John &
Susanna Davis; 27 Oct
1796 (OM)

SHIFFLETT, Pickett &
Lucretia Powell; 25 Jun
1795 (OM)

SHIFLET, John & Ann
Hicks; 15 Sep 1798 (OM)

SHIFLETT, Stephens &
Rachel Hicks; 18 Jan
1795 (OM)

SHORT, Thomas & Eliza
Holloway; 1 Oct 1810
(SpM)

SHORT, William U. &
Fanny Warfield; 5 Sep
1826 (FB)

SHOTWELL, John & Sarah
Worldey; 26 Jun 1725
(StM)

SHOULTRICE, John L. &
Sally Davis (d/o

William Davis); 13 Sep
1804 (FB)

SHOVELER, Frances &
Charlotte Porch (d/o
Easham Porch); 11 Apr
1805 (FB)

SHROPSHIRE, John & Mary
Part---; 4 Dec 1757
(OB)

SHROPSHIRE, John & Mary
Porter; 21 Dec 1757
(OB)

SHROPSHIRE, John & Mary
Porter; 4 dec 1757 (OM)

SIBLEY, J.L. & Mary
Hewlitt; 11 Feb 1837
(FB)

SILL, James & Mildred
Puzey (d/o Alden
Puzey); 9 Jun 1823 (FB)

SILVEY, Stephen &
Frankey Dean; 14 Oct
1785 (OB)

SILVEY, Stephen &
Frankey Dear; 14 Oct
1785 (OM)

SIMMONDS, Ephriam &
Sarah Hanes; 25 Feb
1797 (OM)

SIMMONDS, James (of
Lancaster) & Olivia
A.F. Doggett (d/o
Lemuel Doggett); 14 Nov
1839 (SpM)

SIMMONS, Ephriam & Mary
Pew; 13 Apr 1740 (StM)

SIMMS, Richard & Betty
Bridwell; 15 Oct 1750
(StM)

SIMPSON, Aaron & Mary
Mollican; 16 Mar 1810
(SpM)

SIMPSON, Aaron & Mary
Mullican; 14 Mar 1810
(OB)

SIMPSON, Abraham &
Sarah Mullican; 23 Dec
1810 (SpM)

SIMPSON, Abraham &
Sarah Mullican; 27 Dec
1810 (SpB)

SIMPSON, Daniel &
Elizabeth Jones; 3 May
1800 (OM)

SIMPSON, John & Ann
Eliza McGee; 7 Feb 1849
(SpM)

SIMPSON, Josiah & Ann
Stanard; 8 Jul 1813
(FB)

SIMPSON, William & Ann
THompson (d/o George
Thompson); 8 Dec 1798
(OM)

SIMPSON, William &
Delphia Simpson; 30 May
1819 (SpM)

SIMPSON, William &
Philadelphia Simpson;
28 May 1819 (SpB)

SIMS, Brooks & Polly
Boswell (d/o Charles
Boswell); 22 Nov 1813
(OM)

SIMS, Howard &
Catherine Henry; 11 Apr
1831 (FB)

SIMS, Nathaniel &
Susannah Johnson; 18
Aug 1796 (OM)

SIMS, Nimrod & Nancy
Bowling; 21 Sep 1820
(FB)

SIMS, Reuben & Frances
Graves; 11 Nov 1812
(OM)

SIMS, William & Tannie
Walker (d/o Elizabeth
Walker); 24 Feb 1796
(OM)

SISSON, ____ & Millie
Braham; between 1771 &
1774 (OM)

SISSON, C. & Milly
Branham; 20 Jul 1771
(OB)

SKINKER, Samuel &
Margaret Julian; 28 Nov
1803 (FB)

SKINKER, William (fpc)
& Sarah Nickens (fpc);
19 Oct 1820

SKINNER, John & Sarah
Roe; 15 Sep 1743 (StM)

SKIPWITH, Humberston &
Lelia Robertson; 5 Apr
1830 (FB)

SLAUGHTER, Francis &
Ann Lightfoot; 3 June
1729 (SpB)

SLAUGHTER, Robert Jr. &
_____; 3 June 1723
(SpB)

SLAUGHTER, Samuel &
Virginia Stewart; 11
Nov 1817 (SpM)

SLEET, George & Ann
Lee; 22 Sep 1825 (OB)

SLEET, George & Ann
Lee; 23 Sep 1825 (SpM)

SLEET, James & Euphan Smith; 5 Jan 1733 (SpB)

SLEET, John & Frances Wright (d/o William Wright); 22 Jan 1800 (OM)

SLEET, Weedon & Patsy Petty (d/o George Petty); 21 Oct 1799 (OM)

SMALL, Noah & Nancy Hughlett; 9 Feb 1824 (FB)

SMALLEY, William & Martha Alsop; 17 Jan 1819 (SpM)

SMALLWOOD, Charles & Barbary Sansley; 5 Jun 1809 (SpM)

SMALLWOOD, James & Betsey Jackson; 6 Feb 1816 (SpB)

SMALLWOOD, James & Betsy Jackson; 6 Feb 1816 (SpM)

SMALLWOOD, James & Frances Sweeney; 23 May 1776 (StM)

SMILEY, William & Ester Norwell; 1 Jun 1776 (OM)

SMITH George W. & Jane Wilson; 23 Dec 1824 (SpM)

SMITH, Absolem & Justine Chandler (d/o Joseph Chandler); 25 Oct 1781 (OM)

SMITH, Ambrose & Elizabeth Chandler; Feb 1800 (SpM)

SMITH, Austin & Mary Milen Buck; 25 Feb 1829 (FB)

SMITH, Benjamin & Fenton Brooke; 13 Dec 1832 (FB)

SMITH, Charles & Jane Morton (d/o Elijah Morton); 19 Jun 1783 (OM)

SMITH, Charles & Jane Morton (d/o Elijah Morton); 19 Jun 1783 (OB)

SMITH, Charles H. & Evelina Stone (d/o W.F.Stone); 13 Nov 1811 (FB)

SMITH, Colby & Sally Kendall; 9 Jan 1797 (OM)

SMITH, David & Eleanor Frazer (d/o Bridget Frazer) 6 Aug 1807 (FB)

SMITH, Edward & Rose Warren; 26 Aug 1786 (OM)

SMITH, Edwin & Elizabeth Thomas; 29 May 1845 (SpB)

SMITH, George & Elizabeth Abell; 19 Dec 1798 (OM)

SMITH, George & Elizabeth Luggett; 26 Jan 1760 (OM)

SMITH, George & Elizabeth Suggit; 26 Feb 1760 (OB)

SMITH, George & Ophelia A. Williams; 14 Feb 1825 (FB)

SMITH, Gulildmus &
Rebecca Coleman; 13 Jun
1810 (SpM)

SMITH, Henry & Hester
Stone; 21 May 1749
(StM)

SMITH, Henry & Margaret
Spicer; 23 Sep 1729
(StM)

SMITH, Henry & Virginia
E. Taylor; 25 Jun 1833
(FB)

SMITH, James & Patty
Cleveland; 9 Nov 1775
(OM)

SMITH, James & Polly
Dillard; 9 Feb 1803
(SpM)

SMITH, John & Alice
Wolfe (d/o Grace Fenton
Wolfe); 30 Mar 1819
(FB)

SMITH, John & Ann
Yarentharp; 7 Mar 1748
or 1749 (StM)

SMITH, John & Anne
Yarentharp; 7 Mar 1748
or 1749 (StM)

SMITH, John & Elizabeth
Warren; 24 Mar 1785
(OB)

SMITH, John & Elizabeth
Warren; 24 mar 1785
(OM)

SMITH, John & Jane
Smith; 14 Sep 1775 (OM)

SMITH, John & Mary
Stribling; 8 Jan 1778
(StM)

SMITH, John & Milly
Stewart; 17 Feb 1800
(SpM)

SMITH, John & Nancy
Sutton; 22 Oct 1798
(OM)

SMITH, John & Pleasant
Rose; 30 Sep 1725 (StM)

SMITH, John & Sukey
Smith (d/o Raife &
Sukey Smith); 20 Apr
1796 (OM)

SMITH, John H. &
Margaret Buch (d/o
Anthony Buch); 29 Jun
1826 (FB)

SMITH, John M. &
Virginia S. Holladay;
21 Nov 1850 (SpM)

SMITH, Joseph & Mary
Shropshire; 3 Apr 1746
(StM)

SMITH, Mourning & Sally
Steward; 1 Jan 1805
(SpM)

SMITH, Mourning & Sally
Steward; 1804 (SpB)

SMITH, Nathan & Betsey
Washington; 4 Apr 1790
(StM)

SMITH, Oswald & Joice
Quisenberry (d/o
William Quisenberry);
22 Dec 1800 (OM)

SMITH, Peter & Mary
Rose; 15 April 1800
(SpM)

SMITH, Robert & Ann
Conners (of
Spotsylvania Co.); 15
Jul 1777 (OM)

SMITH, Robert & Ann
Middleton; 19 Jun 1845
(FB)

SMITH, Robert &
Margarett Pritchard; 28
Feb 1838 (FB)

SMITH, Robert (of
Maryland) & Hannah
Walker (w/o ?); 5 Dec
1812 (FB)

SMITH, Samuel & Dorcas
Douglass; 24 Jun 1774
(OM)

SMITH, Will & Tammy
Southard; 22 Dec 1815
(SpM)

SMITH, William & Ann
Bowker, 20 Apr 1749
(SpB)

SMITH, William & Ann
Moore; 17 Oct 1809
(SpM)

SMITH, William & Betty
Barbee; 1 Jan 1750
(StM)

SMITH, William & Judith
Farish; 13 Apr 1795
(SpM)

SMITH, William &
Lucinda Smith (d/o
Joseph Smith); 2 Jun
1783 (OM)

SMITH, William & Mary
C. Porter; 16 Oct 1799
(OM)

SMITH, William (of
Rockingham Co.,Va.) &
Lucindy Smith (d/o
Joseph Smith; 2 Jun
1783 (OB)

SMITH, William M. &
Harriet C. Wishart; 31
Jul 1843 (FB)

SMITH, William P. & Ann
O. Moore; 17 Oct 1809
(SpB)

SMITH, William P. &
Marian M. Seddon (d/o
Susan P. Seddon);28 May
1839 (FB)

SMITHERSAND, James S. &
Isabella Walker; 11 Dec
1808 (SpB)

SMITHEY, Fielding &
Phebe Alsop; 10 Jun
1803 (SpM)

SMOCK, Esme & Sarah H.
Richards; 16 Oct 1813
(FB)

SMOCK, William & Sarah
White (w/o ?); 16 May
1818 (FB)

SMOOT, Cabel & Martha
McShamrock; 10 Sep 1795
(OM)

SMOOTS, John & Polly
Fleek; 7 Oct 1799 (OM)

SNOW, Berd & Polly
Mayhugh (d/o Polly
Watson); 12 Jan 1797
(OM)

SNOW, John & Elizabeth
Lower (d/o Peter
Lower); 4 Mar 1800 (OM)

SNOW, Thomas &
Elizabeth Morgan; 4 Oct
1810 (FB)

SNYDER, William K. &
Mary Pope (w/o ?); 27
Feb 1821 (FB)

SOLAN, John & Martha
Ann King; 5 Jan 1849
(FB)

SOMERVILLE, Walter &
Mary H. Briggs (d/o D.
Briggs); 9 Oct 1817
(FB)

SORREL, James & Emiley
Lewis; 27 May 1819
(SpM)

SORREL, John & Cassee
Bell; 2 Dec 1818 (SpM)

SORRELL, Carter &
Elizabeth Penny; 30 Sep
1817 (FB)

SORRELL, James & Emily
Lewis; 22 May 1819
(SpB)

SORRELL, James P. &
Emily Mardes (d/o
William Mardes); 9 Nov
1831 (FB)

SORRELL, John & Lucy
Coyle; 5 Jan 1813 (SpM)

SORRELL, John Jr. &
Lucy Coyle; 4 Jan 1813
(SpB)

SORRILL, Reubin & Mary
Ann Pendleton; 24 Dec
1821 (SpM)

SOUTHARD, James &
Elizabeth Perry; 25 Jul
1826 (SpM)

SOUTHARD, James M. &
Lucy Ann Frazer; 14 Oct
1840 (FB)

SOUTHERARD, Thomas &
Mary Collins; 4 Oct
1826 (SpM)

SOUTHERLAND, Alexander
& Dinah Howard; 22 Dec
1823 (SpB)

SOUTHERLAND, Alexander
& Dinah Howard; 24 Dec
1823 (SpM)

SOUTHWORTH, Henry &
Isabella Martin; 16 Jun
1814 (SpM)

SOUTTER, James T. (of
Norfolk, Va.) & Agnes
G. Knox (d/o William A.
& Sarah C. Knox); 29
May 1832 (FB)

SPELLMAN, James U. &
Martha L. Baggett (d/o
Judith G.Baggett); 5
Sep 1839 (FB)

SPICER, Benjamin & Caty
A. Snell (d/o Robert
Snell); 9 Jan 1800 (OM)

SPICER, George & Sarah
Skidmore; 1 Jul 1744
(StM)

SPICER, Joseph &
Margaret Swillivan; 14
Sep 1741 (StM)

SPICER, Martin &
Elminey Staicus; 29 Oct
1846 (FB)

SPILMAN, Thomas U. &
Ann Cox (d/o George
Cox); 9 Jan 1832 (FB)

SPINDLE, John & Lucy
Sale; 13 Apr 1795 (SpM)

SPINDLE, John & Polly
Massay; 4 Aug 1801
(SpM)

SPINDLE, John D. &
Sarah Ann Calistra
Luck; 18 Dec 1827 (SpM)

SPINDLE, William A. &
Melinda Damaby; 24 Dec
1819 (SpM)

SPINKS, John (s/o Enoch
& Grace Spinks) &
Rosamund Corbin; (StM)

SPOTSWOOD, Elliot &
Sarah Dandridge
Littlepage; 11 Apr 1808
(SpM)

SPRADLIN, John &
Elizabeth Foster (d/o
Lucy Foster); 10 May
1798 (OM)

STAGE, David R. &
Maryan Mooney; 29 May
1777 (OM)

STAIARS, _____ &
Clary I. Massey; 4 Aug
1829 (SpM)

STAMPER, John &
Susannah B. Young; 7
Mar 1787 (FB)

STANARD, Beverley &
Elizabeth Beverley
Chew; 19 Apr 1750 (SpB)

STANARD, John &
Caroline Matilda Chew;
23 Aug 1815 (FB)

STANARD, John C. &
Sarah T. Thornton; 15
Sep 1829 (SpM)

STAPLES, James & Jane
Owens; 12 Feb 1778
(StM)

STAPLES, William &
Frances Rawlett; 18 Feb
1790 (StM)

STAPP, Achilles &
Margaret Vawter (d/o
Mary Vawter); 27 Nov
1782 (OM)

STAPP, Achilles &
Margaret Vawter (d/o
Mary Vawter); 27 Nov
1782 (OB)

STAPP, Thomas & Betsy
Barbage; 4 Jan 1779
(OM)

STARION, Jacob & Sarah
Sane; 5 Sep 1822 (SpM)

STARKE, Seyman H. &
Mary E.H. Day; 3 Apr
1833 (SpM)

STAUNTON, Beverly &
Jemimah Stanton (d/o
Betty Stanton); 20 Mar
1786 (OM)

STEEL, William & Anne
Prestridge; 27 Apr 1742
(StM)

STEELE, Samuel & Mary
McQuiddy; 24 Nov 1786
(OM)

STEPHANSON, Richard S.
& Amanda M. Herndon; 3
Feb 1818 (SpM)

STEPHEN, Benjamin &
Agnes Nelson; 28 May
1799 (OM)

STEPHENS, Alexander L.
& Mary L. Cox; 24 Dec
1840 (SpM)

STEPHENS, Edmund &
Agnes Robinson (d/o
Agnes Robinson); 31 Dec
1796 (OM)

STEPHENS, Edmund &
Delphy Neale; 1 Jan
1846 (FM)

STEPHENS, James &
Disney Gaines; 12 Jan
1795 (OM)

STEPHENS, John & Mary Whiting; 24 Feb 1725 or 1726 (StM)

STEPHENS, Richard A. & Julia A. McWhirt; 27 Dec 1839 (SpM)

STEPHENS, William & Sally Jordan (d/o Joseph Jordan); 5 Jun 1813 (FB)

STEPHENSON, Charles & Susan Hancock; 30 May 1809 (OM)

STERLING, John & Catherine Ashby (d/o Margaret Ashby); 5 Jul 1837 (FB)

STERLING, Richard & Marian Harrison; 1 Aug 1840 (FB)

STEVENS, Benjamin & Matilda Stevens; 23 Dec 1819 (SpM)

STEVENS, George & Catharin Dipsey; 10 Aug 1810 (SpM)

STEVENS, Hugh & Mary Doggett; 19 Sep 1818 (FB)

STEVENS, James & Alice Grayson; 26 Aug 1744 (SpB)

STEVENS, James & Ann Allen; 31 Jan 1849 (FB)

STEVENS, Monroe & Elizabeth Robinson; 26 May 1847 (FB)

STEVENS, Reuben & Mary M. Moore; 24 Dec 1814 (FB)

STEVENSON, Carter L. & Jane Whitter Herndon (d/o William Herndon); 8 Mar 1809 (FB)

STEVENSON, John & Milly Payne; 23 Dec 1793 (OM)

STEWARD, George & Delphia Pierce; 26 Aug 1808 (SpB)

STEWART, Charles & Harriet Q. Purvis; 1839 (SpM)

STEWART, James & Lucy Massey; 21 Aug 1824 (SpM)

STEWART, James & Mary Bell; 19 Dec 1837 (SpM)

STEWART, John A. & Ellen M. Holladay; 22 Dec 1847 (SpM)

STEWART, Robert & Sarah Shelton; 10 Jun 1823 (SpM)

STEWART, Thomas & Ann Stewart; 9 Sep 1808 (SpM)

STEWART, Thomas & Annie Stewart; 9 Sep 1808 (SpB)

STEWART, William M. & Mary Ann Pare; 18 Nov 1831 (SpM)

STHRESHLEY, James M. & Mary P.B. Fitzhugh; 22 Apr 1828 (FB)

STITH, Griffin & Frances Townshend Washington (d/o Lawrence Washington & Elizabeth Dade); 14 Jun 1788 (StM)

STITH, John & Anne
Washington; 11 Dec 1783
(StM)

STITH, Robert & Mary T.
Washington; 29 Jul 1773
(StM)

STOCAS, Armstead &
Sally McTyre (aka
Mackentier); 24 Jan
1824 (FB)

STOCKDELL, John Jr. &
Sally Duvall; 2 Nov
1786 (OM)

STOKES, Moses & Susan
Strother; 3 Mar 1770
(OB)

STOKES, William & Lucy
Silvey; 15 Feb 1797
(OM)

STONE, Edward & Mary
Cropley; 2 Sep 1846
(FB)

STONE, George &
Catherine Schofield; 1
Jul 1716 (StM)

STONE, George & Mary
Toul; 4 Jun 1726 (StM)

STONE, Henry & Nancy
Golden (d/o William
Golding); 10 Nov 1786
(OM)

STONE, John & Elizabeth
Burton (d/o James
Burton); 9 Apr 1799
(OM)

STONE, Sanford A. &
Eliza A. Anthony; 10
May 1844 (SpB)

STORKE, John (s/o
William & Elizabeth
Storke) & Frances Hooe;
21 May 1750 (StM)

STORY, John & Anne
Steed; 18 Feb 1759
(StM)

STRATTEN, Allen & Mary
McGee; 21 Jan 1841
(SpM)

STRAUGHAN, John & Mary
Sanders (d/o Nathaniel
Sanders); 21 Jul 1783
(OB)

STRAUGHAN,John & Mary
Sanders (d/o Nathaniel
Sanders); 21 Jul 1783
(OM)

STREAT, William &
Malinda Scott; 27 Oct
1814 (SpM)

STREAT, William M. &
Melinda Scott; 24 Oct
1814 (SpB)

STRIBLIN, Colclough
(s/o Joel & Hester
Stribling) & Mary
Hodge; 6 Oct 1749 (StM)

STRIBLING, Thomas &
Elizabeth Peck; 8 Mar
1752 (StM)

STRIBLING, Thomas &
Jane Thomas; 17 Nov
1729 (StM)

STRICKLER, John &
Martha Crawford (w/o ?)
1 Jun 1820 (FB)

STRINGFELLOW, Robert &
Catherine Stiglar; 15
May 1762 (StM)

STROTHER, Anthony &
Behethlem Storke; 25
Aug 1733 (StM)

STROTHER, William & Ann Kavanaugh; 11 Jun 1775 (OM)

STROTHER, William & Evelina West; 26 Apr 1832 (FB)

STRUBECK, George & Susannah Sidney Graham; 2 Oct 1812 (FB)

STRUTLOW, John & Mary Southard; 1833 (SpM)

STRUTTON, John & Elizabeth Sorrel; 23 Feb 1809 (SpB)

STRUTTON, John & Elizabeth Sorrell; 27 Feb 1809 (SpM)

STRUTTON, John & Mary Southard; 16 Apr 1833 (SpB)

STRUTTON, William & Elizabeth Moxley; 3 Apr 1799 (SpM)

STUART, Alexander & Ann Reid (w/o ?); 3 Aug 1796 (OM)

STUART, Alexander & Mary Turner; 23 Dec 1739 (StM)

STUART, Charles & Frances Washington; 23 Feb 1752 (StM)

STUART, Charles & Helen Wray; 31 Oct 1783 (StM)

STUART, Charles B. & Maria Thornton; 29 Feb 1820 (FB)

STUART, Charles B. & Maria Thorton; 29 Feb 1820 (SpM)

STUART, James & Elizabeth Maxwell; 16 Apr 1806 (FB)

STUART, James & Margaret Reins; 24 Mar 1724 or 1725 (StM)

STUART, John Alexander & Mary Wray; 17 Nov 1785 (StM)

STUBBLEFIELD, George & Evalina J. Waller; 1 Mar 1813 (SpB)

STUBBLEFIELD, George & Sarah Morrison; 15 Aug 1775 (OM)

STURMAN, F. & Eleanor Benson (d/o John Benson); Feb 1802 (FM)

STYERS, Leonard & Elizabeth Wolfe (d/o L. Wolfe); 27 Mar 1800 (OM)

SUDDITH, Benjamin & Mary Sebastian; 24 Feb 1752 (StM)

SUDDITH, Joseph & Jemima Skidmore; 18 Aug 1751 (StM)

SUDDUTH, Joseph & Margaret Sebastian; 13 Oct 1735 (StM)

SUDDUTH, Robert Jr. & Sarah Walker; 26 Jan 1741 or 1742 (StM)

SUINZ, Nimrod & Nancy Bowling; Sep 1820 (SpM)

SULLIVAN Abraham & Sarah Ann Wilkins; 31 Oct 1838 (FB)

SULLIVAN, Benjamin &
Fanny Shaugan; 4 Jun
1812 (SpM)

SULLIVAN, Berryman &
Fanny Straughan; 4 Jun
1812 (SpB)

SULLIVAN, Dawson & Lucy
Payne; 13 Jan 1817 (OB)

SULLIVAN, Dawson & Lucy
Payne; 15 Jan 1817
(SpM)

SULLIVAN, George &
Frances Bowling; 1 Jun
1835 (SpM)

SULLIVAN, George &
Lucinda Shelton; 30
_____ 1843 (SpB)

SULLIVAN, John & Adah
Skinner; 17 Apr 1788
(StM)

SULLIVAN, Richard B. &
Frances A. Pierce; 24
Aug 1843 (SpM)

SULLIVAN, Spencer S. &
Mary M. Williams (d/o
Elizabeth Williams); 20
Mar 1833 (FB)

SULLIVAN, Weber & Fanny
Ag___d; 22 Nov 1816
(SpM)

SULLIVAN, Wiley & Fanny
Hoard; 18 Nov 1816
(SpB)

SUTHARD, Allen & Mary
Ledlow; 3 Jan 1807
(SpM)

SUTHARD, James & Mary
J. Perry; 25 Feb 1835
(FB)

SUTHERLAND, Dr. John &
Susanna Brent; 15 Sep
1756 (StM)

SUTTON, William & Alice
Brown; 6 Apr 1775 (OM)

SWAN, Alexander & Mary
Ann Gibson; 10 Jul 1821
(SpM)

SWANN, John & Anna
Wilson (d/o William
Wilson); 5 May 1799
(FM)

SWATS, Christian H. &
Sarah A. True; 12 Sep
1850 (FB)

SWEENEY, Morgan &
Pamela Phillips; 27 Jun
1818 (FB)

SWEENEY, Morgan & Sarah
Waddel (daughter-in-
law/o David Almond); 28
Jan 1806 (FB)

SWEENY, Paul & Frances
Williams; 24 Dec 1728
(StM)

SWIFT, Hezekiah &
Elizabeth Southworth;
12 Jan 1810 (SpM)

SWIFT, John & Ellen M.
Bullock; 20 Dec 1839
(SpM)

SWORDE, Robert S. &
Maria Louisa Stanard;
29 May 1846 (FB)

SYLVA, George & Lucy
Poe; 17 Feb 1796 (OM)

TACKETT, Charles A. &
Frances Ford; 25 Oct
1843 (FB)

TACKETT, John E. &
Sophia Ford; 8 Sep 1845
(FB)

TALIAFERRO, Claibane &
Virginia DeBaptist; 22
Oct 1845 (FB)

TALIAFERRO, Francis W.
& Catharine Ware; 20
Oct 1832 (FB)

TALIAFERRO, Hay & Lucy
Thruston; Apr 1791 (FM)

TALIAFERRO, Hay &
Susannah Conway; 14 Mar
1797 (OM)

TALIAFERRO, James &
Mahallen Ann Walker; 18
Nov 1834 (FB)

TALIAFERRO, John & Amy
Stockdell; 12 May 1771
(OM)

TALIAFERRO, John & Ann
Stockdell; 12 May 1772
(OB)

TALIAFERRO, Lewis W. &
Polly Stanard; 6 Sep
1809 (FB)

TALIAFERRO, Nicholas &
Ann Taliaferro; 3 Oct
1781 (OM)

TALIAFERRO, Peachy
R.(s/o Richard H.
Taliaferro) & Sarah F.
Adams; 10 Nov 1825 (FB)

TALIAFERRO, Warner T. &
Leah Seddon (d/o Thomas
Seddon); 27 Oct 1825
(FB)

TALIAFERRO, William &
Maria West; 17 May 1842
(FB)

TALLEY, Overton & Lydia
Atkins; 8 Sep 1807
(StB)

TAMPLE, John & Mary ann
Canterberry; 29 Jan
1775 (OM)

TANDY, Henry & Sarah
Ann Davis; 16 Dec 1824
(SpM)

TANDY, Henry Jr. &
Betsy Adams; 28 Nov
1796 (OM)

TANDY, Roger & Mary
Adams; 7 Dec 1795 (OM)

TANDY, Thomas A. & Lucy
A. Turnley; 25 Nov 1824
(SpM)

TARR, William &
Clementine Garner; 15
Oct 1836 (FB)

TATT, Richard &
Elizabeth Johnson; 7
Oct 1732 (SpB)

TATUM, Thomas & Nancy
Evans; 26 Dec 1794 (OM)

TAYLOR, Absolem &
Frances Smith (d/o
Jeremiah & Elizabeth
Smith); 25 May 1796
(OM)

TAYLOR, Albert T. &
Jane Alice Cridlin (d/o
William Cridlin); 1 Aug
1849 (FB)

TAYLOR, Alexander &
Hannah Brooks; 24 Feb
1757 (StM)

TAYLOR, Dudley & Ruther
Johnston; 26 Mar 1796
(SpB)

TAYLOR, Edmund & Nancy Thornton; 16 Jul 1800 (OM)

TAYLOR, Elijah & Dilla Walker; 26 Feb 1795 (OM)

TAYLOR, Evan & Ann W. Batley (w/o ?); 6 Mar 1830 (FB)

TAYLOR, Henry & Margaret Jones (d/o Isaac Jones); 25 Oct 1843 (FB)

TAYLOR, Ivan & Alice Thompson; 1 Jan 1824 (FB)

TAYLOR, J. & Elizabeth Conway; Sep 1802 (FM)

TAYLOR, James & Deliah Staunton; 20 Dec 1775 (OM)

TAYLOR, James & Nanna Anderson; 27 May 1799 (OM)

TAYLOR, James A. & Mildred Wren; 7 Feb 1839 (FB)

TAYLOR, James Jr. & Frances Moore; 21 Dec 1795 (OM)

TAYLOR, John & Elizabeth Kavanaugh; 25 Sep 1782 (OM)

TAYLOR, John & Elizabeth Kavenaugh; 25 Sep 1782 (OB)

TAYLOR, John & Elizabeth Pearson; 8 Oct 1795 (OM)

TAYLOR, John & Lucy Brooke; 20 Nov 1823 (FB)

TAYLOR, John & Mary Jarrell (d/o James Jarrell); 21 Dec 1782 (OM)

TAYLOR, John & Mary Jarrell (d/o John Jarrell); 21 Dec 1782 (OB)

TAYLOR, John & Mildred Hughlett (sister of Beder Hughlett); 6 Aug 1817 (FB)

TAYLOR, John & Sally Garner; 7 Jan 1790 (FM)

TAYLOR, John (Dr.) & Mary Gordon (d/o Samuel Gordon); 12 Sep 1834 (FB)

TAYLOR, Joshua T. & Maria Louisa Long; 26 Feb 1850 (FB)

TAYLOR, Larkin & Elizabeth Hume; 2 Jun 1808 (OM)

TAYLOR, Reuben & Rebecca Moore; 11 Feb 1783 (OB)

TAYLOR, Reuben & Rebecca Moore; 11 Feb 1783 (OM)

TAYLOR, Stanton & Elizabeth Stanton (d/o George Bingham); 23 Jan 1800 (OM)

TAYLOR, Thomas Jr.(s/o Thomas Taylor Sr. b.d. 19 May 1793) & Margaret Pearson (sister of Catharine August) 17 May 1817 (FB)

TAYLOR, Thomas Sr. &
Fanny Reveer; 13 Dec
1820 (FB)

TAYLOR, Thornton &
Eleanor Baxter (d/o
Thornton Baxter); 6 Nov
1835 (FB)

TAYLOR, W. & Sally
Burnley; Sep 1805 (FM)

TAYLOR, William & Lucy
Lewis Thom; 16 Oct 1834
(FB)

TAYLOR, William & Mary
Ann Allison; 21 Dec
1833 (FB)

TAYLOR, William &
Susannah Gibson; 26 Nov
1795 (OM)

TAYLOR, Zachariah &
Alice Chew; between
1771 & 1774 (OM)

TAYLOR, Zachary & Alice
Chew (d/o Thomas Chew);
20 Jul 1771 (OB)

TEAZEDALE, Martin C, &
Martha J. Waller; 8 Mar
1849 (SpM)

TENNANT, John & Dorothy
Paul; 27 Mar 1730 (SpB)

TERRELL, Edward & Peggy
Willis; 24 Nov 1760
(OB)

TERRELL, John & Caty
Miller; 10 Sep 1794
(OM)

TERRELL, Joseph N. &
Anne I. Chewning; 18
Sep 1845 (SpM)

TERRELL, Joseph P. &
Maria H.W. Noel; 18 Jun
1845 (FB)

TERRELL, Keeling &
Frances Lewis; 19 Nov
1806 (SpM)

TERRIER, Thomas &
Elizabeth Batchelder; 8
Jan 1824 (FB)

TERRILL, _____ & Susan
Middlebrook; 4 Oct 1812
(SpM)

TERRILL, Edmund & Ann
T. Morton; 19 Jan 1813
(OB)

TERRILL, Edmund & Ann
T. Morton; 19 Jan 1813
(SpM)

TERRILL, Edmund & Peggy
Willis; 24 Nov 1760
(OM)

TERRILL, James & Susan
Middlebrook; 1 Oct 1812
(OB)

TERRILL, Oliver & Susan
Elizabeth Proctor; 26
Sep 1832 (FB)

TERRILL, Reuben & Mary
Walker; 14 May 1771
(OB)

TERRILL, Reuben &
Millie Walker; between
1771 & 1774 (OM)

TERRILL, Robert (s/o
John Terrill & Ann
Quarles) & Ann Mallory
(d/o Uriel Mallory &
Hannah Cave); 22 Feb
1797 (OM)

TERRILL, William & Ann
Daniels; 23 Nov 1780
(OM)

TERRY, John & Lucy
Oaks; 24 Dec 1795 (OM)

TERRY, Overton & Sarah
Garnett; 29 Mar 1808
(OM)

THACKER, Chickely &
Hanah Clowdor; 3 Mar
1730 (SpB)

THACKER, Will & Ann
Southwarth; 30 Dec 1813
(SpM)

THATCHER, Elisha &
Betsy Saunders; 16 Mar
1800 (FM)

THAYER, Barnabus B. &
Sarah W. Cowne (d/o
Balinger Cowne); 19 Dec
1842 (FB)

THOMAS, Barbour & Mary
Taylor; 22 Mar 1787
(OM)

THOMAS, Charles S. &
Ann Margaret Hull; 1
Nov 1827 (SpM)

THOMAS, James & Fanny
Long; 20 Apr 1821 (SpM)

THOMAS, James & Jane
Pedler; 13 Nov 1835
(FB)

THOMAS, John & Mary
Thomas; 19 Feb 1762
(StM)

THOMAS, Massey & Mary
Price; 28 Nov 1731
(StM)

THOMAS, Nicholas S. &
Ellen E. Carter; 20 Jul
1827 (SpB)

THOMAS, Nicholas S. &
Ellen E. Carter; 24 Jun
1827 (SpM)

THOMAS, Richard &
Mildred Taylor; 24 Aug
1753 (OB)

THOMAS, Robert &
_____; 9 Apr 1757 (OB)

THOMAS, Robert & Ann
Moore; 9 Apr 1757 (OM)

THOMAS, Robert & Anne
Moore; 9 Apr 1757 (OB)

THOMAS, Robert & Polly
Smith (d/o Joseph
Smith); 7 Aug 1793 (OM)

THOMAS, Roland & Jane
Thurston; 5 Apr 1757
(OB)

THOMAS, Roland & Jane
Thurston; 5 Apr 1757
(OM)

THOMAS, Rowland & Jane
Thurston; 5 Apr 1757
(OB)

THOMAS, William &
Elizabeth Woolfolk (d/o
Joseph Woolfolk); 7 Apr
1778 (OM)

THOMAS, William & Mary
White; 13 Dec 1785
(StM)

THOMAS, William H. &
Ann E. Riley; 26 Sep
1842 (FB)

THOMPSON, Andrew & Mary
Rose; 2 Jan 1787 (StM)

THOMPSON, David &
Elizabeth Brockman (d/o
Samuel Brockman Jr.);
19 Aug 1784 (OM)

THOMPSON, David &
Elizabeth Brockman; 19
Aug 1784 (OB)

THOMPSON, Joel & Sarah
Thompson (d/o Elizabeth
Thompson); 8 Jan 1798
(OM)

THOMPSON, Philip Rootes
& Sarah Hamilton; 18
Dec 1838 (FM)

THOMPSON, Robert &
Elizabeth Hart; 3 Jan
1823 (SpM)

THOMPSON, Thomas &
Frances Robinson; 7 Nov
1809 (OB)

THOMPSON, Thomas &
Frances Robinson; 9 Nov
1809 (SpM)

THOMPSON, William &
Acquiles Breeding; 3
Apr 1785 (OM)

THOMPSON, William &
Acquilia Breeding; 13
Apr 1785 (OB)

THOMPSON, William & Ann
Washington; 5 Aug 1785
(StM)

THOMPSON, William
Theodocius & Jane
McNeal; 30 Jun 1795
(OM)

THOMSON, Edward & Alice
Smith; 4 Dec 1723 (StM)

THOMSON, James E. &
Caroline M. Fitzhugh
(d/o Francis Fithugh);
17 Mar 1830 (FB)

THOMSON, Joseph D. &
Catharine Gordon; 30
Oct 1818 (FB)

THOMSON, Rhodes & Sally
Vivion (d/o John
Vivion); 13 Oct 1778
(OM)

THOMSON, Richard &
Elizabeth Oxford; 3 Jun
1724 (StM)

THONICI, Anthony & Lucy
Long; 4 Jun 1824 (SpM)

THORBURN, Robert D. &
Helen M. Howison; 16
Dec 1830 (FB)

THORNTON, Anthony R. &
Mildred B. Walker; 29
Dec 1810 (FB)

THORNTON, GEorge &
Nancy Webb; 31 Dec 1800
(OM)

THORNTON, George W. &
Margarett Hamilton; 8
Dec 1846 (SpM)

THORNTON, James &
Elizabeth Rawlins; 21
Oct 1815 (SpM)

THORNTON, Jesse & Ann
Bohen (d/o Benjamin &
Ann Bohen); 22 Jul 1784
(OB)

THORNTON, Jesse & Ann
Bohon (d/o Benjamin &
Ann Bohon); 22 Jul 1784
(OM)

THORNTON, John &
Mildred Gregory; 28 Oct
1740 (SpB)

THORNTON, John & Polly
C. Carey; 2 Aug 1804
(SpM)

THORNTON, John S. &
Susan H. Gordon; 30 Nov
1815 (FB)

THORNTON, Luke & Lucy
Sleet; 27 Jun 1799 (OM)

THORNTON, Luke & Sarah
Sleet; 24 Jun 1799 (OM)

THORNTON, Presley &
Alice Thornton; 19 Oct
1785 (StM)

THORNTON, Presley &
Elizabeth Thornton; 26
Mar 1784 (StM)

THORNTON, Thomas S. &
Isabella Layton; 17 Sep
1838 (FB)

THORNTON, William & Ann
Pritchard; 15 Feb 1844
(FB)

THORNTON, William &
Martha Stuart; 11 May
1775 (StM)

THORNTON, William G. &
Charlotte Hamilton; 6
Mar 1834 (FM)

THORTON, Francis &
Frances Gregory; 3 Sep
1736 (SpB)

THORURN, James D. & Ann
M. Howison (d/o Samuel
Howison); 5 Jan 1826
(FB)

THRAILKELD, William H.
& Ann Towles; 28 Aug
1827 (SpM)

THURMAN, Nathan &
Tabitha Lowry; 4 Sep
1796 (OM)

THURSTON, William
Plumer & Lucy M.
Taliaferro; 11 Jun 1773
(OB)

THURSTON, William
Plumer & Lucy Mary

Taliaferro; 11 Jun 1771
(OM)

TIBBS, Daniel & Jane
Belfour; 11 Oct 1838
(FB)

TILLER, John & Lucy
Keaton; 17 Feb 1800
(SpM)

TILLER, William & Polly
Brookes; 17 Dec 1832
(SpM)

TIMBERLAKE, James B. &
Sarah A. Walker; 24 May
1843 (FB)

TIMBERLAKE, John & Jane
L. Peyton; 8 Feb 1836
(FB)

TIMBERLAKE, John W. &
Mary Garetson; 29 Jun
1805 (FB)

TIMBERLAKE, Joseph &
Elizabeth Benson (d/o
John Benson); 20 Sep
1815 (FB)

TIMBERLAKE, Richard H.
& Amelia H. Andrews; 15
Nov 1827 (SpM)

TIMONS, Thomas &
Susanna Owens; 14 May
1749 (StM)

TINDAR, James & Molly
Shadrack (d/o Tobe
Shadrack); 29 Jan 1785
(OB)

TINDAR, James & Molly
Shadrick (d/o Jobe
Shadrick); 3 Feb 1785
(OM)

TINDER, Jesse & Aleaper
Abell; 11 Dec 1786 (OM)

TINE, James & Ann
Newton; Apr 1813 (SpM)

TINEL, John & Mary
Hyles; 28 Apr 1836
(SpM)

TOLSON John & Catharine
Mills (d/o James
Mills); 18 Apr 1837
(FB)

TOMILSON, George &
Elizabeth White (d/o
Henry White); 24 Nov
1785 (OB)

TOMLINSON, George &
Elizabeth White (d/o
Henry White); 24 Nov
1785 (OM)

TOMLINSON, John &
Mildred White; 20 Jun
1780 (OM)

TOMPKINS, Joseph D. &
Jane Ford (d/o Patsy
Ford); 14 Jun 1836 (FB)

TOMPKINS, Robert R. &
Elizabeth Fitzgerald
(d/o James H.
Fitzgerald); 7 Apr 1835
(FB)

TOOMBS, George W. &
MArtha Williams; 19 Nov
1828 (SpM)

TOOMBS, Joab B. &
Catherine Perry; 1835
(SpM)

TOOMBS, John & Frances
Stevens; 22 Jan 1801
(SpM)

TOOMBS, John & Loretta
King; 1832 (SpM)

TOOMBS, Thomas C. &
Mary Stevens; 2 Nov
1833 (SpM)

TOSTER, James & Sarah
Payne; 10 June 1803
(SpM)

TOUL, William & Mary
Porter; 15 Oct 1722
(StM)

TOWLES, Therit & Ann M.
Smith; 1 Jan 1811 (SpM)

TRAINER, William &
Catharine Bryant (d/o
Rosannah Bryant); 21
Oct 1829 (FB)

TRAINER, William &
Catharine Bryant; 22
Oct 1829 (FM)

TRIBBLE, George & Mrs.
Nancy Bell; 29 Mar 1832
(SpM)

TRIBBLE, George & Peggy
Collins; 7 Jun 1815
(SpM)

TRIBBLE, George L. &
Angelina Cleire; 7 Dec
1847 (SpM)

TRIBBLE, William &
Patsy Collins; 15 Aug
1815 (SpM)

TRIBBLE, William A. &
Mary Ann Fulcher; 21
Dec 1848 (SpM)

TRICE, George W. &
Sarah Perry; 18 Oct
1827 (SpM)

TRIGG, Daniel & Sally
Abbott; 15 Nov 1799
(SpM)

TRIGG, Joseph W. &
Amanda M. Pervis; 1 Jun
1848 (SpM)

TRIGGER, Henry & Ellen Lawson (sister of Catlett Lawson); 25 Apr 1850 (FB)

TRIPLETT, John R. & Louisa R. Stone; 19 May 1813 (FB)

TRIPLETT, William S. & Ann O. Jenifer; 17 Jan 1844 (FB)

TRUE, Edward E. & Lucinda Lawson; 26 may 1847 (FB)

TRUE, Fielding & Ann Brooks; 31 Aug 1829 (SpM)

TRUE, Martin & Ann King; 19 Sep 1804 (SpM)

TRUE, Martin & Frances Burger; 26 Nov 1797 (SpM)

TRUE, Walter A. & Ann E. Mullen; 28 Sep 1846 (FB)

TRUE, William & Susannah Jane Curtis; 5 Jul 1837 (FB)

TRUPELL, William & Katherine Wilson; 17 Jan 1820 (SpM)

TRUSLOW, Jn. & Lucy Vaughan; 30 Dec 1812 (SpB)

TRUSLOW, John & Martha True (d/o Fanny True); 2 May 1842 (FB)

TRUSLOW, Robert & Orphy L. Fugett; 27 Oct 1847 (FB)

TRUSLOW, Thomas & Zilpah Skinner; 19 Jan 1789 (StM)

TUMLEY, Edmund & Polly Duerson; 13 Nov 1817 (SpM)

TUMLEY, John & Melinda Castle; 13 Dec 1821 (SpM)

TUPMAN, Francis & Sarah Lucas; 4 Jul 1787 (FB)

TUPMAN, Thomas G. & Louisianna Wardell; 13 Jan 1825 (FB)

TUPMAN, William B. & Ann Slater; 21 Sep 1826 (FB)

TURNER, Edward & Polly Wharton; 23 Dec 1794 (SpB)

TURNER, George & Martha Frazer; 28 Jun 1832 (SpM)

TURNER, George & Philadelphia C. Frazer; 3 Jan 1828 (FB)

TURNER, James A. & Susan Q. Johnson; 9 Dec 1845 (FB)

TURNER, Thomas & Catey Brown; 31 Jan 1787 (OM)

TUTT, Richard C.(of Spotsylvania Co.) & Peggy Garnett (w/o Thomas Garnett); 20 Apr 1800 (StM)

TUTT, Thomas & Margaret W. Garnett (daughter-in-law of Richard J. Tutt); 27 Feb 1816 (FB)

TWENTYMEN, Benjamin (of Orange Co., Age 70 Years) & Betty Nulty (Age 50 Years); 26 Jan 1790 (FM)

TYLER, Thomas & Elizabeth Settle; 5 Jan 1787 (StM)

TYLER, William W. & Fanny A. Stevenson; 10 Oct 1839 (FB)

TYRE, Lewis (fpc) & Elizabeth Mouth (fpc); 31 Jul 1821 (SpM)

UNDERWOOD, Ambrose & Mary McWhirt; 23 Sep 1815 (SpB)

UNDERWOOD, Ambrose & Mary McWhitt; 25 Sep 1815 (SpM)

UNDERWOOD, John & Jane Hill; 1 Nov 1837 (FB)

UNDERWOOD, John & Margarett Williams; 18 Oct 1802 (SpB)

UNDERWOOD, John & Margarit Williams; 21 Oct 1802 (SpM)

URQUHART, Charles & Finella Duncanson (d/o James Duncanson); 2 Jun 1785 (FB)

VAINT, William & Katherine Raddish; 27 Aug 1723 (StM)

VASS, Vincent & Elizabeth Manning (w/o ?); 24 Aug 1783 (OB)

VASS, Vincent & Elizabeth Manning (w/o ?); 29 Aug 1783 (OM)

VAUGHAN, Edmund G. & Ann M. Shepherd; 30 Dec 1827 (SpM)

VAUGHAN, Joseph & Nancy Turner (d/o Ann Turner); 23 Aug 1798 (OM)

VAUGHAN, William & Eliza Jane Norton; 24 Dec 1850 (FB)

VAWTER, James & Mary Rucker; 19 Jun 1784 (OB)

VAWTER, William & Ann Ballard; 16 Jan 1774 (OM)

VAWTER, William & Anne Ballard; 16 Jan 1774 (OM)

VAWTER, William & Mary Rucker (d/o Mary Rucker); 19 Jun 1784 (OM)

VEACH, Lander & Peggy Thorpe; 5 Jan 1787 (OM)

VESSELS, James & Elizabeth Parker; 27 Sep 1843 (FB)

VINCENT, Thomas & Elizabeth Pennal; 3 Apr 1749 (StM)

VOSS, Nicholas & Mary Spotswood (d/o T. Spotswood); 30 Apr 1794 (OM)

WADDELL, James Alexander & Cornelia Lomax; 29 Jan 1846 (FB)

WADDELL, James Gordon & Lucy Gordon; 22 May 1797 (OM)

WADDLE, James A. &
Louisa Chewning; 19 Feb
1821 (FB)

WAGON, William &
Elizabeth Lewis; 18 Apr
1827 (FB)

WAITE, William H. &
Sarah P. Landram; 25
Jan 1846 (SpM)

WALKER, Benjamin &
Polly Sims; 9 Nov 1795
(OM)

WALKER, Harris &
Margaret Caldwell; 26
Feb 1826 (FB)

WALKER, James & Jane L.
Lowery; 4 Jan 1849 (FB)

WALKER, James N. & Mary
Sorrelle; 12 Mar 1829
(FB)

WALKER, John B. &
Permelia P. Paine
(native of New York);
24 Mar 1847 (FB)

WALKER, Soloman & Sarah
Breeden; 15 Aug 1800
(SpM)

WALKER, Thomas &
Meseniah Powell (d/o
Mary Powell); 18 Aug
1783 (OB)

WALKER, Thomas &
Misiniah Powell (d/o
Mary Powell); 18 Aug
1783 (OM)

WALKER, William G. &
Mary Ellen Taylor; 15
Oct 1845 (FB)

WALLACE, Gustavus B. &
Elizabeth Mcfarlane; 8
Oct 1845 (FB)

WALLACE, John &
Margaret McDarment; 15
Sep 1824 (SpM)

WALLACE, John H. (Dr.)
& Mary N. Gordon (d/o
Samuel Gordon); 27 Sep
1828 (FB)

WALLACE, Richard &
Elizabeth Brown; 17 Mar
1807 (SpM)

WALLACE, Richard & Mary
Louisa Ames (d/o Nany
Ames); 6 Feb 1840 (FB)

WALLER, John B. &
Frances M. Long; 20 Dec
1825 (SpM)

WALLER, Benjamin & Lucy
Carter; 2 Aug 1804
(SpM)

WALLER, Churchwell G. &
Mary V. Ellis; 19 Dec
1844 (SpM)

WALLER, Edmond & Mary
Pendleton; 18 Oct 1740
(SpB)

WALLER, George &
Harriet Alexander (d/o
Lewis Alexander); 3 Oct
1820 (FB)

WALLER, John B. & Jane
M. Smith; 19 Jan 1826
(SpM)

WALLER, Jos. & Maria
Roy; 5 Jul 1813 (SpM)

WALLER, Richmond S. &
Sarah Duerson; 13 Oct
1825 (SpM)

WALLER, Robert &
Elizabeth McWhirt; 21
May 1825 (SpB)

WALLER, Robert &
Elizabeth McWhirt; 22
May 1825 (SpM)

WALLER, Robert Page &
Julia W. Mercer; 12 May
1825 (FB)

WALLER, Thomas & Lyddia
Chandley; 17 Nov 1809
(SpM)

WALLER, William & Amy
Johnson; 19 Apr 1803
(SpM)

WALLER, William & Ann
A. Lucas (d/o Zachariah
Lucas); 19 Dec 1822
(FB)

WALLER, William & Ann
Beverly; 21 Jun 1738
(SpB)

WALTER, James &
Elizabeth Y. Atkins
(d/o Spencer J.
Atkins); 1 Jun 1815
(OM)

WALTERS, George & Nancy
Harvey; 30 Oct 1800
(OM)

WALTON, Francis &
Elizabeth Speers; 22
Dec 1799 (OM)

WARD, Henry & Mary
Rankins; 14 Jun 1775
(StM)

WARD, James & Anne
Willis; 29 Jun 1777
(StM)

WARD, John & Alice
Symonds; 9 Apr 1729
(SpB)

WARE Thomas & Catharine
Reat; 1 Apr 1807 (FB)

WARFIELD, Alexander &
Fanny Sacrae (d/o
Thomas Sacrae); 11 Feb
1804 (FB)

WARING, Thomas & Phiana
H. Mathews; 29 Dec 1825
(FB)

WARING, William &
Levinia Crutchfield; 27
Apr 1826 (SpM)

WARNER, John & Ann
Walker; 26 May 1775
(OM)

WARREN, William & Ann
Bowen; 15 Dec 1819 (FB)

WARTON, John & Patsey
McWhirt; 12 Feb 1801
(SpM)

WASHINGTON, Bailey &
Catherine Storke; 12
Jan 1748 or 1749 (StM)

WASHINGTON, Buckerton &
Ann Syls Smith; 7 Dec
1795 (SpM)

WASHINGTON, Bushrod Jr.
& Henrietta Brayne
Spotswood; 25 Jul 1806
(SpM)

WASHINGTON, Henry &
Mildred Pratt; 12 Mar
1779 (StM)

WASHINGTON, Henry Jr. &
Elizabeth Storke; 18
May 1743 (StM)

WASHINGTON, John &
Betty Massey; 17 Nov
1749 (StM)

WASHINGTON, John &
Catherine Washington;
23 Dec 1759 (StM)

WASHINGTON, John &
Eleanor Massey; 24 Dec
1787 (StM)

WASHINGTON, John & Mary
Storke; 23 Nov 1738
(StM)

WASHINGTON, Lawrence &
Catherine Foote; 5 Oct
1774 (StM)

WASHINGTON, Lawrence &
Elizabeth Dade; 31 Jul
1751 (StM)

WASHINGTON, Nathaniel &
Sarah Hooe; 17 Dec 1767
(StM)

WASHINGTON, Thornton &
Frances Washingto; 2
Apr 1786 (StM)

WASHINGTON, Townshend &
Elizabeth Lund; 22 Dec
1726 (StM)

WASHINGTON, William
Augustine & Sally
Tayloe (d/o John Tayloe
of MT. Airy); May 1799
(FM)

WASS, Henry & Lucy
Jackson; 30 Dec 1824
(SpM)

WATERS, Alexander &
Mary Ninnes; 24 Jul
1833 (FB)

WATSON, Abner &
Elizabeth Dear (d/o
Catherine Dear); 11 Oct
1786 (OM)

WATSON, Benjamin &
Frances Jacobs; 23 Aug
1824 (OB)

WATSON, Benjamin &
Frances Jacobs; 26 Aug
1824 (SpM)

WATSON, Isaac & Susanan
Robbards; 4 Apr 1799
(OM)

WATSON, James & Catey
Lamb; 3 Jul 1800 (OM)

WATSON, John & Sarah
Addison; 27 Feb 1790
(StM)

WATSON, Nehamiah & Lucy
Mallery; 26 1805 (SpM)

WATTS, Johnson & Suckey
Davis (d/o Joseph
Davis); 20 Jul 1785
(OM)

WATTS, Johnson & Sukey
Davis (d/o George &
Elizabeth Davis); 20
Jul 1785 (OB)

WATTS, Julius & Mary
Eve (d/o Ann Eve); 22
Dec 1785 (OM)

WATTS, William &
Elizabeth Beazley (d/o
James & Ann Beazley); 4
Jun 1778 (OM)

WAUGH, John & Jane
Massey; 22 Apr 1761
(StM)

WAUGH, John & Mary
Watts Ashton; 4 Nov
1790 (StM)

WAUGH, Laurence &
Sidney Smith Roddy; 13
Dec 1821 (FB)

WAUGH, Lawrence &
Lavinia W.
Wigglesworth; 25 Oct
1830 (FB)

WAUGH, Richard &
Elizabeth Brown; 11 Nov
1782 (OB)

WAUGH, Richard &
Margaret Brown; 11 Nov
1782 (OM)

WAYT, Charles B. &
Eliza M. Whitehurst; 15
Feb 1837 (FB)

WAYT, James & Sarah C.
Rose; 7 Jan 1837 (FB)

WAYT, Jesse & Peggy
Ballard; 24 Dec 1799
(SpM)

WAYTE, George & Mary
Cuppenhaven; 30 May
1831 (FB)

WAYTES, William H. &
Mary Ann Ballard; 22
Jan 1829 (SpM)

WEATHERLEY, William &
Frances Crooks; 22 Nov
1805 (SpB)

WEATHERLY, William &
Francis Cook; 24 Nov
1805 (SpM)

WEBB, George & Lucy
Hinkston; 19 Oct 1735
(SpB)

WEBB, Jesse B. & Mary
Cooper; 10 Oct 1830
(SpM)

WEBB, Jesse B. & Mary
Cooper; 7 Oct 1830 (OB)

WEBB, Joseph & Clara
Evans; 27 Mar 1839 (FB)

WEBB, Richard B. &
Nancy Trilton; 25 Feb
1808 (SpM)

WEBB, William &
Margaret Atkins; 27 Jan
1798 (OM)

WEBB, William & Sarah
Leathers (d/o John
Leathers); 13 Jan 1785
(OM)

WEBB, William & Sarah
Leathers (d/o John
Leathers); 13 Jan 1785
(OB)

WEBB, William Bennett &
Martha Lancaster (d/o
John & Susannah
Lancaster); 22 Sep 1806
(OM)

WEBB, William
Crittendon & Jane
Buckner; 8 Jul 1783 .
(OB)

WEBB, William
Crittendon & Jane
Buckner; 8 Jul 1783
(OM)

WEBB, William Jr. &
Patsy Smith; 23 Jan
1797 (OM)

WEBBER, John &
Elizabeth Hoard; 25 Dec
1813 (SpM)

WEBSTER, George L. &
Lucinda Minor; 13 May
1827 (SpM)

WEBSTER, William & Mary
Ann Burk; 19 Sep 1818
(SpM)

WEEMS, Thomas & Elen
Boores; 22 Dec 1832
(FM)

WEEMS, Thomas & Ellen
Boores; 22 Dec 1832
(FB)

WEIR, George & Ellen
Jones; 7 Jun 1837 (FB)

WELCH, John & Mary
Hudson; 16 Nov 1727
(StM)

WELCH, Robert &
Elizabeth Yates; 12 Aug
1729 (StM)

WELLFORD, Beverley R. &
Mary Alexander; 4 Feb
1824 (FB)

WELLFORD, John S. &
Jane Henderson; 14 Mar
1820 (FB)

WELLFORD, Robert &
Fanny L. Stevenson; 24
May 1839 (FB)

WELLS, Charles & Mary
Edwards; 10 Dec 1733
(StM)

WELLS, James & Fennetta
Reynolds (d/o Joseph
Reynolds); 5 Dec 1793
(OM)

WELLS, John & Frances
Barnfather; 18 Jun 1723
(StM)

WELLS, Martin & Sarah
Marshall; 28 Jan 1797
(OM)

WELLS, Samuel & Susanna
Brandigan; 8 Jul 1723
(StM)

WELLS, Thomas & Mary
Clark (d/o John Clark
Sr.); 6 Dec 1793 (OM)

WELLS, William & Nancy
Sams (d/o John Sams);
31 Nov 1801 (OM)

WELLS, William T. &
Sarah Pullen; 20 Apr
1839 (FB)

WELSHIRE, Bemjamin &
Sally Jones; 20 Dec
1797 (SpB)

WEST, Baylor & Mary
Ellen Chapman (d/o
Page Thornton); 5 Feb
1845 (FB)

WEST, Isaac & Fanny
Stribling; 11 Jul 1812
(FB)

WEST, James & Patsy
Richardson; 23 Oct 1833
(FB)

WEST, Thomas Bowling &
Louisa Mildred
Phillips; 23 Nov 1842
(FB)

WESTON, Thomas & Ann
Moore; 4 Feb 1786 (FB)

WHALING, Aleander L. &
Ann V. Haydon; 2 Dec
1850 (FB)

WHARTON, Benjamin &
Lucy Chandler; 16 Sep
1813 (SpM)

WHARTON, James & Ann
Haydon; 19 Nov 1823
(SpB)

WHARTON, James & Ann
Haydon; 20 Nov 1823
(SpM)

WHARTON, John & Patsey
McWhirt; 12 Feb 1801
(SpB)

WHARTON, John L. &
Elizabeth Shepherd; 21
Feb 1832 (SpB)

WHARTON, Joseph & Sally
Jones; 18 Jan 1805
(SpB)

WHARTON, Joseph & Sally
Jones; 24 Jan 1805
(SpM)

WHARTON, Leanard &
Betsy Goss; 24 Dec 1803
(SpM)

WHARTON, Leonard &
Betsey Goss; 17 Dec
1803 (SpB)

WHARTON, Samuel & Ann
Williams; 6 Dec 1737
(SpB)

WHARTON, William &
Sarah Pruitt; 3 Oct
1806 (SpB)

WHARTON, William &
Sarah Pruitt; 9 Oct
1806 (SpM)

WHARTZ, Nathanial &
_____ Suthard; 23 Apr
1829 (SpM)

WHEATLEY, George & Mary
Henry; 3 Dec 1729 (SpB)

WHEELER, John Addison &
Virginia Long; 18 Aug
1846 (FB)

WHEELER, William & Mary
M. Godfrey; 9 Nov 1837
(FB)

WHISTON, Francis C. &
Eliza F. Garnett; 10
Apr 1819 (FB)

WHITCRAFT, John & Mary
Magdelene Declore; 25
Sep 1716 (StM)

WHITE, Alexander &
Priscilla Flower; 30
Apr 1775 (StM)

WHITE, Alfred &
Charlotte Corr; 11 Dec
1844 (FB)

WHITE, Ambrose L. &
Frances Ragan; 27 Jan
1830 (FB)

WHITE, Amtron L. &
Frances Rayan; 28 Jan
1830 (FM)

WHITE, Anderson & Mary
Brauner; 14 Oct 1794
(StM)

WHITE, Anderson & Sarah
Bullock; 21 Jan 1803
(SpM)

WHITE, Bartlett &
Elizabeth Mardus; 2 Mar
1792 (StM)

WHITE, Charles C. &
Mary Alsop; 1 Dec 1828
(SpM)

WHITE, George & Sarah
Cooper; 21 Dec 1799
(SpB)

WHITE, George & Sarah
Cooper; 25 Dec 1799
(SpM)

WHITE, Henry &
Elizabeth Peacock; 16
Sep 1803 (FB)

WHITE, Joathan &
Elizabeth Townsend; 16
Nov 1786 (OM)

WHITE, Joel & Frankey
Rucker (d/o John
Rucker); 28 Jul 1785
(OB)

WHITE, Joel & Frankie
Rucker (d/o John
Rucker); 28 Jul 1785
(OM)

WHITE, John & Dolly
Peed; 3 Jan 1790 (StM)

WHITE, John & Elizabeth
Smith; 12 Nov 1730
(StM)

WHITE, John & Mary
Prager; Nov 1832 (SpM)

WHITE, Jonathan & Nanny
Martin (of
Fredericksburg); 8 Aug
1776 (OM)

WHITE, Josiah & Mary
Sale; 7 Feb 1812 (SpM)

WHITE, Josias & Emily
Powell; 4 Jul 1820
(SpM)

WHITE, Lovel & Sarah
Thomas; 14 Dec 1749
(StM)

WHITE, Nathan Skipwith
& Mary Burgess; 15 Apr
1759 (StM)

WHITE, Richard & Catey
Oliver (d/o Tabitha
Oliver); 20 Feb 1783
(OB)

WHITE, Richard & Caty
Olliver (d/o Tabitha
Olliver); 20 Feb 1783
(OM)

WHITE, Robert &
Margaret Fortune; 14
Jul 1828 (FB)

WHITE, Will & Lucy
Mason; 19 Oct 1815
(SpM)

WHITE, William & Mary
Brockman (d/o Samuel
Brockman); 10 Sep 1782
(OM)

WHITE, William & Mary
Brockman (d/o Samuel
Brockman); 10 Sep 1782
(OB)

WHITE, William & Peggy
Pullman; 10 Oct 1804
(SpM)

WHITEHURST, Henry M. &
Eliza M. Towles; 20 Jan
1831 (FB)

WHITING, Bela &
Elizabeth B. Herdon; 17
Dec 1812 (SpM)

WHITING, John &
Elizabeth Scags (d/o
Catharine Boores); 29
Jul 1812 (FB)

WHITING, John & Mary
McBean (of King George
Co., Va.); 10 Aug 1791
(StM)

WHITING, John & Mildred
Jones; 26 Dec 1788
(StM)

WHITING, John & Nancy
Gouldie; 25 Oct 1785
(StM)

WHITING, Maxfield &
Lettice Johnson; 3 Feb
1753 (StM)

WHITING, Samuel & Jane
Kelly; 29 Aug 1744
(StM)

WHITING, Samuel & Sarah
Hall; 5 Oct 1750 (StM)

WHITLEDGE, John &
Elizabeth Overhall; 15
Sep 1733 (StM)

WHITLEDGE, Nathaniel &
Frances Overhall; 27
Oct 1733 (StM)

WHITMORE, William &
Molly Carver; 5 Jan
1781 (StM)

WHITTEMORE, John M. &
Martha E. Lucas; 17 Jan
1831 (FB)

WHOLFREY, Thomas &
Fanny Almond; 14 May
1812 (SpB)

WHOLFREY, Thomas &
Fanny Almond; 14 May
1812 (SpM)

WHORTON, John &
Elizabeth Shepherd;
1832 (SpM)

WICKHAM, Willliam &
Lucy P. Taylor; 11 Jan
1848 (SpM)

WIGGINS, _____ & _____
Rogers; 12 Aug 1787
(StM)

WIGGINTON, Henry &
Margaret Bridwell; 12
Nov 1750 (StM)

WIGGONTON, James &
Sarah Botts; 9 Feb 1756
(StM)

WIGLESWORTH, Claiborne
& Lavinia Ward Farish;
26 Oct 1818 (FB)

WIGLESWORTH, John &
Lucy Lewis; 24 Sep 1812
(SpM)

WIGLESWORTH, Mansfield
& Henrietta B.
Dickenson; 15 Oct 1829
(SpM)

WIGLESWORTH, Thomas &
Matilda Foster; 1 Dec
1803 (SpM)

WILKERSON, James &
Sarah Fagg; 19 Sep 1809
(SpB)

WILKERSON, James Henry
& Catharine L. Chapman;
28 Dec 1846 (FB)

WILKINSON, James &
Sarah Fagg; 19 Sep 1809
(SpM)

WILKINSON, John &
Katherine Copely; 14
Aug 1743 (StM)

WILKINSON, Samuel &
Mary Cotes; 9 Dec 1734
(StM)

WILKISON, John & Sarah
Ross; 13 Nov 1730 (StM)

WILLET, David & Polly
Baughon; 21 Mar 1799
(OM)

WILLIAM, Burnett &
Eliza Correl; 1771 (OB)

WILLIAMS, Bland & Susan
Bell; 24 Nov 1831 (FB)

WILLIAMS, Francis &
Nanny Harvie; 5 May
1776 (OM)

WILLIAMS, Francis &
Sally Rogers; 3 Mar
1795 (OM)

WILLIAMS, George &
Alice Fowler; 31 Dec
1734 (StM)

WILLIAMS, George &
Peggy McClone; 5 Jul
1814 (SpM)

WILLIAMS, Henry A. &
Mary Elder; 23 Feb 1843
(FB)

WILLIAMS, Jacob &
Elizabeth Miller; 3 Dec
1747 (StM)

WILLIAMS, Jacob & Mary Delaney; 25 Mar 1786 (OM)

WILLIAMS, James & Elizabeth Bruce; 3 Jun 1795 (OM)

WILLIAMS, James & Margaret Smith; 12 Dec 1815 (FB)

WILLIAMS, James & Molly Price; 24 Apr 1782 (StM)

WILLIAMS, James & Sally Thompson (d/o John Thompson); 5 Aug 1800 (OM)

WILLIAMS, James L. & Ann Beach; 31 Aug 1837 (FB)

WILLIAMS, James M. & Mildred Williams; 17 Jul 1825 (SpM)

WILLIAMS, James T. & Martha J. Roio; 17 Dec 1850 (SpM)

WILLIAMS, John & Agnes Simpson; 16 Nov 1797 (SpM)

WILLIAMS, John & Elizabeth Reeves (d/o Mary Reeves); 3 Feb 1810 (FB)

WILLIAMS, John & Elizabeth Rumsey; 5 Mar 1778 (OB)

WILLIAMS, Joseph & Anne Smallwood; 24 Apr 1819 (FB)

WILLIAMS, Paul & Eliza W. Gayles; 26 Nov 1812 (SpM)

WILLIAMS, Richard & Elizabeth Smock (d/o William Smock); 21 Dec 1820 (FB)

WILLIAMS, Richard & Sarah Beazley (d/o Mildred Williams); 2 Jan 1798 (OM)

WILLIAMS, Robert M. & Matilda Ingram; 25 Nov 1829 (FM)

WILLIAMS, Robert M. & Melinda Ingram; 24 Nov 1829 (FB)

WILLIAMS, Tandy & Elizabeth Jane Parker; 20 May 1850 (FB)

WILLIAMS, Thomas & Ann Floyd; 23 Dec 1744 (StM)

WILLIAMS, Thomas & Hannah Tarkelson; 8 Jan 1831 (FB)

WILLIAMS, Thomas & Helen Morphew; 4 Sep 1723 (StM)

WILLIAMS, Thomas & Janet Johnson; 13 Nov 1744 (StM)

WILLIAMS, Walter & Catharine G. Edmondson; 7 Oct 1837 (FB)

WILLIAMS, William & Mildred Duncomb; 8 Dec 1743 (StM)

WILLIAMS, William T. & Ann Newby (d/o J. Newby); 17 Dec 1817 (FB)

WILLIAMSON, Thomas & Milly Bledsoe (d/o

Aaron Bledsoe); 29 Mar 1796 (OM)

WILLIAMSON, Walter & Mildred Dade; 1 Mar 1755 (StM)

WILLIBY, Tandy & Polly Chiles (d/o James Chiles; sister of Walter Chiles); 29 Apr 1815 (OM)

WILLIE, Washington & May Crump; 20 Oct 1841 (FB)

WILLIS, Benjamin N. & Charlotte U. Briggs; 8 Nov 1838 (FB)

WILLIS, Henry & Elizabeth Gregory; 29 Apr 1743 (SpB)

WILLIS, John & Elizabeth Plunket; 17 Jan 1734 or 1735 (StM)

WILLIS, John & Sally Thomas; 27 Apr 1771 (OM)

WILLIS, John & Sally Thomas; 27 Apr 1772 (OB)

WILLIS, Lewis & Elizabeth Brumfield, 16 Jun 1810 (FB)

WILLIS, Moses & Elizabeth Thomas (d/o Joseph Thomas Sr.); 20 Apr 1781 (OM)

WILLIS, Reuben & Ann Garnett; 17 Sep 1776 (OM)

WILLIS, William H. & Eliza White; 9 Jun 1846 (FB)

WILLOUGHBY, James & Elizabeth Williams Luck; 25 Nov 1807 (SpM)

WILLOUGHBY, Joseph & Susan Lewis; Oct 1822 (SpM)

WILLOUGHBY, William & Lucy Stevens; 15 Jan 1824 (OB)

WILLUGHBY, John B. & Lucy Hicks; 6 Jan 1835 (SpM)

WILSON, Abraham & Sally Ann Crutchfield; 28 Jan 1847 (SpM)

WILSON, Benjamin & Alinda McDonald; 27 Feb 1757 (StM)

WILSON, David & Lucy U. Batchelder; 22 Nov 1832 (FB)

WILSON, Jeremiah & Agnes Wiglesworth; 28 May 1811 (SpM)

WILSON, John & Ann Asberry; 16 Aug 1748 (StM)

WILSON, John & Ann Lambert; 28 Oct 1759 (StM)

WILSON, John & Jane Wood; 12 Feb 1750 or 1751 (StM)

WILSON, John & Sally Perry; 21 Dec 1820 (SpM)

WILSON, John & Sarah Brooks; 7 Feb 1752 (StM)

WILSON, Reuben & Eliza
Dillard; 3 Mar 1804
(SpM)

WILSON, Reubin & Eliza
Dillard (d/o Francis
Dillard); 3 Mar 1804
(FB)

WILSON, Richard & Anne
Smith; 31 Oct 1722
(StM)

WILSON, Robert H. &
Mary June Lucy; Dec
1850 (SpM)

WILSON, Thomas H. &
Eliza T. Dickenson; 11
Oct 1836 (SpM)

WILSON, Walker & Eliza
Haley; 23 Jan 1816
(SpM)

WILSON, William & Maria
Doggett; 4 Jan 1808
(SpM)

WINDER, Edward & Jane
Ward (w/o James Ward);
Feb 1790 (FM)

WINSLOW, Benjamin &
Susanah Beverly; 22 Nov
1726 (SpB)

WINSTON, Jn B. & Judith
T. Duoby; 1802 (SpM)

WINSTON, John B. &
Indeth T. Duorley; 1
Oct 1802 (SpM)

WINTERS, William & Caty
Hooe; 1 Nov 1781 (StM)

WIRT, William & Betty
S. Payne; 19 Mar 1845
(FB)

WITHERS, Walter &
Margaret M. Baggott; 8
Mar 1841 (FB)

WITHERSPOON, John &
Mary Boston; 20 Dec
1774 (OM)

WITTSHIN, Benjamin &
Sally Jones; 21 Dec
1797 (SpM)

WOIRHAYE, Francis &
Nancy Hancock (d/o
William Hancock); 22
Feb 1817 (OM)

WOLFE, Thomas R. &
Maria B. Temple; 24 Jul
1843 (FB)

WOLINGFORD, John W. &
Jane Williams; 31 Aug
1842 (FB)

WOOD, Alexander &
Catherine Goodloe; 4
Jun 1799 (SpM)

WOOD, Elijah & Jane
Powell; 30 Jun 1722
(StM)

WOOD, Elliot & Mary
Conner; 19 Oct 1775
(OM)

WOOD, Henry & Mary
Weatherspoon; 16 May
1780 (OM)

WOOD, John & Nancy
Johnson (d/o Benjamin
Johnson); 27 Jun 1805
(FB)

WOOD, Jonathan &
Elizabeth Barefoot; 28
Nov 1729 (SpB)

WOOD, Joseph & Margaret
Bell (d/o Mary Bell);
22 Mar 1781 (OM)

WOOD, Silas & Julia
Anne Brock; 17 Apr 1816
(FB)

WOOD, Singleton & Eliza Jane Mackay (d/o Maria L. Mackay); 24 Jun 1840 (FB)

WOOD, William & Jane James; 5 Oct 1809 (SpB)

WOOD, William & Jane James; 5 Oct 1809 (SpM)

WOODFORD, William & Elizabeth Cock; 3 Aug 1732 (SpB)

WOODS, Aaron & Ann Grigsby Grinnan; 8 Aug 1831 (FB)

WOODSON, Freeborn & Elia Garner; 23 Dec 1841 (FB)

WOOLDRIDGE, Archibald & Elizabeth B.C. Stanard; 9 Jul 1811 (SpM)

WOOLDRIDGE, Archibald & Julia Ann Virginia Stanard; 25 Jan 1826 (SpM)

WOOLFOLK, Augustine & Frankie Thomas; 28 Aug 1777 (OB)

WOOLFOLK, Thomas & Mrs. Elizabeth Ellis (w/o ?0; 11 Aug 1828 (OB)

WORMELEY, John T. & Virginia F. Holt; 17 Sep 1833 (FB)

WORMLEY, Warner L. & Maria Hall; 2 Dec 1807 (FB)

WORTON, William & Margaret Hamilton; 26 Feb 1724 or 1725 (StM)

WRAY, Jacob & Mary Ashton; 13 May 1761 (StM)

WREN, James & Catherine Brent; 27 Mar 1753 (StM)

WREN, Lewis & Eliza Pilcher; 20 Sep 1842 (FB)

WREN, Thomas & Malinda Mills; May 1815 (FM)

WREN, William & Caty Fagg; 22 Feb 1807 (SpM)

WRENN, Albert W. & Catharine E. Benson; 14 Feb 1838 (FB)

WRENN, William A. & Susan A. Luck; 28 Nov 1850 (SpM)

WRIGHT, Alexander & Agnes S. Robinson; 15 Apr 1823 (SpM)

WRIGHT, Alexander & Lucy Pitcher; 24 Jan 1820 (OB)

WRIGHT, Augustine & Mary Lindsay (d/o Mary Lindsay); 21 Dec 1799 (OM)

WRIGHT, Dabney & Sally Bell; 26 Aug 1809 (OM)

WRIGHT, Edward & Frankey Powell (d/o John Powell); 24 jan 1787 (OM)

WRIGHT, Francis & Anne Massey; 7 Dec 1737 (StM)

WRIGHT, James & Letty Humphries; 22 Dec 1847 (SpM)

WRIGHT, James & Sarah
Rouser; 28 Feb 1785
(OB)

WRIGHT, James C. & Jane
Southard; 13 Oct 1842
(FB)

WRIGHT, James C. & Lucy
Ann Burden (d/o
Elizabeth Burden); 16
Apr 1828 (FB)

WRIGHT, Jefferson &
Salley Wright; 5 Dec
1828 (OB)

WRIGHT, John &
Elizabeth B. Horn; 10
Nov 1836 (SpM)

WRIGHT, John &
Elizabeth Sebree; 23
Jan 1797 (OM)

WRIGHT, John & Margaret
Jones; 5 Nov 1783 (OB)

WRIGHT, John & Margaret
Jones; 5 Nov 1783 (OM)

WRIGHT, John & Salina
Crawford; 5 Apr 1847
(SpM)

WRIGHT, John H. & Lucy
Quisenberry; 25 Feb
1828 (OB)

WRIGHT, John H. & Lucy
Quisenberry; 7 Mar 1828
(SpM)

WRIGHT, John Lee & Mary
Kitchen; 8 Aug 1751
(StM)

WRIGHT, John S. &
Charlotte Pendleton
(d/o Robert Pendleton);
27 Oct 1818 (FB)

WRIGHT, Larkin & Lucy
James; 26 Oct 1799 (OM)

WRIGHT, Stapleton C. &
Jane P. Sorrell; 16 Apr
1828 (FB)

WRIGHT, Thomas & Ann
("Nancy") Norwood; 19
May 1807 (FB)

WRIGHT, William & Mary
Brent; 18 Oct 1753
(StM)

WRIGHT, Willis & Lucy
Fortson; 15 Aug 1800
(SpM)

WROTEN, George W. &
Sarah W. Rollow; 28 May
1850 (FB)

WROUGHTON, Stewart &
Mildred Layton (d/o
John Layton); 23 Jul
1827 (FB)

WROUGHTON, Stewart &
Sarah King; 13 Jan 1845
(FB)

WYTHE, George & Ann
Lewis; 26 Dec 1747
(SpB)

YALIS, Henry & Mary
Goodloe; 1813 (SpM)

YARBY, Thomas &
Harriott Pratt; 6 Aug
1828 (SpM)

YATES, Charles & Betsy
Loyd; 12 Mar 1810 (OB)

YATES, Charles & Betsy
Loyd; 15 Mar 1810 (SpM)

YATES, Gerod & Matilda
Crawford; 10 Dec 1815
(SpM)

YATES, James & Mary
Green; 19 Nov 1745
(StM)

YATES, James & Sally
Sanford (d/o Pierce
Sanford); 29 Jan 1799
(OM)

YATES, John B.(s/o
George Yates of
Rappahannock Co. Va.) &
Elizabeth Murray (d/o
Elizabeth Murray); 23
May 1833 (FB)

YATES, Michael & Milly
Goodloe; 8 Feb 1810
(SpM)

YATES, Robert &
Elizabeth Dade; 17 Feb
1750 or 1751 (StM)

YATES, Robert (probably
s/o Robert Yates &
Elizabeth Dade) & Jane
Dade; 11 Apr 1777 (StM)

YEARBY, Thomas &
Harriott Pratt; 6 Aug
1818 (FM)

YEATMAN, John W.(b.d.17
Feb 1803) & Mary Ann
Boyle; 16 Dec 1824 (FB)

YERBY, Thomas (s/o Mrs.
Brent, b.d. 12 Oct
1791) & Elizabeth
Catlett ; 12 Oct 1812
(FB)

YONG, Richardson &
Elizabeth Lewis; 28 Feb
1805 (SpM)

YOUNG, Edwin & Frances
Wright (w/o ?); 19 Dec
1785 (OM)

YOUNG, Edwin & Frances
Wright; 19 Dec 1785
(OB)

YOUNG, Henry &
Elizabeth Burnett; 17
Jul 1845 (FB)

YOUNG, Jacob & Mary Ann
Smith; 4 Aug 1801 (SpM)

YOUNG, James & Susannah
Smith; 17 Nov 1807
(SpM)

YOUNG, John & Frankey
Grady (d/o Samuel
Grady);17 Oct 1795 (OM)

YOUNG, John James &
Sarah E. Crutchfield;
12 Sep 1837 (FM)

YOUNG, Lawrence &
Catherine Martin; 7 Jul
1800 (OM)

YOUNG, Otis & Lucinda
Williams; 28 Dec 1837
(SpM)

YOUNG, Walter & Sarah
McKenzie; 13 Apr 1808
(SpM)

YOUNG, William &
Elizabeth Griggs; 29
Aug 1746 (StM)

YOUNG, William &
Melinda Ferrell; 20 Oct
1825 (FB)

YOUNG, William &
Mildred Douglass; 29
Nov 1781 (OM)

ZACHARY, Benjamin &
Frankie White; 10 Dec
1775 (OM)

184

186

Brockman, Nancy......107	Brown, Cytha.........103
Brockman, Nelly......23	Brown, Elizabeth.....104
Brockman, Nelly......45	Brown, Elizabeth.....165
Brockman, Polly......108	Brown, Elizabeth.....2
Brockman, Rebecca....12	Brown, Elizabeth.....167
Brockman, Sarah......14	Brown, Emily........24
Brockman, Sukey......67	Brown, Frances.......119
Brockman, Susan......130	Brown, Jane.........46
Broderick, Sarah.....30	Brown, Linny.........120
Brooke, Fenton.......147	Brown, Louisa........16
Brooke, Helen.......76	Brown, Lucy.........83
Brooke, Lucy........157	Brown, Margaret.....168
Brooke, Mary R.L.....13	Brown, Mary Ann......36
Brooke, Nancy.......113	Brown, Mary.........133
Brookes, Polly......161	Brown, Mary.........73
Brooks, Ann.........163	Brown, Nancy.........139
Brooks, Betsy........84	Brown, Nancy.........32
Brooks, Clarissa T...138	Brown, Parthenia.....64
Brooks, Hannah.......156	Brown, Sara.........38
Brooks, Rachel......113	Brown, Sarah........65
Brooks, Sarah........174	Browne, Margarett M..47
Brooks, Susanna......113	Browne, Maria.......117
Brown, Agnes.........94	Browne, Milly S......110
Brown, Alice........155	Brownlow, Frances....138
Brown, Ann..........86	Bruce, Catherine.....61
Brown, Caty.........163	Bruce, Elizabeth.....173
Brown, Christian.....71	Bruce, Mary.........2

189

190

198

215

217

Martin, Sarah........89	Massey, Mary.........47
Masey, Lucy A.E......138	Massey, Parthenia....47
Mason, Betsey........52	Massey,Sigismunda M..2
Mason, Eliza.........110	Mastin, Amy..........72
Mason, Elizabeth.....28	Mastin, Martha.......47
Mason, Lucy..........171	Mastin, Mary.........129
Mason, Margaret......31	Mastin, Rachel.......142
Mason, Mary..........128	Mastin, Rachel.......143
Mason, Mary..........29	Matheny, Mary........74
Mason, Nancy C.......132	Mathews, Phiana......166
Mason, Nancy.........81	Matthew, Grisel......112
Mason, Susanna I.....35	Matthews, ____......94
Mason, Susannah......127	Matthews, Charlotte..84
Massay, Polly........150	Matthews, Mary.......72
Massey, Anne.........176	Maury, Matilda H.....57
Massey, Behethland...26	Mauzy, Margaret......81
Massey, Betty........166	Maxwell, Elizabeth...154
Massey, Clary I......151	May, Milly...........28
Massey, Eleanor......111	May, Sarah...........30
Massey, Eleanor......167	Mayers, Catherine....122
Massey, Elizabeth....38	Mayfield,____........22
Massey, Elizabeth....47	Mayhugh, Polly.......149
Massey, Elizabeth....72	Mays, Elizabeth......52
Massey, Ellen........130	Mazes, Sarah.........8
Massey, Jane.........167	McBean, Mary.........171
Massey, Lucy.........152	McCaill, Jane........120
Massey, Mary A.......118	McCalley, Ann........83

226

233

234

237

239

242

244

76

246

254

ADDENDUM

The first edition of this book generated several comments from researchers that I found interesting and helpful. In two instances, a researcher found documentation that affected the name found on the record in the county or city. This is not surprising considering the casual attitude many early clerks had regarding how accurately they recorded their information. There were also a couple of typographical errors that researchers or I found. I am including the comments and the corrections in this addendum. Regard the material here as an alternate to that found in the main text. There is one additional name not included in the first publication (see item below marked "addition"). The page numbers where the original data can be found is included to the right of the entry. Please see the underlined entries. If what is in the main text confuses rather than clarifies, this addendum may help.

COLEMAN, Ormgum & Nancy Sorrell; 27 Mar 1834 (SpM) PG 39

COLLAMS, John W.S. & Ann M. Bullock; 13 Sep 1827 (SpM) PG 40

CORE, Thomas S. & Ann Dounvant; 18 Dec 1823 (SpM) Addition

HARRIS, Edward I. & Mary F.S. Fox; 10 Jan 1832 (SpM) PG 78

HART, Archibald & Ann Carmichael; 19 Oct 1815 (FB) PG 79

HART, Arthur & Evelina C.S. Goodwin; 26 Oct 1843 (FB) PG 79

HART, John & Harriet Green; 16 Oct 1815 (FB) PG 79

HART, William & Elizabeth Turnley; 16 Feb 1819 (SpM) PG 79

HOWARD, Bloxam & Agnes A. Pendleton; 17 Jan 1831 (SpM) PG 87

GOODALL, James & Elizabeth Davis; 10 Apr 1793 (OM) PG 69

LIZER, William & Pennely Davenport; 16 Jun 1825 (SpM) PG 105

MANSELL, John & Mary Pulliam; 1 May 1820 (SpM) PG 108

MAURY, Richard K. & Lucy Hunton; May 1824 (SpM) PG 111

MCCARTY, Nathaniel & Frances Suthard; 23 Apr 1829 (SpM) PG 170

PEALLE, William B. & Frances M. Parker; 26 May 1826 (SpM) PG 128

SULLIVAN, Wiley & Fanny Hord; 22 Nov 1816 (SpM) PG 155

WEBSTER, George L. & Lucinda Minton; 13 May 1829 (SpM) PG 168

WIGLESWORTH, Mansfield & Hardinia B. Dickerson; 15 Oct 1829 (SpM) PG 172

WINSTON, John B. & Judith T. Duoby; 1 Oct 1802 (SpM) PG 175

Other Heritage Books by Therese A. Fisher:

CD: Heritage Books Archives: Virginia Marriage Records

*Marriage Records of the City of Fredericksburg, and of
Orange, Spotsylvania, and Stafford Counties, Virginia, 1722-1850*

*Marriage Records of the City of Fredericksburg,
and the County of Stafford, Virginia, 1851-1900*

*Marriages in the New River Valley, Virginia:
Montgomery, Floyd, Pulaski, and Giles Counties*

*Marriages in Virginia: Spotsylvania County, 1851-1900
and Orange County, 1851-1867*

Marriages of Caroline County, Virginia, 1777-1853

Marriages of Orange County, Virginia, 1747-1880

Marriages of Orange County, Virginia, 1757-1880

Skeletons in the Closet: 200 Years of Murders in Old Virginia

*Vital Records of Three Burned Counties: Births, Marriages, and Deaths of
King and Queen, King William, and New Kent Counties, Virginia, 1680-1860*

Made in the USA
Middletown, DE
26 February 2024

50256406R00156